D1588164

The American Journalists

THE STORY OF A PAGE

J. L. Heaton

ARNO
&
The New York Times

Collection Created and Selected
by Charles Gregg of Gregg Press

Reprint edition 1970 by Arno Press Inc.

LC# 75-125698
ISBN 0-405-01677-8

The American Journalists
ISBN for complete set: 0-405-01650-6

Reprinted from a copy in
The Columbia University Library

Manufactured in the United States of America

THE STORY OF A PAGE

Very truly yours

Joseph Pulitzer

THE
STORY OF A PAGE

THIRTY YEARS OF
PUBLIC SERVICE AND PUBLIC DISCUSSION
IN THE EDITORIAL COLUMNS OF
THE NEW YORK WORLD

BY
JOHN L. HEATON

HARPER & BROTHERS PUBLISHERS
NEW YORK AND LONDON
MCMXIII

I-N

THE WORLD, AS ESTABLISHED BY JOSEPH PULITZER
MAY 10, 1883:—

"AN INSTITUTION THAT SHOULD ALWAYS FIGHT FOR PROGRESS
AND REFORM, NEVER TOLERATE INJUSTICE OR CORRUPTION,
ALWAYS FIGHT DEMAGOGUES OF ALL PARTIES, NEVER BELONG TO
ANY PARTY, ALWAYS OPPOSE PRIVILEGED CLASSES AND PUBLIC
PLUNDERERS, NEVER LACK SYMPATHY WITH THE POOR, ALWAYS
REMAIN DEVOTED TO THE PUBLIC WELFARE, NEVER BE SATIS-
FIED WITH MERELY PRINTING NEWS, ALWAYS BE DRASTICALLY
INDEPENDENT, NEVER BE AFRAID TO ATTACK WRONG, WHETHER
BY PREDATORY PLUTOCRACY OR PREDATORY POVERTY."

CONTENTS

CONTENTS

CONTENTS

CONTENTS

INTRODUCTION

JOSEPH PULITZER bought *The World* from Jay Gould in May, 1883, and on the tenth day of the month assumed control of its columns. He was thirty-six years old. He did not live to complete thirty years in the ownership of the paper. He died in his sixty-fifth year, upon his yacht, *Liberty*, in the harbor of Charleston, South Carolina.

Mr. Pulitzer's chief concern in the management of *The World* was the conduct of its editorial page. Details of business management never engaged his attention longer than was necessary. He was a great news editor, with a marvelous instinct for seizing upon what was vital in passing events; but neither did he devote to the presentation of the news his most earnest attention.

His was the journalism of influence, of advocacy, of direction. He recognized in public opinion the power in modern government, the builder of modern civilization. It was his ambition to voice public opinion. It was his duty, as he saw it, to inform public opinion, to oppose public opinion, and even patriotic impulse, when he saw it to be in the wrong. To this duty he gave his constant thought with a singleness of purpose intensified by infirmity.

An examination of the conduct of the editorial page of *The World* for thirty years is a study of a stirring epoch. The public advocacy of *The World* has in many ways affected American history. At some points it has made history.

THE STORY OF A PAGE

THE STORY OF A PAGE

I

THE NEW "WORLD"

1860–1883

Mr. Pulitzer's Salutatory—Curious History of "The World"—Religious Daily Paper and Copperhead Organ—Its Suppression for Four Days in 1864—General Conditions in 1883 in New York City and the Nation—Civil-service Reform in Its Infancy; Ballot Reform Not Begun—The Conditions of Journalism in New York—Bennett, Greeley, Brooks, Webb, and Bryant Gone—The Unique Position of "The Sun"—Brief Sketch of Mr. Pulitzer's Career—His Platform—"The World" Utterly Changed Over Night—Its Dedication to "The Cause of the People."

WITHOUT previous announcement the following leading editorial appeared in the New York *World* on the 11th of May, 1883:

The entire World newspaper property has been purchased by the undersigned, and will, from this day on, be under different management—different in men, measures and methods—different in purpose, policy and principle—different in objects and interests—different in sympathies and convictions —different in head and heart.

Performance is better than promise. Exuberant assurances are cheap. I make none. I simply refer the public to the new World itself, which henceforth shall be the daily evidence of its own growing improvement, with forty-eight daily witnesses in its forty-eight columns.

There is room in this great and growing city for a journal that is not only cheap but bright, not only bright but large, not only large but truly democratic—dedicated to the cause of the people rather than that of purse-potentates—devoted more to the news of the New than the Old World—that will expose all fraud and sham, fight all public evils and abuses—that will serve and battle for the people with earnest sincerity.

In that cause and for that end solely the new World is hereby enlisted and committed to the attention of the intelligent public.   JOSEPH PULITZER.

The newspaper for which this inspiring challenge was issued was an odd figure in American journalism, with a curious history.

In 1860 a one-cent religious daily newspaper was begun in New York by Alexander Cummings and others, chiefly Philadelphians. It was called *The World*. It refused to print police or theatrical news or theatrical advertising; and by its small size, feeble management, and lack of popular support it seemed doomed to early death in spite of the wealth and standing of its founders. After a brief and costly career upon its chosen lines it was merged with the *Courier and Enquirer;* and, though the latter was a consolidation of two well-known journals, the shorter title, by some happy chance or stroke of foresight, was placed first in the new name.

The World and Courier and Enquirer was bought in 1862 by August Belmont, S. L. M. Barlow, and other influential Democrats sympathetic with the "Albany regency." They placed it under the editorial charge of Manton Marble, who became in time its owner. During the Civil War *The World* was an organ of the New York Copperheads, as extreme opponents of the war policies of the government were called. In May, 1864, it was one of two or three New York newspapers that published the bogus Presidential proclamation issued for stock-jobbing purposes through the late Joseph Howard, which, in the name of President Lincoln, appointed a day of national fasting and prayer and called for four hundred thousand more soldiers. A guard was thrown into *The World* office on May 18, and for four days its publication was suppressed. Its editor was arrested, and was to have been imprisoned, like Howard, in Fort Lafayette, but was soon released.

Mr. Marble surrounded himself with able writers, but his newspaper was not a success. In 1876 he sold it to a group of men headed by Thomas A. Scott, president of the Pennsylvania Railroad. It was then known simply as *The World*. Scott put in charge of the paper William Henry Hurlbert, a writer of extraordinary brilliance and keenness. Of its character in Mr. Hurlbert's time St. Clair McKelway, the veteran editor of *The Brooklyn Eagle*, has written:

It upheld Horatio Seymour when he insisted on the gold standard for New York State in a time of irredeemable paper currency. It warred on William M. Tweed's criminal alteration of the city charter from behind which he practised highway robbery to the tune of millions in the name of law. It made now and then a stand for better municipal results by informal fusion of parties. But it never sought the art of commanding a living by the approbation and confidence of the masses, for the tendency of its management inclined to the satisfaction of the capitalists with its steadiness, and to the applause of the carping, the cynical, the sciolistic, and the pessimistic by its selection and treatment of topics. Its mistaken sense of humor comprised the discussion of serious matters from a comedy side and the discussion of trivial matters from a serious side.

The lack of a serious purpose handicapped the venture heavily, and it languished until Scott's death. His estate sold it to Jay Gould, with the natural result that it lost money steadily, was distrusted by the people, and was unable even to represent effectively the policies or to serve the interests of its owner. In April, 1883, it had less than ten thousand circulation in New York City. It was known to be for sale, and possessed a membership in the Associated Press, but newspaper men of other towns who were tempted to try their fate in the metropolis fought shy of a property so heavily handicapped by its record.   No man could hope to succeed with it who had not the genius to discern and the force to carry out a plan of divorcing it at once, and with conspicuous completeness, from its former courses.

Conditions of time and place supplied the opportunity for a great popular journal.   The city and that part of the country which could be easily reached from New York were a tempting field for the political reformer.

Hard hit by the Civil War and by the panic of 1873–77, New York had grown for twenty years less rapidly than has been its wont both before and since that period.   The ten years of penny-pinching that saved its credit after the Tweed Ring's downfall had left it bare of modern improvements.   The streets were ill-paved and dirty. Healthful tenements did not exist; the people of the congested districts were housed in old residences subdivided into dark rooms, where disease worked ceaselessly to pile up a death-rate almost approaching that of St. Petersburg.   Public morals and public decency were upon a low plane.   Along Chatham Street sailors and countrymen were nightly robbed in low dives more like Port Said than like the New York of to-day.   The connection between vice, the criminal gang, the higher police officials, and the political boss was an evil against which *The World* was to wage unceasing war during thirty years of gradually improving conditions.   Political corruption was not so costly to the public purse as in Tweed's time, but it was almost as harmful to the moral sense of the community.   Power was shared by rival Democratic "halls," among which Tammany was again forging to the front, and by Republican bosses always ready for deals with the Democratic factions.   Franklin

Edson was Mayor of New York, filling out the brief term of an unprogressive administration.

Hard times had compelled children to go earlier to work, so that the total school registration of the state had risen but little in twenty years. The insane were kept in county almshouses, often a source of excessive profit to individuals and almost always neglected. Drunkenness was far more common than now. Preventive medicine was in its beginning, except as to smallpox, which vaccination had not yet made a rarity. Ten hours was a day's work in the building trades. Street-car employees toiled fifteen or sixteen hours. So late as 1886 those of New York and Brooklyn struck for twelve hours a day.

The turning-point for political decency in New York State and City had been reached in 1871, through the assault on the Tweed Ring and the storming of its Albany outposts. But in the federal government the Civil War had drawn after it a train of evil consequences which were as yet scarcely lessened. Judges of high federal courts had been driven from the bench by threat of impeachment. Congressmen had trafficked in appointments. The triumph of the first Pacific railroad had been turned into shame by the disclosure that, as Senator Hoar said, "every step of that mighty enterprise had been taken in fraud."

In the Presidency Grant had proved a disappointment. His very virtues, his simple-mindedness, his trust in his friends and his friends' friends, made him a gull for grafters. His private secretary was involved in the Whisky Ring scandals; his Secretary of War, Belknap, was impeached for bribery and resigned under fire. The Vice-President and the Speaker of the House were implicated in questionable railroad transactions.

The fraud that counted in Rutherford B. Hayes as President had so inflamed the anger of the majority that civil war might once more have broken out had Tilden been less patient in his patriotic desire to avoid conflict. For years longer the country was fated to endure the belated disputes of reconstruction; in the North the waving of the "bloody shirt," in the South impassioned protest against negro domination upheld by federal bayonets, was the political highroad to preferment.

Hayes, unpopular with politicians and handicapped by a clouded title, was brushed aside after four years by stronger men. The movement for the third-term nomination of General Grant met the renewed onset of the friends of James G. Blaine, and, between the two, in the fiercest national convention then of record, James A. Garfield became the compromise candidate. As President, Garfield intensified the faction fight between the Grant and Blaine forces and was shot down by Guiteau. Chester A. Arthur, who succeeded him, was desirous of winning a renomination by a creditable administration. A former associate of local bosses in New York, who made light of corruption at the polls and who had been removed from office by President Hayes, he had been chosen to placate the Grant faction, and the Blaine men would have none of him. His was the crippled administration that in 1883 was drawing to a close. By forcing the nomination of Charles J. Folger for Governor of New York in 1882 Arthur had caused the revulsion of public feeling that swept Grover Cleveland into office by an unprecedented majority and made him one of the conspicuous leaders of the national Democracy.

The attempt of Grant in 1870, and again of Hayes, to introduce the merit test in political appointments had failed, and not until 1883 was the Pendleton bill passed, which applied the examination method to fourteen thousand unimportant federal offices. Consulships and diplomatic appointments and important posts in the home administration were held at the disposal of political and financial power and became the fruitful source of faction.

The people had no adequate way of imposing their will
upon their public servants. Nowhere in the United
States was there a secret ballot. The citizen might
prepare with "pasters" or other crude devices his "vest-
pocket vote," but he was balanced on election day by
some poor fellow who for fear of loss of employment or
by some knave who for a fee marched to the polls holding
in sight the folded ticket the district captain put into his
hands. Not until after five years of *The World's* new
ownership was the Australian ballot introduced into any
state. The first effective blow was thus struck at the
buying of votes and the intimidation of voters when the
buyer could no longer be certain that the seller would
stay bought, and when the intimidator could be fairly
sure that his victim would betray him.

In such a state of public affairs the short cut to many reforms lay through a change in the national administration.

The journalistic forces that could be marshaled for that
or any other public purpose were weak compared with what
they are to-day. The principal newspapers of New York
sold at four cents. A small journal of great circulation,
The Evening News, was the organ of Tammany and of
the sporting interests, but had no standing in the nation.
The group of editors whose able personal journalism
had enlivened New York in the Civil War period had
passed. Bennett and Greeley, James Brooks, of *The
Express*, and William Cullen Bryant, of *The Evening Post*,
had died within the six years from 1872 to 1878. James
Watson Webb, of the old *Courier*, yet lingered, a man
past eighty, long retired from journalism. *The Times*
and the *Tribune*, rapidly recovering under Whitelaw
Reid's editorship from the ruin that threatened it in 1872
when Horace Greeley was the Liberal Republican and
Democratic candidate for President, competed for the
favor of Republican readers. It seemed as if journalism
had reacted from its feverish activity during the anti-

slavery agitation, the war and reconstruction, and was unconsciously awaiting the new issues, new leadership, and new methods which should revivify it.

In the prevailing condition of journalistic conservatism two strong personalities were conspicuous, those of E. L. Godkin of the *Evening Post,* a journal of small circulation but wide influence, and Charles A. Dana of the *Sun.* The *Sun,* sold for two cents a copy, had a circulation surpassing that of the other morning papers, and was a masterpiece of intelligent compression, with pungent editorial comment which made it on the Democratic side the foremost power in journalism in the East. But *The Sun* was not in full sympathy with Democratic doctrines, and failed to represent the party. It had referred to General Hancock while candidate for the Presidency in 1880 as "a good man weighing two hundred and forty pounds," and it was about to oppose another Democratic candidate.

That Mr. Pulitzer saw the tactical advantage which this opening gave is certain, for he saw most things; and he had been *The Sun's* Washington correspondent for a brief but active period. But the driving-power which sent the immigrant young man of thirty-six years to try conclusions in the metropolis was his desire for wider leadership, his wish to grasp the great journalistic opportunities of the metropolis.

Born in Hungary in 1847, Joseph Pulitzer had come to America in 1864, and at seventeen had enlisted in the First New York Cavalry. He served eight months—to the end of the war. At twenty-one he was a reporter on the *St. Louis Westliche-Post* under Carl Schurz; at twenty-two, a member of the Missouri Legislature; at twenty-five, a member and the secretary of the Cincinnati Liberal Republican convention which nominated Horace Greeley for President; at twenty-seven, a member of the Missouri constitutional convention; at thirty-three, the founder of the *St. Louis Post-Dispatch.*

This feat was the baptism of his blade. It drew to him the attention of newspaper men throughout the country and gained thus early their confidence and the expectation of high achievement. It was a success accomplished without adequate resources, yet without faltering in his determination to follow the rule of absolute independence —an almost bankrupting independence that took him within about three hundred dollars of his total cash resources before he succeeded in establishing, upon the same lines that he later followed with *The World*, a newspaper that has since wielded an immense power in the Middle West.

There was not a conservative hair upon Mr. Pulitzer's head or a conservative ounce of blood within his body. He was a born independent. But where Carl Schurz and others with whom he had taken part in the Liberal Republican movement looked back with longing to the Republican party, as in imagination they could see it "builded closer to their hearts' desire," Mr. Pulitzer had ceased to expect political reforms at its hands. He was an independent; the logic of the situation and his own instinct for opposition made him an independent Democrat.

What was the political creed of this rising power in American journalism at the moment when he grasped his great opportunity? He printed it on May 17, 1883, under the title "*The World's* Platform":

1. Tax luxuries.
2. Tax inheritances.
3. Tax large incomes.
4. Tax monopolies.
5. Tax the privileges of corporations.
6. A tariff for revenue.
7. Reform the civil service.
8. Punish corrupt office-holders.
9. Punish vote-buying.
10. Punish employers who coerce their employees in elections.

2

But Mr. Pulitzer had not waited six days to sound his challenge, nor one. To make *The World* trusted of the people it was necessary to change its character utterly over night. How well he succeeded there is a vivid record from a non-professional witness. Writing from Mount Pocono, Pennsylvania, June 4, 1912, to *The World*, Ryerson W. Jennings, of Philadelphia, said:

Crossing the Chestnut Street bridge in Philadelphia many years ago, I bought from a bright-eyed newsboy the first number of the New York *World* under Joseph Pulitzer's management. I saw at a glance that the emancipation of the newspapers of this country had commenced, and the people were to get the news of the day in an uncolored form; that great wrongs were to be righted; that light was to be let in where darkness covered it; that crooked things were to be made straight.

Never, indeed, was transformation more radical. Mr. Pulitzer was naturally obliged to work with the news staff that Mr. Hurlbert had collected, though he began at once to make additions from the local field, enlisting many clever writers. But the change in tone was instantly perceptible. The old black head-line carrying the title was changed to one nearly resembling that used to-day. Heavy head-lines over articles were replaced by lighter, smaller, more modest type. Big and deep head-lines in the New York press, a blemish to many critics, were no invention of *The World*. They came later, and gradually. In the much more important matter of the treatment of the news there was a revolution. An experienced man scanning the first page of *The World* for May 10 and May 11, 1883, could see at a glance that in the interim a master had come. More interest, more earnestness, more heart and thought appeared throughout.

But the greatest change was in the editorial page. Anxious as Jay Gould was to get rid of a useless property, he had nearly defeated the negotiations for the sale of *The World* by stipulating that one or two editorial writers be retained.   Mr. Pulitzer preferred to urge new measures with new men, and some diplomacy was necessary to smooth away the difficulty.   An earnestness of purpose which Gould writers might have found it embarrassing to assume took the place of the old cynicism.   An eagerness to attack corporate and political rascality foreign to *The World* of May 10th, which defended them or ignored them or joked about them, appeared in *The World* of May 11th. Men about town who had read Hurlbert's beautifully written but cynical articles rubbed their eyes in amazement.   Many such men promptly dropped the paper; Mr. Pulitzer did not share the fears then common with newspaper men undertaking such tasks of reorganization lest they should lose old readers before gaining new ones.   Deserters were more than made good by men in sympathy with the new editor's aims.

Journalists were quick to note the transformation, usually with disapproval, as men are wont to disapprove portents that war against the familiar and accustomed. A shrewd impression was that of the *Philadelphia Chronicle* of May 14th:

The change which is apparent to-day on every page of the New York *World* in its tone, character, and style is a most gratifying one.   There is force and vitality in its utterances, something of the snap, the breeze, and the racy flavor of the West, from which its new owner, Mr. Joseph Pulitzer, comes.   The same space which formerly was devoted to the verbose discussion of one or two leading topics now contains short and crisp articles on a half-dozen or more subjects, and there is something positive and emphatic in its deliverances that is truly refreshing when compared with the elegant but uninfluential literary estheticism that marked its previous control.   Above all, the sardonic leer and avaricious grin of Mr. Jay Gould are no longer discernible in its columns.

Violently, harshly, conspicuously, unmistakably turned in a new direction and plainly ''dedicated to the cause of the people,'' the new *World* was launched upon a career which its rivals prophesied would be brief.

II

TRUE DEMOCRACY

1883–1884

"The World's" Energetic Beginning—Not a Jack Cade of Journalism—
Political Conditions in New York City—Preparing for 1884—The Fighting
Issues—The "Southern Brigadier" Still a Bugaboo—The Seymour Tariff
Plank of 1868—"Randall Democrats" and Reformers—Mr. Tilden as
New York's "Favorite Son"—"Resolved, That We Must Have Money."

IT was necessary to *The World's* success to make it clear
at once that it was no longer the tool of Jay Gould. It
was necessary to its owner's plan that he should make
it equally clear that *The World* would be no Jack Cade
of journalism.

Under the heading "True Democracy" the first issue
under Mr. Pulitzer's control mapped the course he intended to pursue:

Democracy, sometimes from ignorance, more frequently
from malice, has been represented as radicalism and destructive-
ness. It is nothing of the kind. True democracy, based on
equal rights, recognizes the millionaire and the railroad magnate as just as good as any other man and as fully entitled
to protection for his property under the law. But true democracy will not sanction the swallowing up of liberty by property
any more than the swallowing up of property by communism.

There was no lack of specific occasions to make good
a promise to espouse true democracy. If in the crucial
first months of its career it scored the "scandalous mis-
management" of the New York Central Railroad, *The*

World denounced as hotly the sham radicalism of Ben Butler in Massachusetts, which was so soon narrowly to miss involving the whole country in misfortune. If it attacked the Ramapo Water Company's scheme to exploit the city, prelude of a more famous later fight, it also assailed the "silver kings" for the manipulation that gave currency to the trade-dollar. If it exposed star-route frauds in the Post-office Department, neither had it any mercy for greenbackism or repudiation. If it explained why the police could not break into Wall Street gambling-houses and cart away the apparatus because "The law makes a distinction in gambling; faro is forbidden, roulette is ruled out, poker is prohibited, but margins are sanctioned by law, and corners are legitimate," it also lost no opportunity of disclaiming tolerance for dangerous methods of gaining popular aims.

It was fortunate for the new venture that 1883 was an off year in politics. With its limited circulation and feeble equipment it could have done little then to further its policies. Indeed, there was but scant time to prepare for the struggle of the following year. To the weakening of the dominant party, and especially to the exposure of corruption and the building up of a public sentiment that would cure the evil, it devoted its keenest invective.

It was Democracy in the nation which *The World* sought to foster as the first condition of reform. For a time it waged no war against local organizations of Democracy. If the federal government was to be turned over to other hands there was need in New York of the help of every Democratic faction, and none of these factions was so potent for harm, even locally, as the Republican machine with its allies commonly in power in Washington and Albany.

Tammany Hall had been chastened by the fate of its members who, with Tweed, had filched from the people and had fled their wrath, and John Kelly, its boss, was generally considered as honest as he was obstinate. He had favored reform, and for that reason was the logical leader of the Hall after the débâcle.

Irving Hall bore no good repute, but was the weakest of the three.

The County Democracy generally acted with the up-state Democrats. Such men as Abram S. Hewitt and Edward Cooper were prominent in its counsels, and it furnished most of the reform mayors that followed Tweed's downfall. Though Samuel J. Tilden was friendly with Kelly, the County Democracy most nearly represented his policies. Yet, in spite of the general acceptance of this faction as best representing New York Democracy, *The World* protested in the interest of harmony against the Robert Roosevelt resolution which in 1883 passed the state committee by a bare majority, committing that body in advance to accept as "regular" the seventy-two delegates of the County Democracy in the state convention. The party nominations in that year were unimportant, but with 1884 in view *The World* urged harmony in national matters upon the factions.

Besides turning its searchlight upon rottenness in the party in power *The World* had to meet in the preliminary tactics of the Presidential campaign three questions of importance: the question of the tariff, the question of the candidates, the question of Southern rights within the Union and the "bloody shirt."

It may seem strange that at so recent a date the "Southern Brigadier" was still a bugaboo. But the issue had its practical effect and must be considered. Its survival might be a perversion of justice and common sense, but its influence in swaying the people could not be ignored. In the South the white aristocrat and former slaveholder was the natural leader of the people until Democracy could adjust itself to new conditions. Carpet-baggism had unleashed upon the late Confederate states the most shocking corruption, which honest Southern men could less easily forgive than the hard blows dealt in the war. The nation had need of the sense of honor and the political acumen of the best men of the South. How was it to resume the employment of them in the public service?

The Republicans had sharpened sarcasm as a shrewd weapon against themselves by their readiness to take up Mahone and Riddleberger, who won a brief success in Virginia, fusing the Republicans and a portion of the Democracy for "readjusting" the state debt. As *The World* remarked of "Two Kinds of Rebels" the "fiercest Southern brigadier is a patriotic American citizen, entitled to enjoy equal rights with the patriots of Ohio or Massachusetts and to hold public office, provided he will ally himself politically with the Republican party."

As to the tariff *The World* pinned its faith to the Seymour doctrine of 1868. Upon a pronounced tariff-for-revenue plank, such as Frank Hurd and other extremists were urging, the Democrats could not win; and to win, for the house-cleaning that might follow victory, was a duty. Even the issue of a lower tariff was not quite so clearly defined as it has since become. Not until nearly a decade later did the trust movement get fully under way, which was to "kill competition and capitalize the corpse."

A moderate reduction of the tariff could only be looked for from Democrats, and only from the reforming wing of the Democracy. During the Ohio campaign of 1883 *The World* especially commended the tariff plank adopted by the Democrats. After the election in October it reminded the Republicans that their alarm lest the tariff be lost sight of was unfounded, and said:

An election has been held this week in Ohio. The Democrats met last June to nominate candidates and construct a platform. In the platform was the following plank:

"We favor a tariff for revenue, limited to the necessities of a government economically administered, and so adjusted in its application as to prevent unequal burdens, encourage productive interests at home and afford just compensation to labor, but not to create or foster monopolies."

Upon a full vote of the State, after more than three months' thoughtful consideration, the people of Ohio have indorsed this tariff plank by over 12,000 majority.

It has won a glorious victory in Ohio this year. It will win a yet more glorious victory in the Union next year.

The World's championship of the Ohio platform was more than a stirring voice in the preliminary struggle of 1883. It heartened the national Democracy for the greater contest. It blazed the way for Grover Cleveland's tariff policy and message.

Bound up with the tariff was the question of the candidates. With the House of Representatives Democratic and a great wave of discontent sweeping the country, there was a chance for Democratic success at the polls in the Presidential year if the party could be restrained from blundering. The first Democratic President after the war must come from the genuinely Democratic wing of the party, and not from the "assistant Republicans," of whom Samuel J. Randall, of Philadelphia, was the chief representative. Months before the Speakership contest in December we find *The World* on May 17th making its position unmistakable:

We oppose Mr. Randall's election because he is not in accord with the Democracy in its opposition to the encroachments of corporate monopolies. It is unquestionably true that there is a monopolistic wing of the Democratic party. It is equally true that its principles and objects are offensive to the great mass of the party. Mr. Randall's interests are identified with the monopolies of his own State, and his sentiments are friendly to them rather than to the people.

Such considerations, in which the position of the tariff reformers was masked behind the popular cry of anti-monopoly, prevailed, and the election of John G. Carlisle as Speaker in December, 1883, put the reformers in control of the party. This wing of the party in the autumn elections had won encouraging victories. In its search for Democratic Presidential material and to recruit the ranks for the coming struggle *The World* had entered heart and soul into the campaigns of Leon Abbett for Governor in New Jersey and George Hoadly in Ohio. Thus it gave notice of its intent to be not a local but a national power, and it aided greatly in their campaigns. The political revolt which in 1882 had swept a Democratic House of Representatives into office still had the force to secure the choice of these two strong Democratic governors in states counted upon by the Republicans in Presidential years.

More pivotal were the two great doubtful states of New York and Indiana. No election, it was held, could be carried without their electoral votes. The attempt of 1880 to win upon a tariff-for-revenue plank, with a candidate who assured the.country that the tariff was a local issue, had so disastrously failed that there was little danger of its repetition. But there was danger of an attempt to angle for New York's vote by the nomination of Mr. Tilden, the unseated victor of 1876, never a robust man and now nearing his seventieth year. Of this movement *The World* said on August 28th:

The western Democratic sentiment reported in our special correspondence from Saratoga as in favor of the old ticket is based on what old Bill Allen would call a "barren ideality." This sentiment takes the shape of asserting that the old ticket was defeated by fraud. This is true. Then it asserts that the fraud can be rebuked only by nominating the victims of that fraud. This is a fallacy. The real victims of the fraud were not the two eminent citizens who were cheated out of their offices, but the millions of honest Democratic voters who were cheated out of their votes.

Throughout this year of preparation *The World* made it clear that it was ready to support Mr. Tilden if he were nominated, but it cast about for other material— first and far foremost, of course, Grover Cleveland, the "tidal-wave" Governor of New York, then John G. Carlisle, Governor Hoadly, and others, as they successively rode upon the crest of some wave of public triumph.

And always, day after day, it poured upon the Republican party the full fire of its batteries. The extracts that follow, taken at intervals throughout the year, may do more than illustrate the skill of its attack. They may remind us how vital was the need of such advocacy in a period of great political unrest:

Will not the people remember that Roscoe Conkling — in intellect a giant among pygmies, in public life an honest man in the midst of corruption and rascality—has been retired by his own party to private life? That Bristow, who exposed the Whisky Ring frauds, has been politically killed by the Republican organization? That Dorsey, Brady, "Lo" Sessions, and A. D. Barber—the two former on trial, the two latter under indictments that will, probably, never be tried—are still active and powerful in the Republican organization?— *June 5, 1883.*

The party Judge Foraker represents has been plundering the Government for twenty-three years. Its plunder commenced with war contracts, shoddy uniforms, shoddy blankets, and "cooked-up" rifles without any connection between the lock and the barrel. It has been continued through whisky rings, subsidy rings, Treasury rings, Interior Department rings, Credit Mobilier rings, Washington District rings, public-building rings and star-route rings, down to the star-route trial farce and raids upon the Treasury by some of the Government lawyers.—*June 26, 1883.*

From time to time the leaders of the Republican party hold conventions in which they formulate certain moral axioms and platitudes which they call the platform of the party.

The real platform of the party, however, is expressed in private and personal letters exchanged between these leaders after the mummery of the convention is over. This, the real platform, may be written in one line—"We want money."

Blaine writes to Dorsey that in failing to send money to Maine he is "imperiling the whole campaign."

Allison writes to Jewell: "Money must be had and sent to Indiana."

Stewart Woodford writes to Jewell from West Virginia: "With $25,000 Sturgis and Atkinson can make an effective campaign."

John F. Lewis, Mahone's lieutenant, writes: "The expenditure of $50,000 will insure the electoral vote of Virginia for Garfield and Arthur. 'Help us, Cassius, or we sink.'"

Mr. Henderson, of Iowa, writes to Dorsey: "Put money in thy purse."

Richard Smith, of the Cincinnati Gazette, who has been called the Good Deacon Richard Smith, was alive to the need of money. He writes: "There should be $50,000 judiciously placed in each of these States [Ohio and Indiana] within the next ten days." . . . Everybody wanted money. What did they want it for?

The Republican party claims to have saved the nation, to have paid off the debt, settled the finances and pensioned the soldiers. It has held power for twenty-odd years. It has taken credit to itself for the prosperity of the country; has had all the support of capital, of protected interests, of the army of office-holders and of all privileged classes.

Yet when a national election came around, when a great national battle was to be fought, the grand old party could find only one battle-cry. Danger of defeat changed all its boasting into abject terror and its platform shrank to a single line:

Resolved, That we must have money.—*August 30, 1883.*

"J. Warren Keifer, of Ohio, is a corrupt and shameless man," said the Republican Times yesterday.

On the same day the party of moral ideas—the grand old party—voted almost unanimously for J. Warren Keifer, of Ohio, for Speaker of the House of Representatives.—*December 4, 1883.*

Such hammering won public approval. Within one week from the time when Mr. Pulitzer, taking hold of a moribund journal of high literary quality but negligible influence, promised to "serve and battle for the people with earnest sincerity" he had shaped a course which was to hearten Democracy and hasten political independence; within six months the success of his venture was assured; within a year it was a marvel in the journalistic field; within eighteen months it had caused the election of the first Democratic President since the Civil War, as that President appreciatively acknowledged.

III

GROVER CLEVELAND

Mr. Cleveland's Remarkable Rise to Political Power—Tilden's Weakness as a Candidate—Cleveland and Hoadly as a Ticket—"No Free Whisky" —Blaine and Republican "Principles"—Theodore Roosevelt's Dilemma— Tammany's Unavailing Opposition — "We Love Him Most for the Enemies He Has Made" — Butler and the Prohibitionists — The Fisher Letters — "Rum, Romanism, and Rebellion" — "Belshazzar's Feast"— "The World" Not a Cleveland Organ—Mr. Cleveland's Public Tribute to "The World"—Mr. Pulitzer's Insistence Upon Independence.

STEPHEN GROVER CLEVELAND was born in Caldwell, New Jersey, March 17, 1837. There were nine children in the family, and after the death of his father, a Presbyterian clergyman, straitened means prevented the future President from obtaining a college education. He became office-boy in a Buffalo law firm, and in 1859 was admitted to the bar. In 1863 he was elected assistant district attorney in Erie County, and in 1869 sheriff. In 1873 he resumed the practice of the law. In 1881 he was nominated for Mayor of Buffalo and elected as a Democrat in a community usually Republican. He was not especially ambitious; political tasks came to him unsought and were accepted in the line of public duty. He was an excellent mayor, upright and painstaking.

In 1882 the Republican party in New York was rent by the Stalwart-Halfbreed war, and President Arthur was accused of forcing upon the state convention the nomination for governor of Charles J. Folger, a man of ability but devoid of magnetism, his Secretary of the Treasury and a Stalwart. The Democrats named the reform

Mayor of Buffalo, and Mr. Cleveland was elected by 192,854 votes. In Albany he had made an excellent record by his messages, and especially by his vetoes, when the young journalist who was to elect him President came to New York.

Throughout 1883 *The World* watched Cleveland's course with keen appreciation of its strength and honesty. Here was Presidential material placed where it was most available, in the greatest debatable state. But New York's favorite son was still the cheated Tilden. The sentimental appeal of his wrongs at the hands of the Electoral Commission was almost irresistible.

As early as June 2, 1883, *The World*, stating its faith in "principles, not personalities," said:

Mr. Tilden is still a fine intellectuality. He represents a sentiment. He has a great party behind him. . . . He has the admiration of thousands who see and feel and know nothing else except that he was fairly elected in 1876. He has enormous wealth. But with all that he has no more chance of ever again becoming President than Napoleon III. had of regaining the French crown after Sedan.

Revolutions never go backward.

Mr. Tilden's Sedan was when he consented to the Electoral Commission. His Chiselhurst is Graystone.

During the summer *The World* continued to point out Mr. Tilden's weakness. He "practically ceased to be a leader when he lost the Presidency. Since then his mouth has been closed, and he utterly refused to advise and lead his party on any question." Here appears the new editor's usual insistence upon leaders and ideas. "Mr. Tilden," the argument continued, "has claims upon the sympathies of Democrats. He is a real thinker. But he is not a party leader on any issue of the hour. His great effort is to conceal his ideas. After all, ideas lead parties, not men."

A leader of a more modern type, bolder and more uncompromising, appealed to *The World*. "Does any Republican really believe," it asked, "that Grover Cleveland, elected in 1882 by 193,000 majority over the Republican candidate, and with a clean record for honesty, capacity, and economy in his administration of the State government, could be defeated in New York in 1884?"

Again in October *The World*, conceding that Mr. Tilden was still master of the nomination, but contemplating the possibility of his withdrawal, spoke of him as a maker of Presidents:

Mr. Tilden might name George Hoadly. But will not his shrewdness shrink from the needless risk of the October election in Ohio?

Mr. Tilden may make choice of Grover Cleveland, having an eye to the vital importance of strength in New York.

In this event is it not probable that the next Democratic Presidential ticket may be graced by the names of the two greatest Governors in the United States—greatest in brains, in character, in the magnificence of their victories—Grover Cleveland, of New York, and George Hoadly, of Ohio?

Cleveland and Hoadly was, in fact, *The World's* "slate." As to the issues of the campaign, they were clearly indicated after the 1883 election. The Treasury surplus had become so great as to threaten the Republican party with the necessity of revising the tariff as a revenue measure. In January, 1884, the New York *Sun*, on behalf of the Randall or high-tariff Democracy, suggested the removal of internal-revenue taxation as a Democratic policy. *The World* was quick to brand this proposal under the heading of "No Free Whisky." To this it added the ringing popular cry: "Turn the rascals out!" It urged the Democratic House of Representatives, which was making an excellent record for economy and efficiency, to provide campaign material by exposing corruption:

It has been admitted by the ex-secretary of the Republican National Committee that in the election of 1880 the State of Indiana was carried for the Republicans by bribery and corruption. Investigate!

It has been admitted by the Republicans that a corruption fund of $400,000 was raised in New York City, which was carried to Indiana and used to "induce men to change their opinions and their votes." Investigate!

It has been charged that the present United States Minister to France, Levi P. Morton, bought his appointment with the share he contributed to that fund and his efforts in securing other subscriptions. Investigate!

It has been charged that two prominent speculators interested in suits before the Supreme Court of the United States involving millions of dollars paid $100,000 toward Garfield's election expenses in consideration of his pledge to make appointments to that court acceptable to them, and that a judge friendly to them (Stanley Matthews) was actually appointed in conformity with the bargain. Investigate!

As early as April 7th *The World* foresaw that "the chances are that the candidate of the Republican party will be James G. Blaine." It felt for his claims a certain sympathy "Because he is manifestly the choice of the great bulk of his party and has the Federal patronage and the machines against him. Because he was the choice of the majority of Republicans in 1876 and 1880, and on each occasion was cheated out of the nomination by machine methods."

When the Republican national convention met Mr. Blaine proved to be the leader in popular favor. Manipulation could no longer balk his candidacy, and he was without great difficulty nominated June 6th on the fourth ballot. *The World* was under no illusions as to his strength:

Before the canvass is fully opened it will be clear to the plainest understanding that James G. Blaine represents not only the machine of the Republican party, but the demoralizing and corruptive power of Wall Street, the money interests, the monopolies, corporations, and all protected, privileged, special classes. All that is reprehensible and base in our demoralized political system will naturally rally to his support.

Will he be defeated?

That is clearly in the hands of Democrats.

If the Democratic candidate for the Presidency should be precisely what Mr. Blaine is not—a man of the highest judicial mind, the most elevated character and purposes—he would doubtless attract the support of many self-respecting independent Republicans, carry New York and other doubtful States and be elected.

Of the fighting issues *The World* had said:

The Republican platform starts with a truism which no person will attempt to gainsay:

"The Republicans of the United States, in national convention assembled, renew their allegiance to the principles upon which they have triumphed in six successive Presidential elections."

Among those principles are the coercion of a number of the States at the point of the Federal bayonet.

The arbitrary use of the enormous Federal patronage designedly increased by Republican administrations as a means of perpetuating the power of the party.

The corrupt appliance of money wrung from public officers by compulsory assessments, or collected from dishonest Government contractors, favored corporations, and pampered national banks.

The theft of the Presidency by aid of fraud and forgery when beaten by the people.

The unblushing purchase of elections with an enormous corruption fund raised by the sale of Supreme Court judgeships, Cabinet offices and diplomatic appointments.

Colonization of voters, false counting and other offenses against the purity of the ballot-box.

These are the "principles" upon which the Republican party

3

has "triumphed," despite the desire of the people to drive it from the Government, and these are the "principles" on some of which it founds the desperate hope of a continuance of power.

Many eminent Republicans repudiated the nomination of Mr. Blaine because his record would not bear scrutiny. Carl Schurz, Benjamin H. Bristow, George William Curtis, Charles W. Eliot, and Franklin MacVeagh led into the ranks of those political independents whom it was the fashion to call "Mugwumps" a group of the best men of the party. Some of these had followed Greeley in 1872; some were for the first time breaking away from party trammels. Among these latter the country looked with interest for the name of a young New York assemblyman who had hotly opposed Blaine in the convention. They looked in vain. Theodore Roosevelt decided to accept Blaine, but not without careful balancing of opposing considerations. It was the political crisis of his life; at the early age of twenty-five he turned to the machine men of his party, with whom for almost thirty years he was generally to stand in agreement.

Attention turned to the Democratic convention. Mr. Tilden's expected refusal to accept a nomination came in a letter to Daniel Manning, chairman of the New York State Democratic Committee. The way was clear for Cleveland. *The World* on June 17th again presented the claims of the man of "Manifest Destiny":

The name of Grover Cleveland has suggested itself naturally to Democrats as presenting pre-eminent availability. As Governor of the State Mr. Cleveland has displayed a straightforward, unpretending desire to do his duty, without regard to political consequences and without affectation of demagogism. . . . When a blathering ward politician objects to Governor Cleveland because he is more a "Reformer" than a "Democrat" he furnishes the best argument in favor of his nomination and election.

And again on the following day: "Grover Cleveland is available, not assailable." On July 3d, just before the Democratic national convention was to meet, an article appeared telling "Why *The World* Likes Cleveland." It ran as follows:

He is a poor man.

He came from plain, common people.

He has no so-called aristocratic lineage or illustrious ancestry, but owes everything he is to his own efforts and his own character. . . .

He is a poor politician because an absolutely honest, conscientious reformer.

He has no lifelong political record to defend or explain. . . .

He does not believe that even a moderate protective tariff is unconstitutional and "legalized communism." Quite the contrary.

He does not speculate in stocks, does not build railroads, did never sit with Blaine as an associate in the same directory. Quite the contrary.

He is not popular with the local "machines" and "politicians" whose special interests he has disregarded whenever the public welfare demanded it.

He is certain of a larger Independent and disaffected Republican vote than any other Democrat yet born.

He is more apt to carry New York, Connecticut and New Jersey than any other Democrat who can be named.

He is certain to make a good President—not brilliant and "magnetic," but repulsive to the rascals who are preying upon the Government and who must be driven out of Washington.

He is certain to make a very bad President—for all the jobbers and corruptionists and on-the-make partisans.

There was need of such advocacy; Tammany, under command of .John Kelly, opposed Cleveland, and the opposition came from the greatest Democratic stronghold of the country. The Hall could not deliver the delegates of the state under the unit rule; Greater New York was yet unmade; Brooklyn commonly acted with the rural

Democrats against Tammany; but Tammany was a power. "Personal Comfort" Grady (the late Thomas F. Grady, whom Mr. Cleveland's request to John Kelly had kept out of the New York Legislature of 1884) made a speech against Cleveland on the floor of the convention. It was then that Gen. E. S. Bragg, of Wisconsin and of the "Iron Brigade," made his famous retort: "We love him most for the enemies he has made."

The Cleveland forces were heartened by *The World's* advocacy and by assurance from Daniel Manning and others of Cleveland's strength in New York, and on July 10th he was nominated upon the second ballot, with Thomas A. Hendricks, of Indiana, his leading convention opponent, as his running-mate.

The Anti-Monopoly party convention, on May 14th, and that of the National party, legatee of the Greenbackers, on May 28th, nominated Benjamin F. Butler for President. On June 30th, after Blaine's nomination, *The Sun*, foreseeing the success of Cleveland at Chicago, had announced that it had a candidate, "which his name it is Butler," who could beat Blaine. Really Butler's candidacy was in Blaine's favor, as calculated to draw its support largely from the Democratic ranks.

The Sun's defection was serious. It was a very able paper, nominally Democratic, and had warmly supported Mr. Cleveland in 1882. *The Sun's* powerful opposition, continued throughout the campaign, made *The World* the mainstay of the Cleveland forces in the pivotal state.

But if Democracy had an enemy in Butler, Republicanism with Blaine was pursued by a Nemesis of its own. The Republican platform of New York in 1883 had promised to submit to the people a prohibitory amendment to the state constitution. The promise was broken in the session of 1884, Mr. Roosevelt having introduced as a sop a high-license bill that failed to pass. This evasion caused much ill-feeling among New York Prohibitionists allied with the Republicans, and there was every prospect that the Prohibition candidate, John P. St. John, would get a considerable vote. To make matters worse for Blaine, his own state on September 8th voted upon constitutional prohibition. Maine had had statutory prohibition since 1854, but the friends of the policy wanted it pegged down in the constitution, where it could not be repealed by act of legislature. Mr. Blaine dodged a vote in his home city, and these extracts from *The World* show how quickly his opponents seized upon the fact:

The Republican party of Maine yesterday indorsed by a large majority the proposed amendment to the Constitution which forever prohibits within the State the manufacture or sale of intoxicating liquors—cider excepted. This measure was submitted by a Republican legislature. It was indorsed by the Republican party, and in consideration of this Neal Dow, the great Prohibition apostle, advised his followers to abandon the Prohibition ticket and help Mr. Blaine by electing his State ticket.—*September 9.*

(Blaine's) pretense, made in his jubilee speech after the close of the polls, that the Prohibition question should be kept out of politics, and that for that reason he "decided not to vote at all on the question," is a stupid and shallow fraud. Mr. Blaine was voting as a citizen of Maine, in a State election, on State issues.—*September 10.*

As for Butler, "to believe that he could secure enough votes to insure Blaine's election would be to suppose that the working-men of the country are destitute of brains or that the Democratic party is destitute of honesty." In the result St. John received in New York State 24,999 votes and in the nation 151,809; Butler in New York 16,955 and in the entire country 133,825. In inflicting damage upon the two great parties they were nearly balanced.

A grave issue in the Blaine campaign arose out of the usual methods of corruption.   On August 5th *The World* said:

The fact that the "Stand and Deliver" Committee of the Blaine managers is applying to Government employees at their residences for campaign funds instead of at their offices proves beyond dispute that the political blackmailers are sensible of the illegality of their action.

Larger sums were contributed by financiers from interested motives.   "There is no safety for business or capital," said *The World*, "if the Republican party method of buying elections with money contributed by monopolies is allowed to continue until the wrath of the people rises irresistibly against it."

But the strongest issue with the people was that which had driven so many Independents to revolt—the financial recklessness of Mr. Blaine in former years.   He had been cartooned by *Puck* as "The Tattooed Man" of the Republican Great Moral Show—tattooed with evidence of the carelessness of his conduct while Representative and Speaker—and Republican campaign glee clubs had been driven to the expedient of singing "The Tattooed Man Our President Shall Be."   *The World* unearthed the Blaine-Warren Fisher correspondence.   Unpleasant reading about a candidate for President of the United States was this letter from Fisher to Blaine, written in April, 1872:

I have loaned you at various times, when you were comparatively poor, very large sums of money, and never have you paid me one dollar from your own pocket, either principal or interest.   I have paid sundry amounts to others to whom you were indebted, and these debts you have allowed to stand unpaid like the notes which I hold.   I have placed you in positions whereby you have received very large sums of money without one dollar of expense to you, and you ought not to forget the act on my part.   Of all the parties connected with the Little Rock & Fort Smith Railroad no one has been so fortunate as yourself in obtaining money out of it.

A pitiable chapter in American history is the Blaine campaign. Not without sympathy for a man who possessed so many admirable qualities and who was still to render valuable public service can one read to-day the lashing which *The World* gave Mr. Blaine:

But now comes another batch of telltale letters. In them Blaine, the Speaker of the House of Representatives, the plumed knight, crawls a beggar at the feet of contractors and railroad jobbers. He solicits money from Fisher and Josiah Caldwell. "If you leave this burden on me it will crush me," he cries. He draws unauthorized drafts on Fisher. "As a wholly innocent third party, doing my best to act as a sincere and steadfast friend to both of you," he says, "I ought not to be left exposed to financial ruin and personal humiliation."

"I am in a very painful and embarrassed situation, growing out of my connection with the Fort Smith enterprise," he writes to Fisher; and he prays him for $36,000 land bonds and $9,000 first mortgage "which," he says, he "needs and must have." He continues to dun these railroad speculators for favors, a persistent beggar, until Mr. Fisher is compelled to write to him and tell him practically that he is a dead-beat and can have no more.

It may be wondered how any man of whom such words could be written came so near being elected President. Mr. Blaine had long been the idol of the Republican in the ranks. He made a magnificent personal canvass. He was magnetic. He was able. He was aided by the prestige and power of a party which had behind it six Presidential victories in succession; by a large and compact body of office-holders; by the use of money when money could be used far more effectively than now; by the fact that many Northern men still believed that the country was menaced by "Confederate Brigadiers." It was true, as cynical Republicans said, that "there was one more President in the 'bloody shirt.'"

For, barring accident, Blaine was elected as the campaign closed.

That accident came on October 29th, when a number of clergymen waited upon Mr. Blaine in New York to assure him that the moral sentiment of the city was not shocked by the disclosures concerning him. The Rev. Dr. Tiffany was to have delivered a prepared address. Some of the ministers objected to being represented by Dr. Tiffany, and after a silly wrangle it was suggested that the oldest man present should do the talking. This was Dr. Burchard, of the Murray Hill Presbyterian Church, he who immortalized himself in American politics by saying, "We are Republicans, and don't propose to leave our party and identify ourselves with the party whose antecedents have been Rum, Romanism, and Rebellion."

It is said that Mr. Blaine, quick to catch a political point, started at these words and thought of replying upon the spur of the moment, but quickly concluded that it was wiser to let them pass, hoping that they would do little harm so late in the campaign. *The World* next morning caused him to regret his decision by publishing the remark with caustic comment. "How do the Democrats," it asked, "and especially those of Irish birth and descent who are said to be willing to support Mr. Blaine, relish this picture of the party to which they have adhered for years?" The thrust was effective, for especial efforts had been directed to organizing Irish-American clubs for Blaine. It was claimed in his behalf that if elected he would gratify the Celtic hatred of Albion by "twisting the lion's tail," and the bait had been swallowed. Now the work was all but undone.

Powerful in its crude vigor was a cartoon, entitled "Belshazzar's Feast," which *The World* printed in the height of the Burchard excitement. It portrayed the Republican chiefs in the robes of ancient revelers at the banquet of privilege with Blaine himself in close conference with Jay Gould, Commodore Vanderbilt and others. The newspaper cartoon was then an innovation in New York, and the "feast" caused a well-remembered sensation.

Cleveland won in New York State, which was decisive, by but 1,047 votes. The defection of Roscoe Conkling's Stalwart friends in Oneida County and elsewhere was held responsible for the result. A more cynical view was turned regretfully upon the pocket borough of Supervisor John Y. McKane in Gravesend, now a part of New York City, where some hundreds of votes were notoriously for sale. It was a common remark in Republican circles, "if we had known how close it was going to be we could have bought the McKane vote and won hands down." For some days the claim was made that Blaine was elected. The Democratic girls in Vassar College who paid their bets by giving a feast to the Republican girls upon the election figures of the *Tribune* were not the only ones of their party faith deceived.

Some Democrats, alarmed by the persistency of Republican newspapers in claiming a victory, expressed fears that the Republicans would count in Blaine as they had counted out Tilden. *The World* reminded such pessimists that:

General Grant is not at the head of the Government, with a General Augur in command of United States bayonets in the States to be stolen, and a Don Cameron as Secretary of War. Wells, Packard and Kellogg are not in control of an infamous Returning Board of thieves and forgers in New York, Indiana, or any of the disputed States. Ferry, of Michigan, is not President of the Senate.

For *The World* the election of Cleveland was more than an ordinary political victory. The young venture drew the attention of the country. Its swift leap into prominence and power gratified the public taste for the mar-

velous and the unexpected. Its contemporaries of the
press, trained in the school of partisan politics, assumed
that President Cleveland would look to *The World* as his
personal organ; most of them considered the position
desirable.

Such relationship to the new administration was
promptly disclaimed. "The World," it said, the day after
election, "seeks no favors, patronage or office, and asks
but one thing of President Cleveland. That is to redeem
the promises he made, and which The World made on his
behalf, that he would lead the nation away from corruption and to a restored, a reformed, a regenerated real
republic."

But the theory of organship would not so easily be
refuted. A month after election the *Boston Traveler*,
familiar with the relations between newspaper - offices
and custom-houses, said, "If Governor Cleveland has
an official organ, one authorized to speak for him and
to outline his policy, that organ is the New York
World."

The World replied that it felt complimented by the
credit given it for effecting a needed change in the government. But it did not believe in one-man power or one-
man newspaper organs. "The World," it said, "is chained
to no conqueror's chariot. It will gladly and zealously
support all that is good in President Cleveland's administration. But it would oppose anything that should be
clearly wrong or mistaken. We regard the editorship of
The World as a great public trust, as Mr. Cleveland regards the Presidency."

What powerfully appealed to Mr. Pulitzer's imagination, what he wished to impress upon the country, was the
romance of Mr. Cleveland's swift rise as a result of direct
appeal to the people and trust in them. Thus after the
induction into office of the new President in the following
March he wrote:

Grover Cleveland, who is now President of the United States, was four years ago almost unknown outside the city of Buffalo. He had not yet been elected Mayor of that city. He had never figured in the nation's politics; his reputation, whatever it may have been, was local, and his career uneventful.

He is now the Chief Magistrate of fifty-five millions of people, by their own choice, and it is certain that they selected him without reference to his ambition.

The marvelous rise from obscurity to pre-eminence of such a man has all the interest of a romance. It would be hard to find a parallel to it in history. Four years is a short time in which to make such a prodigious passage, and the romance has its significance, for it shows that, after all, ours is a government of the people and for the people, and the fitness and faithfulness that shall administer the Government aright ought to be one of the proudest results of a nation like ours.

Nearly nineteen years later, writing at Princeton to *The World* **for publication in its twentieth anniversary number, Mr. Cleveland thus testified to its "services to Democracy" in the campaign of 1884:**

I never can lose the vividness of my recollection of the conditions and incidents attending the Presidential campaign of 1884: how thoroughly Republicanism was intrenched; how brilliantly it was led; how arrogant it was; and how confidently it encouraged and aided a contingent of deserters from the Democratic ranks. And I recall not less vividly how brilliantly and sturdily The World then fought for Democracy; and in this the first of its great party fights under present proprietorship it was here, there, and everywhere in the field, showering deadly blows upon the enemy. It was steadfast in zeal and untiring in effort until the battle was won; and it was won against such odds and by so slight a margin as to reasonably lead to the belief that *no contributing aid could have been safely spared. At any rate, the contest was so close it may be said without reservation that if it had lacked the forceful and potent advocacy of Democratic principles at that time by the New York "World" the result might have been reversed.*

Upon the receipt in Hamburg of copies of *The World* **containing this tribute Mr. Pulitzer cabled on May 29th, for publication the following morning:**

Mr. Cleveland has spoken of The World's service to the Democratic party, and particularly of its decisive "advocacy of Democratic principles," upon an occasion critical indeed to him and to the Democracy. Many other distinguished gentlemen have generously, yet mistakenly praised The World's services to the Democratic party.

I say mistakenly because, whatever benefit Mr. Cleveland and the Democratic party received, The World never for one moment during the last twenty years considered itself a party paper. It promised to support truly Democratic principles, truly Democratic ideas, and it has done so, and will do so, with entire independence of bosses, machines, candidates and platforms, following only the dictates of its conscience.

Five years later, upon *The World's* twenty-fifth birthday, May 10, 1908, the idea finds repetition:

What is truly Democratic?
Not party, but country. Not party, but humanity. Not party, but liberty. Not party, but equality. Not party, but equal opportunity. Not party, but equal justice.

IV

1885–1886

*The Statue of Liberty, a New Colossus of Rhodes—How "The World"
Raised the Pedestal—Hill and the Mugwumps—Civil-Service Reformers
Dissatisfied with Cleveland—The Hungry Horde of Office-Seekers—Tariff
Reform Delayed by a Divided Congress—Jake Sharp and the Boodle
Aldermen—The Labor Troubles of 1886—Henry George's Candidacy for
Mayor—Theodore Roosevelt's First Defeat.*

In the last years of his life Joseph Pulitzer built a steam-
yacht in the hope of finding upon a craft especially designed
for him the quiet essential to his shattered health.   He
named it *Liberty*.

The name expressed what had been the chief concern
of his life.   It also recalled one of the most famous of *The
World's* early exploits.

In the early seventies Édouard Laboulaye, of Paris,
proposed that a gigantic statue of Liberty Enlightening the
World be presented by the people of France to the people
of America, to "declare by an imperishable memorial the
friendship that the blood spilled by our fathers sealed
between the two nations."   The French people eagerly
took up the plan.   M. Auguste Bartholdi was commis-
sioned to model the statue.   Our government set aside
space for it upon Bedloe's Island, and in 1877 a committee
was formed to raise funds for the base.   Five years later,
at a mass-meeting called by this committee, November
28, 1882, William M. Evarts said of the statue:

It is so vast and stupendous a work that without comparing it to some well-known object the mind is scarcely able to conceive of it. The statue itself, from its base to the top of the torch, is 145 feet high [151 feet 1 inch as erected; with pedestal, 305 feet 6 inches]. It is but 135 feet from the water-level to the highest point in the span of the Brooklyn Bridge, so that this statue, if placed on the water-level, would overtop the bridge ten feet. It is 40 feet square at the base. The great statue known as the seventh wonder of the world, the Colossus of Rhodes, was erected to show the gratitude of the people of Rhodes for the aid given them by a friendly power in their struggles for liberty. That work cost the poor, feeble Rhodians between $400,000 and $500,000—twice as much as the powerful and wealthy American people are called on to provide for the proper erection of the gift of the French nation.

Neither Mr. Evarts's eloquence nor the labors of the committee gave Liberty a place to set her foot; in April, 1883, when the big figure was almost ready to ship from France and work upon the base was begun, there was not nearly enough money to complete it. This was the situation when Mr. Pulitzer arrived in New York.

The Liberty statue appealed to him with singular force. He had not forgotten how, a poor boy entering Boston harbor as an immigrant, he had looked eagerly for the Land of Promise to rise upon the horizon. He could imagine how immigrant boys of future time would look up at the great figure towering over New York Bay, embodying an idea that all could grasp. He felt not sorrow only, but shame that his adopted country did not respond to its opportunity.

Throughout the first year *The World* made frequent attempts to aid the pedestal fund, but its grasp was not then firm enough to undertake so great a task as raising the money. In 1884 it devoted all its energy to the election of a Democratic President. But in the spring of 1885 no obstacle prevented its return to the project, and upon the 15th of March *The World* engaged to raise through its readers the $100,000 needed. It appealed as a "people's paper" to the people of the United States, reminding them that "The $250,000 that the making of the statue cost was paid in by masses of the French people — by the working - men, the tradesmen, the shop - girls, the artisans — by all, irrespective of class or condition. Let us not wait for the millionaires to give this money," it urged. "It is not a gift from the millionaires of France to the millionaires of America."

The money came slowly for a time; considerably less than one dollar each was the average contribution. But by May 15th enough was in hand so that work was resumed by the committee; in four months the fund was sufficient, and by April 23, 1886, the pedestal stood complete. The *Isere* sailed from France June 18th with the statue, cast in sections, and upon her arrival in New York was thus welcomed by *The World:*

Surely peace has wrought no nobler victory in our generation than this. And if to-day the pageant of reception is made imposing by the war-vessels of two governments they are this time only giving obedient and kindly service to the people who have learned to make governments and have outstripped them in fraternal purpose. And this purpose, if carried out in man's intercourse with Liberty and Light, as it has been carried out in this emblematic labor, will yet make war-vessels unnecessary.

There will be no answering salute from those peaceful bastions where Liberty is to plant her feet. There are no cannon on the parapets that the people have reared. But the mute and mighty Goddess for ages, let us hope, will tell her eloquent mission of sentiment there.

The inauguration ceremonies, after the statue was set up, took place in October, 1886, attended by the President and other American high officials, and by a distinguished delegation from France.

Upon bronze tablets at the sides of the central arch of the pedestal facing the sea are two inscriptions:

A GIFT FROM THE PEOPLE OF THE REPUBLIC OF FRANCE
TO THE PEOPLE OF THE UNITED STATES

and

THIS PEDESTAL WAS BUILT BY VOLUNTARY CONTRIBUTIONS
FROM THE PEOPLE OF THE UNITED STATES OF AMERICA

Another reminder of the raising of Liberty's pedestal faces the reader of *The World* each morning.   In the heading of the paper, slightly changed from that first adopted by Mr. Pulitzer in May, 1883, a vignette sketch of Liberty stands between twin globes representing the Western and Eastern hemispheres.

If the task of the spring was the setting up of the Statue of Liberty, autumn brought fresh labors to broaden liberty in political life.

Political interest in New York in the off-year 1885 centered in the contest for Governor.   David B. Hill, of Elmira, elected in 1882 lieutenant-governor for a three-year term, had succeeded Cleveland upon his promotion to the Presidency, and he was nominated by the Democrats for the full term on September 24th.   In view of later events it may seem odd that *The World* should have hailed his nomination as that of a man "in State politics a disciple of President Cleveland."   But it was true, as the article continued, that Hill was "trained under Mr. Cleveland as his,Lieutenant for two years, while the latter was Governor," and that he had "carried out Mr. Cleveland's policy while acting as his successor."

War was declared upon Hill by the Mugwumps on the ground that he was not a civil-service reformer; they were right enough, as the event proved. *The World*

begged the President to come to his lieutenant's assistance.
It reminded him that he had written "columns in letters
to George William Curtis, Dorman B. Eaton and other
Mugwumps," and asked him to send a "letter of twenty
positive lines" to Mr. Hill expressing sympathy with him
in the abuse he was receiving. Such a letter would be
worth "twenty thousand votes to Mr. Hill and the party
that elected Mr. Cleveland."

Mr. Cleveland heightened the Mugwump wrath by
writing a letter. It was a very practical letter. It was
written to a Democratic friend and inclosed the President's
check for one thousand dollars to aid in Hill's election.
This was neither the political assessment of a helpless
office-holder nor a secret contribution of a large sum by a
buyer of legislative privilege; and it was of great indirect service to Mr. Hill. He was perhaps more served
by the Republicans injecting the bloody-shirt issue into
the campaign, a piece of folly less excusable since the
election of a Democratic President had shown that the
nation could survive a change of parties.

The World warmly supported Mr. Hill. It also took
the ground, familiar since to its readers, that "in local
elections party lines should be set aside where Republican
Judges had made an especially honorable record and
while on the bench had shown no party feeling." And
it renewed the bitter sarcasm it had poured out upon those
who resorted to sectionalism as an argument when others
failed them in their weakness.

The victory was complete all along the line. Judge
Sedgwick, a Republican supported by *The World*, was
elected by Democratic votes. Governor Hill was chosen
Governor by a majority of 11,134—small, but many times
more than that of Mr. Cleveland in New York the previous year. The election was a "rebuke of two things—
the bloody shirt and the bloodless Mugwump."

Pleased as *The World* was at its success in an off-year
4

in New York, its main interest was the course of the Democratic administration then beginning in Washington and the promise it held out of economic reform. In the defense of the new administration *The World* had occasion with a frequency which is now surprising to meet the charge that Democracy meant disunion. "Perhaps," it said upon one of these occasions, "if Mr. [Jefferson] Davis, instead of leading the life of a private citizen, had lent his name, which beyond doubt has a certain influence, to a firm of Wall Street brokers, had made himself friendly with the Goulds, Vanderbilts and Fields, of the moneyed classes, and had voted the Republican ticket, he would have been courted by the politicians who now hold him up as a scarecrow and lash themselves into fury whenever his name is mentioned." A month later we find it rebuking a man of such ability and position that he had little excuse for playing the demagogue:

Mr. Evarts asserts that the success of the Democracy "brings us once more to the position of affairs and complexion of sections as we found them in 1860."

Is this true? Is this honest? Is it worthy of a lawyer of reputation? Or is it a blatant, foolish political lie such as should be uttered only by a low, dishonest political demagogue? We leave the American people to judge.

A life unusually prolonged brought Mr. Evarts to a time when he must have blushed to recall such utterances. In 1885 they were of every-day occurrence.

Discussion of the civil-service-reform situation was more difficult; in fact, it was the chief strategic difficulty confronting the new President.

There was a tendency among Mugwumps to go back to the Republican party, now that it had received its rebuke; and this tendency was strengthened by the impatience of the leaders with what they considered Mr. Cleveland's slowness in advancing their reform. A

practical difficulty beset this undertaking in the horde
of hungry Democrats, famished by twenty-four years of
banishment from Washington, who made a wild lunge
for the offices, waylaid the President day and night, and
would not be denied. If some of these men were not
pacified there was danger of political reaction. As *The
World* said:

President Cleveland's Administration is between two fires.
Some Democrats blame him for not turning Republicans out
of office more rapidly and generally. The Independents fret
and worry because he happens to have appointed a few men
to office who are hard workers in the party and labored to make
his election possible.

Between these contending groups *The World*, far more
interested in the reform of the tariff and the checking of
corruption than in other issues, was for a time not without sympathy for the partisan Democratic attitude. It
found its preference consistent with belief in the merit
system. "For the best interests of good government"
it insisted that "before the bars are put up against re-
movals from office there should be something like equality
of both political parties in the public service," especially
as "the Republicans who are in were put there through
political favor, without regard to their qualifications or
merits, while a great portion of persons now appointed
are subjected to a strict competitive Civil-Service examination." Twenty-eight years later President Wilson was
to take a somewhat similar attitude with regard to
fourth-class Postmasters whom a late order of President
Taft had placed in the classified service, and to order
their examination as a test of fitness to retain office.
There was treachery in the departments; there were
employees who looked to party and not to country as
their employer. It was natural enough, considering the
reasons for their employment and the conditions of their

service. Horatio Seymour said that "no prudent business man would employ a bookkeeper who was working against his interests and praying that he should fail." Mr. Cleveland had something like this in mind when he declared that "offensive partisans" must quit public service. Yet so great was the dissatisfaction among Democratic party workers that *The World* was no doubt right in saying after the 1885 election that "if Mr. Cleveland had been a candidate this year instead of Governor Hill the State would have defeated him most overwhelmingly as a rebuke to his Mugwumpism."

But the spectacle of the chief elected servant of the people compelled to devote his time to sifting the claims of petty politicians for patronage was not to be patiently endured. Casting about for a remedy, *The World* proposed "a straight path through the Constitution to Civil-Service Reform." Let Congress, was its idea, by law "cut off from the President all the inferior appointments, vesting them in different heads of departments." So far as the Independents were concerned it set its face against their recognition upon claims of patronage:

The Independents frankly avowed their position. They were Republicans, but not unscrupulous and dishonest Republicans. They declared for the representative Democratic candidate, not because they intended to join the Democrats or hoped to personally profit by their success, but because they preferred country to party. They chose to elect an honest partisan opponent rather than a dishonest partisan associate. They would rather see the Presidential office Democratic than Disgraced.

Under these circumstances we regard it as unjust to the Independents and harmful to the principles they uphold to agitate the question whether they are to receive recognition or reward in patronage from the Democratic Administration. Unjust to them, because it implies self-interest as the motive of their action. Harmful to the principles they represent,

because it imparts to what we believe was unselfish patriotism
the appearance of prompt political payment.

But by 1887 *The World* became convinced that the
attempt to secure at once proportional representation of
the parties in public employment was impracticable, and
that it was safer to leave to time the redress of remaining
inequalities. It was to this change of view that President
Cleveland referred in a letter written August 17, 1887,
to Silas W. Burt and recently unearthed for publication,
in which he asks: "Did you see how quickly *The World*
and some of the rest of the Democratic spoils papers . . .
became champions of civil-service reform under the inspiration of Mr. [George William] Curtis's speech?" *The
World* had never been a spoils paper; it had not criticized
the merit system; it had not sought to delay its introduc-
tion save to the extent indicated; and it needed no speech
of Mr. Curtis or any one else to shape its course.

Except for this temporary divergence of opinion, which
did not touch the essential merit of reform, *The World's*
support of Mr. Cleveland's policies in his first term was
uniform. When the first calendar year closed upon a
Democratic administration in Washington it asked:

Has not the Government grown stronger in the proof that
the people can elect and inaugurate a President of their own
choice? Has not the declining bitterness of sectionalism drawn
closer those fraternal bonds which bind State to State and make
the Union more perfect than ever? Do not the people feel safer
now against the encroachments of monopolies than they did a
year ago?

The "horizontal-reduction" tariff bill of William R.
Morrison, of Illinois, introduced in 1884, was the chief
proposal for reducing the surplus before the country the
following year. The new Congress assembled in December, 1885; the Senate was still Republican, blocking

action; the House was strongly Democratic, but there was discord within the party.

This element of delay and danger was furnished by the Randall assistant Republican group, with its theory that, to stave off action on the tariff, internal-revenue taxes should be swept away. *The World* had no patience with this plan. The country was collecting nearly one hundred million dollars on distilled spirits and fermented liquors. The people did not "desire to see this tax removed and the tariff increased so as to add to the cost of articles of necessary consumption in the poorest man's family," especially when the object of the manœuver was to "build up to yet grander proportions the profits of monopolies."

To dispose temporarily of the surplus Congress passed a compromise resolution providing that the idle money in the Treasury, above all liabilities of the government, above $100,000,000 reserve for the redemption of the legal tenders, and above $20,000,000 to be held as an emergency reserve, should be used to pay bonds. This the President killed in August, 1886, by a pocket veto. The relief of war taxation was the first necessity.

The World heartily indorsed the veto. It was prompt to demand of Attorney-General Garland, of Mr. Cleveland's otherwise strong Cabinet, that he should resign when it became known that he was interested in the stock of the Pan-Electric Telephone Company, and that the contest on the Bell Telephone patents must come before the Department of Justice for consideration. It supported the Reagan interstate-commerce bill, a precursor of the present act. The vote of 158 to 75, which this measure received in the House, showed that "with a change of administration will come a change of policy toward the abuses and despotism of large corporations, and that in future the interests of monopolies will not be allowed to override the interests of the people."

A running fight that began early in 1885 and lasted until the law's delay removed the danger of punishment for most of the thieves was waged by *The World* in 1886–87 upon the "boodle" aldermen who sold Jake Sharp, a notorious promoter, a franchise for the Broadway surface railway.

How the rails came to be laid in this important street after the merchants opposed to the line had obtained an injunction may be read in *The World's* editorial article "Scoundrelism and Vandalism," in which on May 24, 1885, it scored Justices Brady and Daniels of the Supreme Court for action practically removing the injunction. Sharp was waiting for the decision, and within a few hours "the only grand thoroughfare of the city," as it was oddly described, was being torn up by pick and shovel. Merchants on Broadway now regard the street-railway as a friend. There is no need to soften condemnation of the means by which it was legalized or the stock-jobbery which has been loaded upon the line.

The way for the criminal prosecution of the boodle aldermen was cleared in a manner suggesting opera bouffe. Alderman Jaehne, one of the boodle-takers, combined the occupation of a "fence" for stolen goods with the more lucrative one of selling aldermanic franchises. Caught in the less objectionable of these pursuits by a courageous woman whose silverware had taken wing, Jaehne's craven soul yielded under the hammering to which he was subjected, and he confessed, as *The World* summarized his statement, "that since he has been in the Board of Aldermen every vote he has given in favor of a street-railroad franchise has been bought."

In April, 1886, *The World* was able to announce as a "Triumph of Public Opinion" the indictment of "nearly an entire Board of Aldermen on charges of accepting bribes." This "unprecedented event proves the irresistible power of public opinion. Whatever may follow, the fact that all the members of the infamous Board of 1884, except two who were honest, two who are dead, and three who have saved themselves temporarily by absconding, will be brought to the bar of a criminal court and tried before a jury cannot fail to have a purifying effect."

Of the boodle aldermen some went to jail, some took refuge in Montreal with Moloney, the clerk of the board. One, McQuade, was released in 1888 on a technicality after serving twenty months in prison. Punishment was, upon the whole, a disappointment, but *The World's* urgency helped secure a law providing that franchises should be sold at auction for compensation to the city "instead of, as in the past, buying up a sufficient number of Aldermanic votes to pass the franchise over a possible veto and cheating the city."

The World in these years exposed the stock-watering of the elevated railroad lines to prevent their payment to the city of profits in excess of 10 per cent., as provided in the law authorizing construction. The watering was done through the formation of the Manhattan Company as a holding corporation with fresh capital to lease the New York and Metropolitan companies. Other matters which the newspaper urged as an advocate included the Saturday half-holiday, which it gained and for years protected against efforts at repeal by bankers and others; the opening of the park museums on Sunday, then opposed by influential citizens; and the effort to secure some relaxation of the blue laws to permit of playing games on Sunday. In an effort to show the absurdity of a prohibition which is only now beginning to yield *The World* engaged a baseball park at Sunnyside, New Jersey, and chartered a steamboat to take boys' ball clubs there, only to be defeated by the New Jersey blue law.

The most stirring events of 1886 were its labor troubles. In Chicago hard times and anarchistic agitation led to the tragedy of the Haymarket, in which seven policemen were killed and eighty-three persons injured by bombs thrown during an open-air meeting. In New York there were bitterly contested street-car strikes. Impossible for any one with a heart not made of stone not to sympathize with men who were toiling sixteen hours a day while a bought vote in the Board of Aldermen could add two million dollars to the value of the Broadway and Seventh Avenue Railroad franchise; the contrast was too disheartening. But *The World's* sympathy did not lead it to condone disorder. It warned the labor-unions that they would act wisely if they should instruct members that their first duty was to obey the laws.

Out of the labor agitation of the year grew an event that will be remembered—the nomination of Henry George, author of *Progress and Poverty*, for Mayor of New York. *The World* was practically alone in the local journalistic field in treating Mr. George's candidacy with the respect which his ability and honesty, and the just grievances of many who followed him, demanded. "If the working-man's party," it said on August 29th, "is to take a separate political existence and to name its own candidates for office, as the Prohibition party has done, it could not make a better selection for Mayor than Mr. George." Discussing the candidacy on September 26th, it said: "Mr. George's theories will neither make him a bad officer nor a good one." He "would be an experiment, and this, we believe, is the most valid argument that can be brought against him. His philosophy, so long as it does not conflict with the official oath to execute the laws, is immaterial."

"What the George Movement Means" is treated more at length on October 7th:

The George movement is a protest—a deep, disgusted protest, not wholly free from anger—against the evils, abuses and corruptions that are rooted in our politics and bearing fruit in our government. These evils and abuses do not need to be described. They are seen and felt by all who note the condition of public affairs in this city.

For more than twenty-five years the people have sought to secure honest and efficient local government, a decent respect for law, and a proper regard for popular rights through the instrumentality of political parties and of so-called "Citizens'" movements. They have for the most part failed. The long record of Bossing and Stealing, broken only by occasional spasms of virtuous indignation, ends for the present with a city government honeycombed with frauds — with Aldermen in prison, fugitives from justice or awaiting indictment; with a debt of near $100,000,000 and a yearly budget of $33,000,000; and with a management of municipal affairs that has become proverbial for extravagance, jobbery and inefficiency.

While *The World* considered the George theory of land taxation "visionary and harmful," it refused to be stampeded into panic. Abram S. Hewitt was nominated by a combination of the Democratic "halls" to meet the storm, and *The World* gave him its support. The Republican nominee for Mayor was a young man of twenty-eight years beginning to be well known in the city. *The World*, in terms rather amusing, considering Mr. Roosevelt's subsequent course upon the tariff, discussed "Still Another Free-Trader":

The Republican City Convention last night nominated for Mayor the candidate of the Committee of One Hundred, Mr. Theodore Roosevelt. The nominee is a young man of wealth who has had very little business experience, but who is something of a reformer, a very good lecturer and a first-class bear-hunter. . . .

The most distressing thing is that, upon the theory of the Republicans that every man who favors an abatement of the surplus-producing war tariff is a Free-Trader, Mr. Roosevelt will not be able to command the support of the organs that are clamoring for the "American I-dee" in our local politics.

If *The World* had been gifted with prophetic vision it might have added that a greater menace than Henry George had been selected by the Republicans, to turn upon them years afterward.

Mr. George's candidacy threw many men of property into hysteria. Republican votes were swung to Hewitt in such numbers that Mr. Roosevelt received but two-thirds of Blaine's strength in 1884, and little more than three-fourths of the vote cast for the Republican candidate for the Court of Appeals on the same day. The figures as later canvassed were: Hewitt, 90,552; George, 68,110; Roosevelt, 60,435.

It has been persistently held that Henry George was robbed of office; that with a fair election he would have been the Mayor, not Hewitt. Though the disparity of the Hewitt and the George votes as counted seems to forbid such a supposition, the Democratic bosses were united for Hewitt, the Republican bosses were satisfied to see him elected and only desired to keep their machine regular; and the possibilities for crooked work, in the absence of a secret ballot and of safeguards at the counting, were such as do not now exist.

More helpful at the time, more applicable to political conditions for the future, were *The World's* comments upon Mr. George's vote the day after election:

The deep-voiced protest conveyed in the 67,000 votes for Henry George against the combined power of both political parties, of Wall Street and the business interests, and of the public press should prove a warning to the community to heed the demands of labor so far as they are just and reasonable —and that is much further than the majority of citizens have thus far been willing to admit. . . . It is plutocracy that makes socialism. To remove the effect abate the cause.

V

Mr. Pulitzer's Great Misfortune—How a Blind Man Edited a Paper for Twenty-five Years — His Methods of Work — Friendship for Roscoe Conkling—Presentation of the Gladstone Memorial—The Pacific Railroad Frauds — Off-year Election of 1887 and Cleveland's Tariff Message — Harrison's Nomination and Election — The Murchison Letter and the Campaign—The "Great Question" of War Taxation Left Unsettled.

To make *The World* a journal of public opinion its founder had four years of comparative health. Thenceforth he worked under difficulties that to a less ardent soul would have seemed insuperable.

Mr. Pulitzer had always toiled at high pressure for long hours with few intermissions for rest. In 1887 nervous prostration took him from *The World* office, and he was never able to resume desk-work. He was but forty years old. Success in his chosen field was won. He was still in the full tide of physical strength, tall, slender, athletic, a fine horseman, a strong swimmer, passionately fond of travel and of cultured society; and he was physically a broken man. His nervous organization had failed him. His eyesight, never of the best, he was losing altogether. From this time he could never read, though the loss of sight was not so absolute as to prevent him from vaguely distinguishing objects or telling light from darkness.

Gradually out of the chaos of his plans and the bitterness of his despair he evolved the methods that enabled him, wherever he might be, to keep his hand upon the great machine he had set in motion.   In the article upon "Mr. Pulitzer's Journalism," printed two days after his death, a hint is given of what these methods were:

His chief concern centered in the editorial page as the expression of the paper's conscience, courage and convictions.   To that he devoted infinite care and attention.   Sick or well, it was never wholly absent from his thoughts.   When he was well he had it read to him every day, and expressed his opinion about every editorial article—the style in which it was written, the manner in which the thought was expressed, whether the editorial was strong or weak, whether it served any useful public purpose, whether it said the thing that a great newspaper ought to have said.

When ill health made it impossible for him to have the editorial page read every day he would keep the files for weeks, and then, when his condition permitted, he would go over them with painstaking care, always from the point of view of a detached critic, seeking only to determine whether the page was taking the fullest advantage of its opportunities for public service and whether it was measuring up to the high standard that he had set for it.

Nothing was ever allowed to interfere with its independence and its freedom of expression.   There were certain questions about which he became convinced that, in spite of all his efforts, he was possibly prejudiced.   In these matters he exacted a pledge that no suggestions or instructions, or even commands, from him would ever be followed, but that the paper would always say what an independent, untrammeled newspaper ought to say in performing its duties to the people.

Much has been said about Mr. Pulitzer's marvelous news sense.   There was nothing weird or miraculous about it; it was born of an insatiable thirst for information and a restless curiosity about everything of human interest.   He wanted to know.   What?   When?   Where?   How?   He took it for granted that hundreds of thousands of other people wanted to know.

It has been remarked that Mr. Pulitzer's blindness made him a greater man by concentrating his thought.

Concentration, at any rate, was the word that best described his methods of working. Presiding at the quarter-century celebration of *The World* in 1908, Ralph Pulitzer said:

I have in my mind's eye the picture, seen many and many a time, of a man in the throes of sightlessness and suffering, insisting on a paragraph or phrase, just dictated, being read and reread to him over and over again, listening with painful attention to catch and correct any slightest suspicion of misstatement in a fact, any slightest shade of overemphasis in an adjective, any possibility of conveying an impression that was not altogether accurate and scrupulously just.

It was natural that a man forty years old, stricken not quite blind, and suffering mainly from nervous troubles should at first have spent his energies in seeking recovery for normal activities, not in developing ingenious methods for doing his life-work under handicap. Yet in the darkest hours when Mr. Pulitzer was seeking vainly to restore his fading sight and ruined health he never failed to feel the pressure of public questions.

The death of Roscoe Conkling, a sequel of the great blizzard of March 12, 1888, was a personal shock to Mr. Pulitzer in his illness. He admired Conkling for his ability and integrity, and employed him as counsel. In two senatorial elections *The World* had urged Conkling's name upon the Republicans. When Elbridge G. Lapham's term was about to expire it pointed out that "Blaine's overthrow and the destruction of his forces, which could only be held together by plunder, make Roscoe Conkling more a Republican than ever, for he becomes a necessity to the reconstruction of the party and its continued existence." Because Lapham's successor must be a Republican *The World* advised Democrats in the Legislature to unite with a few Republicans "to elect an able and honest Republican." Lapham's successor was William M.

Evarts, whose selection "stamps the Republican party of New York again with Blaine's seal. The hand of Blaine is apparent in the result. . . . Nevertheless, the defeat of the Golden Calf, [Levi P.] Morton, is a great advantage."

Again in 1887 *The World* pressed Conkling upon the attention of the Stalwart Republicans and the Democratic minority. But the Democrats in Albany had not been educated to disregard partisan consistency for public advantage. Nor was the breach between Stalwarts and Half-breeds to be healed by the advancement of either of the leaders of faction. Conkling never forgave Mr. Blaine, the man who in a speech in Congress had compared him with Henry Winter Davis as "Hyperion to a satyr, Thersites to Hercules, mud to marble, dunghill to diamond, a singed cat to a Bengal tiger, a whining puppy to a roaring lion"; who had spoken of "his haughty disdain, his grandiloquent swell, his majestic, supereminent, overpowering, turkey - gobbler strut." Nor was Blaine more ready than Conkling to forgive and forget, though perhaps more inclined to a formal truce.

The World had not long left doubt in the minds of its readers whether it would assail Democratic less vigorously than Republican misconduct. The antics of Tammany in the 1887 Legislature gave opportunity to show its independence. Its members cast a solid vote in favor of the repeal of the Civil Service Reform Act, and opposed higher license fees for liquor-sellers. "The people of this State," said *The World*, "do not want the Civil Service Act repealed. They do want to see diminish the number of places where liquor is sold." Opposed to prohibition and to oppressive Sunday laws as assaults upon personal liberty, it has held to the position of those early years upon higher license. "There are too many dram-shops," was its theory. "The license law is disregarded in a most demoralizing manner. Society has a right to a more adequate reimbursement for the expenses of crime and pauperism caused by the traffic." The Saxton license bill, finally passed by the Legislature under its urging, was a precursor of the present Raines law. It was vetoed by Governor Hill on the ground, which did not satisfy *The World*, that its revenues were to be applied to localities where they did not originate.

In 1886 *The World*, because of its success with the Statue of Liberty pedestal, had been asked to raise a fund in the United States to aid Home Rule in the British parliamentary campaign, and did so. In 1887 a similar fund was provided through its urgings for a memorial to Mr. Gladstone from political friends in America, and on July 9th, at Dollis Hall, his suburban residence near London, the memorial was presented.

Said Mr. Pulitzer upon that occasion:

Mr. Gladstone, 10,689 people of the first city of America ask the first citizen of England to accept this gift. They ask you to accept it as an offering of their sincerest sympathy. They ask you to accept it as a token of their personal admiration. They ask you to accept it as a tribute to your great public services in the cause of civil and religious freedom. They ask you to accept it for your determination that the principles of liberty and justice, which have made England so free and great, shall no longer be denied to Ireland. They ask you to accept it as an evidence that there is an irrepressible sympathy between the liberty-loving masses which is more sincere than that of rulers. They especially ask you to accept it because in your great struggle for Home Rule and humanity for Ireland you represent essentially those American principles of representation, legislation, and political equality by which the greatness of their own country and their own well-being were made possible. . . . Americans know what England has done for liberty and civilization to all mankind. They know how your people have sympathized with every struggle against tyranny in Europe—in Greece as well as in Italy, in Poland as well as in Hungary. . . . They see in their own country forty - six different States and territorial legislatures, besides their federal Congress; they see in Germany twenty-six different legislatures, besides the imperial parliament; they see in Austria-Hungary eighteen state legislatures, besides two general parliaments; they see separate legislatures in Norway and Sweden; they see a council-general in eighty-seven departments of France; they see even in conquered Alsace-Lorraine a legislative provincial committee; they see, besides the Dominion Parliament, seven separate and distinct legislatures in Canada and eight in Australia.

Why, then, refuse a parliament to Ireland? Passions and resentments may suggest an answer; peace and patriotism cannot.

Mr. Gladstone in his reply said that some of his countrymen expressed jealousy of American interference in English affairs. If he was to consider the interference of one nation by the expression of opinion on the affairs of another unjustifiable and intolerable, that sentence would fall heavily upon England, because she had been interfering with everybody's concern throughout the world, instructing countries what they ought to do and how to do it.

Triumph attended in 1887 *The World's* efforts to secure from Congress an official investigation of the relations of the United States government to the land-grant Pacific railways. For two years it had been urging this step, not wholly because the country had been cheated out of an immense sum, but also because the pressure of corrupt interests put a stain upon Congress. Finally in March, 1887, it was able to say that the resolution was in the hands of the President and would be signed. The necessity for inquiry is revealed in comments upon the disclosures later made:

Mr. Huntington now admits, under oath, the expenditure of over $6,000,000 by his company between 1874 and 1885 (with one year missing) for "legal" and "miscellaneous purposes."

5

He says that Franchott, his first agent at Washington, was paid $20,000 a year for his own services in "explaining things" to public servants, and may have been given as high as $30,000 or $40,000 a year, for which no vouchers were asked or given.—*April 29, 1887.*

"I had no idea of corrupting members of Congress or having a penny expended in any other than a lawful way," said C. P. Huntington to an interviewer yesterday. . . . Yet on March 7, 1877, he wrote to "friend Colton": "I stayed in Washington two days to fix up Railroad Committee of Senate." On October 30th of the same year: "I think the Railroad Committee is right, but the Committee on Territories I do not like. A different one was promised me." On January 17, 1873: "It costs money to fix things, so I knew that his [Scott's] bill would not pass. I believe that with $200,000 I can pass our bill, but I take it it is not worth that much to us." And these are some of the words from which Mr. Huntington says "none but an evil mind could extract wrong."—*August 23, 1887.*

It may refresh some memories to recall from the report of this commission of inquiry that the government loaned the Pacific railroads $64,623,512, which, with interest, grew to over $125,000,000 in 1895; that the companies undertook to issue only paid-up stock; that, nevertheless, the stock actually paid for was less than $2,000,000, while the stock sworn to was more than $97,000,000; that the companies issued $172,000,000 of fictitious capital, dissipated more than $107,000,000 which should have been paid to the government, and charged traffic $8,000,000 a year more than would have been necessary to pay a fair profit upon an honest construction price.

The World was not engaged in digging up Pacific railway scandals merely for the sake of setting unpleasant reading before the people. Out of the Huntington sensation it fashioned a club to beat Congress into passing the interstate-commerce law of 1887, the first great act in a line of reform transportation statutes. The force of its presentation of the case for regulation may be shown in an example:

A QUESTION

The Interstate-Commerce bill is opposed by Jay Gould;
> By C. P. Huntington;
> By the Western cattle rings;
> By Philip D. Armour;
> By stock jobbers, large and small;
> By corporations generally;
> By Leland Stanford, the millionaire and corporation Senator.

It is favored by
> The Western farmers;
> The Eastern merchants;
> The boards of trade and transportation;
> Anti-monopolists in general;
> The people.

Ought the Interstate-Commerce bill to become a law or to suffer defeat?

The World's support of Cleveland was varied by admonition, as when, in June, 1887, he did a generous thing at a wrong time by ordering the return of Confederate battle-flags, an order afterward withdrawn. This was a mistake, *The World* bluntly said:

The order was made to include the Union as well as Confederate flags; but the Northern regiments, for the most part, brought their flags home or have since had them returned from Washington. So that the real significance of the action was in the return to Southern States of flags captured in a war for the preservation of the Union.

What better could be done with them? might now be asked. But that question did not sound in 1887 as to-day it might. *The World*, having at heart the greater participation of the Southern soldier in the political life of the nation, held that the flags would better remain "in the keeping of a government that now represents a restored Union of loyal States, rather than be held as symbols of a lost cause in communities that have no lack of mementos."

But the great controversy of 1887 was on public taxation.

After the election of 1886 the Democrats still held the House by a narrow majority of but fifteen votes, while the Republican margin in the Senate was reduced to two. This situation blocked tariff legislation during the remainder of Cleveland's first term. The Republicans, with aid from Randall Democrats, passed an extravagant Dependent Pension bill and River and Harbor bill chiefly to dispose of the surplus and make revenue reduction seem less necessary. With a similar purpose Mr. Randall renewed the proposal to remove the remaining taxes on liquors and tobacco. *The World* supported Cleveland in vetoing the Pension and River and Harbor bills while the surplus continued to pile up.

The off-year elections of 1887, though they could neither alter the complexion of Congress nor give hope of immediate tariff reform, did encourage President Cleveland by their evidence of the strength of Democratic sentiment to send to Congress on December 6th the admirable message which, *The World* said, gave the party "what it has long lacked—an issue and a leader. The issue is tax reform. The leader is the President." The result of the election in the President's own state *The World* had summarized as settling three things:

President Cleveland will be renominated by his party.
Mr. Blaine will not be renominated by the Republicans.
Mr. George will not control the election next year.
New York is the pivotal State. Mr. Cleveland's friends have had a complete triumph. They are entitled to the fruits of the victory. Grover Cleveland is indeed a lucky man; and James G. Blaine may be said to be a dead cock in the pit.

With the issuance of the tariff-reform message *The World* swung wide into the current of the great issue. Three days after the message appeared it thus swept aside discussion of schedules and rates with the question "In a Nutshell." It tells us all we need know of that almost forgotten fight:

Facts:

1. Surplus taxation for the current fiscal year, $113,000,000.

2. The Treasury glutted at the close of the current fiscal year with $140,000,000 taken from private enterprise and stored in public vaults.

3. John Sherman's blundering funding of the public debt forbids bonds to be called or paid, except with his own premium to the bondholder, until 1891, when $230,544,600 become due and payable at their face; and 1907, when $732,440,850 become due and payable at their face.

Proposals:

1. The Democratic policy: Off with the needless taxes on clothing, fuel, shelter, food. Let alone the taxes on whisky, beer, tobacco.

2. The Republican policy: Off with the taxes on whisky, beer, tobacco, so as to keep the war taxes on clothing, fuel, shelter, food.

The tariff measure which Democracy proposed was known as the Mills bill, from Roger Q. Mills, of Texas, chairman of the Ways and Means Committee. As *The World* summarized it, it proposed to "cut off, in round numbers, $78,000,000 of the surplus revenue. Of this amount $54,000,000 is taken from the tariff and $24,000,000 from internal taxes on tobacco. It adds to the free list flax, hemp, jute, salt, tin plate, wool, and a few other articles. The present average rate of the tariff on dutiable goods is 47.10 per cent. The Mills bill would leave it at 40 per cent. The present average rate on articles affected by the bill is 54.16 per cent. The proposed rate would leave it on these articles at 33.36 per cent."

A long, long way from being a "free-trade measure" was the one thus described. Clay's tariff was but 20 per cent.

Public revolt against the tariff had not risen to the height it reached in 1892, after the passage of the McKinley bill, but it was unmistakable. Senator Aldrich said that revenue ought to be cut by $100,000,000. Senator Allison, returning from a trip home to Iowa, reported that "the party which fails to do its share in reducing the tariff taxes will lose in public favor." Yet so wild a proposal as the division of the surplus among the states instead of reducing taxation found favor with John Sherman, Ohio's Presidential candidate, as it had earlier found favor with James G. Blaine, the beaten candidate of 1884.

The issue was made. The selection of candidates remained. · Upon the Democratic side Mr. Cleveland's candidacy was a matter of course. For the Republican nomination there was rivalry. Mr. Blaine, who since 1884 had been in poor health, wrote on January 25th from Florence, Italy, to B. F. Jones, steel manufacturer in Pittsburg and chairman of the Republican National Committee, that his name would not be presented to the convention. His friends continued to urge him with such effect that on May 22d George William Curtis said in a *World* interview that he was "probably the most popular man in the United States." No parallel to the devotion he inspired had been seen in American politics since "Harry of the West."

Yet he was out of the question. "The Republican nomination," *The World* said, on May 31st, "will go to a second-class, not to a first-class man. . . . It will be a Western candidate." The nomination of Benjamin Harrison it thus greeted:

It will be said of Mr. Harrison that he is nominated for his name; that if his grandfather had not been President of the

United States, and his great-grandfather a signer of the Declaration of Independence, he would not have been the candidate. But this is idle talk. . . . He is a prominent citizen of a doubtful State, and he had the support of its delegates, all but unanimously. He has a good soldier record, having gone into the war a Second Lieutenant of volunteers, and having come out of it a brevet Brigadier-General. He is a thoroughly equipped lawyer, and he has experience as a statesman. . . . Moreover, he has always been a practical civil-service reformer and an extreme protectionist.

It is singular how little the argument for tariff reduction has changed in twenty years. How *The World* fought for lower taxes may be briefly shown by citations from its editorial columns as applicable now as the day they were penned:

A Few Definitions

Taxation for surplus is robbery.
A tariff for bounties is robbery.
A tariff is a tax.
"Definition is argument."—*August 27th.*

Republican Paradoxes

That "there is no surplus," but that it was not safe to adjourn Congress until a bill had been reported in the Senate to cut down the taxes $75,000,000. . . .

That America is the greatest, freest, and most prosperous country under the sun, . . . but that without a Chinese-wall tariff America will be at the mercy of a little, crowded island three thousand miles off, which is dependent upon outsiders for food.

That the effect of the tariff is to lower prices, but that without the higher prices which the tariff enables the manufacturer to charge he could not pay higher wages to his working-men.

That prices are as low here as in Europe, but that we should be undersold but for a 47-per-cent. tariff.

That the tariff is not a tax, but that if it is reduced there will be no money for pensions.

That the tariff is a tax, but that "the foreigner pays it."—
October 26th.

The campaign was far different from that of 1884.
The Democrats, entrenched in the White House and the
departments, but blocked by a divided Congress from
accomplishing needed legislation, had the appearance of
power without the substance. Conkling was dead.
Blaine spoke for Harrison, in whose Cabinet he was to
be Secretary of State. Four years had softened the
memory of Republican corruption. Republican civil-
service reformers, satisfied with Harrison's attitude,
had little excuse for leaving their party. David B. Hill's
Democratic state convention in New York, by trying to
dodge the tariff issue, had not bettered Cleveland's
chances. The Republicans did not this time neglect
John Y. McKane, whose pocket vote had alone been
enough to elect Cleveland in 1884. Nor was Mr. Cleveland, his luck for once failing him, to escape his Burchard.
This thankless part was played by the British Minister
in Washington, Sir Lionel Sackville-West, to whom a decoy
letter had been written from California signed "Murchison," affecting to ask advice how former British subjects who
had become American citizens should vote. Falling into
the trap, the minister replied in favor of Mr. Cleveland,
and the publication of the letter threw many voters into
a rage recalling that of four years before, but impelling
them now in the contrary direction. Mr. Cleveland was
obliged to ask for Sackville-West's recall, and he went
from the country a disgusted man.
Of what use was it for *The World* to oppose common
sense to jingoism? Manfully it set at the task. Sackville-West had said in the Murchison letter that the
Democratic party was "still desirous of maintaining
friendly relations with Great Britain." "What party
isn't?" *The World* asked. "Is the Republican party in

favor of war?   If so, it is at least prudent in withholding its declaration until a Democratic Administration can restore the Navy, which the Republican régime permitted to go to decay."

It was good defensive campaigning, but a poor substitute for the smashing blows that had laid Blaine low. Cleveland was beaten in New York by thirteen thousand votes and in the electoral college by sixty-five; yet he had a popular plurality of ninety-eight thousand.   Eleven months had not been long enough to break the protective-tariff superstition.   But the President at least "gave to his party an issue worthy of such a contest.   He lifted the plane of national politics from a petty strife for spoils to a noble contest for principle.   He buried beyond resurrection the dead issues of the past and brought both parties face to face with a living question of the present."

With confidence *The World* faced the future:

The war taxes will be reduced.   The surplus will be stopped. The tariff that enriches the few at the expense of the many will be reformed.   President Cleveland and his party can afford to wait for the vindication of their position in this contest.

Thousands of children born since this was written cast in 1912 their first votes for President, and the "great question" was not yet "settled right."   The tax that "enriches the few at the expense of the many" was still to be lightened upon the shoulders of the people.

VI

1889–1890

Blaine a Great Figure in the Harrison Administration—A "Forward" Policy in Samoa and Hawaii—The Mafia Murders in New Orleans— Mr. Pulitzer's Wiesbaden Despatch — Tammany Returns to Power in New York—A Century of Protection Closing in Gloom—McKinley Bill Stirs Republicans to Revolt—The Débâcle of 1890—The Silver Question Begins to Trouble Democracy.

AFTER the return of the Republican party to power in 1889 the chief political figure in the United States was James G. Blaine.

Beaten candidate for the Presidency, invalid and disheartened, a fatalist in his belief that the stars in their courses fought against his supreme ambition as they had fought against Henry Clay's, Blaine rose by sheer intellect to greater heights of political power and popular favor than he had yet scaled.

Leaving the White House, Grover Cleveland entered upon the practice of the law in New York. Mr. Blaine, by the understanding that secured for Harrison his aid in the campaign, became Secretary of State.

Upon the announcement of this honor for its great antagonist *The World* commented that it was "perhaps inevitable," but that "unless travel and reflection have modified Mr. Blaine's ideas of a foreign policy, and experience and disappointment have chastened his spirit, President Harrison will have reason to regret and the country to deplore this selection." There followed one of the most stormy periods in the conduct of its foreign affairs which the country had known. But Blaine won praise from his severest critics by his clear view of domestic issues when most of the leaders of his party went astray.

The long-drawn-out Samoan troubles, with which "the Monroe doctrine has no more to do than with Cyprus," first brought *The World* into conflict with the Blaine foreign policies, not far different from those of present-day Imperialists. Our participation in the Samoan government would now be well forgotten, along with the crisis that led to it, if that stirring story of tribal war and the plots and counterplots of consuls and beach-combers in an island earthly paradise had not been illumined by the genius of Robert Louis Stevenson.

The World opposed "the absurdity and wrong of American participation in any such business." "The sole question," it said, when the Samoan treaty was announced on January 20, 1890, "is whether or not the United States is prepared to enter into a partnership with Great Britain and Germany in the business of seizing and governing the Pacific islands through the agency of a titular sovereign. And every tradition and principle of the Government is against this preposterous and entangling alliance."

Another forerunner of Pacific imperialism came when in December, 1889, President Harrison suggested that Congress should invite Hawaii to send delegates to Secretary Blaine's Pan-American conference. "May it be," asked *The World*, "that Hawaii is the country which Mr. Blaine has found on the bargain-counter in his shopping-tour for territory?" Its suspicion that the administration contemplated the annexation of the Sandwich Islands proved correct.

Another issue in which *The World* criticized Mr. Blaine at first, though it later softened its asperity, was the fur-seal controversy with Great Britain. Blaine appeared to lay claim to a *mare clausum* bringing under exclusive American control the whole Pribylov archipelago. Later he proved willing to arbitrate the question. *The World* heartily supported all movements that furthered arbitration. Its comment upon the final treaty to settle the sealing dispute, November 12, 1891, was a promise of greater services to peace:

Arbitration is civilization's substitute for the brutality of war.

Arguments cost less than ammunition. Reasoning comes cheaper than throat-cutting.

Justice is all that any civilized nation really wants in any dispute, and justice is much more likely to be the outcome of arbitration than of armed conflict.

In agreeing to submit the Behring Sea question to arbitration the governments of Great Britain and the United States have made their bow to the enlightened sentiment of the people of both countries.

This is civilization. This is progress.

When in March, 1891, the people of New Orleans, exasperated by a number of Mafia murders, lynched several Italian subjects Mr. Blaine did not delay his acknowledgment of the responsibility of the United States to the government and the families of the dead men. Premier Rudini in Rome used the outbreak for political effect, and when Blaine explained what Rudini well knew, that our federal government could not compel a Louisiana jury to convict the slayers of the Italians, Rudini sought to coax European statesmen to join in a declaration that the United States ought to manage its affairs better. *The World* found in Blaine's skilful final reply to Rudini proof that "the 'diplomatic incident' had its origin mainly in the necessities of Italian home politics." Rudini's ministry fell only three weeks after the payment of twenty-five thousand dollars for the families of the slain Italians.

Again in the recognition of the republic of Brazil was Blaine in his element; here *The World* was his hearty sympathizer in congratulating the continent that "no king mocks manhood with the flummery of a court" within its confines.

But Mr. Blaine's wisdom in domestic affairs far outshone his brilliant provocative foreign adventures. He was against the policy of his party in urging the Force bill. He was against its folly in the McKinley tariff. Out of the wreck of Republican hopes in 1890 he alone emerged with prestige enhanced.

The Federal Elections or Force bill was an attempt of the Republican junta to put, in the words of Senator Frye, of Maine, "a bayonet behind every ballot." It was an attempt to restore in the awakening South the conditions which had made carpet-baggism almost a greater curse than the war; to turn over its government to ignorance, spoliation, waste, and greed. Designing men in the North were not above cynically using the negro problem as a means of perpetuating the power to tax the people through the tariff; but there was unquestionably a large body of honest men who felt that the newly enfranchised slave needed the protection of the ballot, and his ballot the protection of the federal government. *The World* reminded Republicans how in 1884 their National Committee had issued from Nashville an "Address to the People of the South," and how they had appealed "with earnest good faith and in the spirit of American fraternity to the intelligence, enterprise, honorable ambitions and American instincts and aspirations of the Southern people." Republican "earnest good faith" was now shown in a measure to put Southern elections for representatives under control of federal agents, creating a power such as "should not be bestowed upon any administration or any party."

Mr. Blaine had been as ready as his party associates

to flaunt the "bloody shirt" in previous years. His common sense now rejected the Force bill, and his hostility and the opposition or luke-warm approval of his followers so delayed its passage that repeal by a Democratic Congress followed before much harm was done.

While these stirring events were going forward in national politics *The World*, now firmly established, planned for its future home a noble building. The beginning of this structure, at first but half its present size, drew from Mr. Pulitzer, then upon a sickbed in Wiesbaden, this message of aspiration, read at the laying of the corner-stone, October 10, 1889:

God grant that this structure be the enduring home of a newspaper forever unsatisfied with merely printing news—forever fighting every form of wrong—forever independent—forever advancing in enlightenment and progress—forever wedded to truly democratic ideas—forever aspiring to be a moral force—forever rising to a higher plane of perfection as a public institution.

God grant that The World may forever strive toward the highest ideals—be both a daily schoolhouse and a daily forum, both a daily teacher and a daily tribune, an instrument of justice, a terror to crime, an aid to education, an exponent of true Americanism.

Let it ever be remembered that this edifice owes its existence to the public; that its architect is popular favor; that its corner-stone is liberty and justice; that its every stone comes from the people and represents public approval for public services rendered.

God forbid that the vast army following the standard of The World should in this or in future generations ever find it faithless to those ideas and moral principles to which alone it owes its life, and without which I would rather have it perish.

In the spirit of this message *The World* in these years interested itself in many matters but remotely connected with politics. It led the movement for the wider in-

struction of the people in evening courses which has resulted in the great free-lecture system. It urged the
appointment of women upon school boards and as police
matrons. It continued to advocate a high-license bill.
It pushed ballot reform to success against obstacles raised
by the bosses of both parties. In this work great aid was
rendered by the Knights of Labor and similar organizations. Perhaps some day a monograph will be written
upon the public services of American labor-unions in
urging political reforms.

A great injustice which *The World* denounced was the
persistent refusal of the New York Republicans to call a
constitutional convention and their neglect to take a
census of the state as by law directed. By these means
they continued to carry the state Senate and to hold or
tie the Legislature, even with a Democratic Governor and
a heavy Democratic popular plurality.

The World continued its running fight to compel the
opening of the Metropolitan and other city museums on
Sundays. In a campaign to bring the Columbian Expo-
sition to New York instead of Chicago it was beaten, in
part because of Senator Platt's unwillingness that local
advantage should come to Tammany Hall, in part because New York business men were not overanxious to
provide money.

The influence of Platt was manifested to the city's
disadvantage in many ways. It long blocked the consolidation of Greater New York. It delayed rapid transit;
finally, in 1891, the first Rapid Transit Commission was
constituted by a deal that kept the appointment of the
commissioners out of the hands of city authorities.
Nor would it have been possible to make such use of the
fear of Tammany had it not been a name repugnant to the
country as a synonym of misgovernment.

That Tammany had again secured a firm foothold was
partly *The World's* fault. Mr. Hewitt, elected in 1886,

though a man of ability and integrity, had failed as Mayor, as perhaps any man was bound to fail with such a mingled crew of tax-eaters behind him. Hence in 1888 *The World* opposed his re-election. Fortune provided Tammany in Hugh J. Grant with a candidate who had easily won a reputation. He had simply been one of the two men in the boodle Board of Aldermen who were demonstrably honest. *The World* supported him for Mayor and opposed the Tammany candidate for district attorney, John R. Fellows, with the justified presentiment that he would waste little energy in pursuing political thieves. Grant and Fellows were elected.

As the Congressional elections of 1890 drew near it became apparent that the administration party had committed its worst blunder since reconstruction in the passage of the McKinley tariff bill.

The country had been warned that some such measure might follow Republican success. The Republican platform of 1888 had upheld high protection even to declaring that the party would make such revisions as would "tend to check imports" and thus reduce income, and would repeal all internal-revenue taxes, including those on whisky and tobacco, rather than "surrender any part of our protective system."

The McKinley bill did not proceed to this extreme. But it did remove the tariff on sugar and substitute a bounty of two cents a pound. By this measure the Republicans demonstrated that the tariff is a tax, paid by the consumer, and turned the surplus into a deficit, with some aid from extravagant expenditures in the Pension Office and elsewhere.

To soften public anger at the McKinley bill, which he denounced as failing to open a market abroad for one bushel of American wheat or one pound of American pork, Mr. Blaine sought to inject into the measure during discussion provisions for reciprocity treaties with nations willing to frame preferential tariffs. President Harrison was less ardent in admiration of a bill which was to provide him with a rival and a successor than were the high-tariff men, intent upon the privileges they had paid for with campaign contributions. He became convinced that Blaine was right and added his persuasions. In the end the reciprocity provisions were accepted.

Blaine reciprocity never lowered the cost of living or forced a market abroad for any considerable American product. In accepting it the "stand-patters" reasoned that it would be easier to negotiate reciprocal treaties than to secure their ratification. Though some treaties of minor consequence were concluded under the McKinley bill, no important benefit was derived. At a later period a familiar comedy was presented by the Hon. John A. Kasson negotiating reciprocity treaties under the Dingley Act, and the Senate uniformly refusing to sanction them.

A "centennial of protection" was closing as the McKinley bill was drafted. The tariff indorsed by Washington had averaged eight per cent. upon a limited range of articles. *The World* said:

At the end of a hundred years the revenue produced by the tariff is $100,000,000 in excess of the needs of the Government. And the coddled infants of that early day, grown into stalwart and hoary monopolies, are exacting a tariff of 47 per cent., or almost six times as much as was required to "protect" them a hundred years ago.

More inauspicious occasion for increasing protection could not have been selected. A world-wide financial depression was approaching. The failure of Baring Brothers at the end of 1890, with liabilities of one hundred and fifteen million dollars, in part assumed by the Bank of England and other institutions to avert a crash, was its beginning, though it did not reach full development until 1893. At such a time a higher tariff could not be

6

followed by the heightened prosperity which alone could make the public tolerant of its exactions.

Nevertheless, the Republicans "practically decreed that their proposed tariff bill shall not be discussed, but shall be passed with only a show of debate. Their judgment in this matter is perfectly sound. The McKinley bill will not bear looking in the face. It is a measure designed to embarrass and restrain trade; to make favored individuals rich at the expense of the mass of the people." Both before and after the passage of the bill on October 1, 1890, *The World* continued to drive home the lesson:

Mr. McKinley and his fellow-partisans have accomplished what Mr. Mills and Speaker Carlisle failed to do; they have completely united the Democratic party in favor of tax reduction through tariff reform.

Only a few days ago a Democratic successor to Samuel J. T. Randall was elected upon a platform favoring "free raw materials" and a reduction in duties. Mr. Vaux holds that "a tariff is a tax," and declares that "the favored class of monopolists to-day does not amount to one thousand individuals who are the immediate beneficiaries of the tax for protection, while the fifty million consumers suffer the burden of paying the tax."—*June, 6, 1890.*

Mr. McKinley, in eulogizing his tariff law, said: "We have looked after our own. That is the sum of our offense." Whom did Mr. McKinley mean by "our own"? Not the wage-earner, for since the passage of the act that bears his name wages have gone down. Not the consumer, for the cost of much that he consumes has gone up.—*June 19, 1891.*

Mr. Niedringhaus, who has made some tin-plate for campaign emblems, has declined to pay the wages asked by the Amalgamated Metal Workers, and meets their strike with a request to the Government to allow him to import Welshmen to man his works.—*August 4, 1891.*

While *The World* thus lashed the McKinley tariff, with evidence of popular appreciation, it neglected no issue that could aid the general result. It assailed the "Czarism" of Speaker Thomas B. Reed, of Maine, whose changes in the rules of the House did much to hasten legislative action, and sometimes the play of the brute force of a majority. It denounced the corruption employed by the Republicans. It repeated again and again the words of William W. Dudley in 1888:

Divide the floaters into blocks of five, and put a trusted man with necessary funds in charge of those five, and make him responsible that none gets away and that all vote our ticket.

When the votes of 1890 were counted *The World* was able to rejoice that "The people have fittingly rebuked the partnership with monopoly and plutocracy into which the Republican party has forced the Government." The House was again Democratic. New York State had gone Democratic for the eighth successive time. McKinley was beaten in Ohio. Oregon had elected, in June, a Democratic governor. Massachusetts chose as governor that promising young Democrat, William E. Russell, but for whose untimely death the course of American politics might have run differently. Rhode Island, New Jersey, Connecticut, Illinois, Indiana, Michigan, Nebraska, Pennsylvania, and Wisconsin were Democratic upon state tickets; Iowa, Ohio, Kansas, Minnesota, and New Hampshire were close. Upon popular vote for Representatives the Democrats had a plurality of eight hundred thousand.

For such an amazing overturn there was more than one reason. The policy of "spending the surplus," in effect announced in President Harrison's message, and the corruption of the "fat-frying" agents of protected interests had much to do with the result. But the chief cause of the revolt was the McKinley Act.

In explaining his party's crushing defeat after the election Speaker Reed said "The Shopping Woman did it."

In the following year there was no marked receding of the wave of indignation. *The World* in July, 1891, stated the issues of the state campaigns to be "the sixty-per-cent. monopoly tariff, the extravagance of the billion-dollar Congress, and the conspiracy against home rule and free elections embodied in the Force and Fraud bill." The country again spoke with emphasis. There were no federal elections, and in many states no candidacies of general interest, but Iowa remained Democratic and Massachusetts re-elected Russell; while in New York the re-election of Governor Hill was of national importance. For the first time he had the Legislature with him. In spite of the maintenance of rotten boroughs by denial of reapportionment the state Senate was Democratic. To this result, with a majority for Hill of forty-eight thousand, an amusing incident had contributed.

J. Sloat Fassett, Hill's opponent for Governor, was speaking in Germania Hall, New York City, on the night of October 20th. The room was intensely hot. To quote from *The World:*

"I wish I could take off my coat," said Mr. Fassett.
"Take it off! Take it off!" shouted the audience, and Mr. Fassett did take it off. Chairman Eidmann, fearing that Mr. Fassett might be dry, offered him a glass of water.
"None of that for me," said Fassett. This caught the audience again in the right spot.

The incident cost Fassett many votes, and his party, perhaps, the Senate.

So the scene was set for 1892. The country was in revolt against privilege. But for a single cloud upon the horizon there was reason to anticipate a complete Democratic victory.

That cloud was the silver question.

Silver, which for two centuries had ruled in price as fifteen or sixteen to one, in weight of gold, had been "demonetized" in 1873 by the cessation of coinage, except for fractional currency. The silver men sought in the Bland Act of 1878 to provide for unlimited free coinage of silver, but the act as passed limited coinage to two million dollars a month for government account. This law was replaced in 1890 by the Sherman Act, which required the Treasury to buy four million five hundred thousand ounces of silver a month and issue against it bullion certificates. But silver advocates had not ceased to demand unlimited coinage at sixteen to one, and both parties coquetted with them. Mr. Bland was a Democrat; Mr. Sherman was a Republican. William McKinley, who was afterward to be a successful candidate upon a sound-money platform, ran for Governor of Ohio in 1891 upon this statement of his position with regard to silver:

> The silver dollar now issued under a limited coinage has eighty cents of intrinsic value in it, so accredited the world over, and the other twenty cents is legislative will—the mere breath of Congress. That is, what the dollar lacks of value to make it a perfect dollar Congress supplies by public declaration and holds the extra twenty cents in the Treasury for its protection.

It would not be uncharitable to conclude that Mr. McKinley's opinions upon the silver question were at that time hazy.

The World nailed him to the policy of the Republican administration and denounced the Sherman Act as introducing into our legislation "the false and dangerous theory that it is the business of the Government to maintain the price of a commodity by compulsory purchase of it—a theory which has already borne fruit in a series of wild warehouse proposals of a socialistic sort."

In its desire to see taxation reduced, economy enforced, and corruption checked in the federal government *The World* was anxious to guide its party away from rash action upon silver.   It favored an international monetary conference upon bimetallism, expecting no result except delay.   It urged moderation upon both factions.   For the time such efforts succeeded.   The tariff again led among issues in 1892.

Then the demand for a debased currency returned to plague American politics for years and to delay attention to the need of a progressive policy upon the tariff and the trusts.

VII

DAVID B. HILL

1891–1892

Mr. Hill's Election as Senator—His Long Tenure of the Governorship—
Disputes Cleveland's Standing as "Favorite Son" of New York—The
Snap Convention — "The World" Forces Cleveland's Nomination — Its
Course During the Homestead Strike—An Incident of Editing at a Dis-
tance—Blaine and Chili; His Retirement—"The Next President Must Be
a Democrat"—Chairman Hackett's Search for "Discreet" Men—Cleve-
land's Election and Its Lessons.

SINCE Daniel Tompkins and George Clinton no Governor has served New York so long as David Bennett
Hill.

Elected Lieutenant-Governor with Mr. Cleveland, Hill
finished his unexpired term and was twice re-elected for
three-year periods.   Chosen Senator in 1891, he remained
in the Governor's chair until the assembling of Congress.

Mr. Hill was an able man, a skilled political manager, an
excellent Governor.   Circumstances made him the natural
successor of Robinson, Tilden, and Cleveland as a leader
of up-state men and a check upon Tammany.   He cared
little for money, though he philosophically accepted the
greed of others as a fact with which a practical politician
must deal.   No instance of profiting by a dishonest act
was brought home to him, unless his acceptance of a
lawyer's retainer from an insurance company seeking
political complaisance merits that description.   He preferred working by conclave and cabal.   He never learned
the lesson, taught by Cleveland and Hughes and Wilson,
of appealing to the people over the heads of politicians.

A better reading of public opinion would have saved him the blunder of the "snap convention" of 1892.

With Cleveland beaten in 1888, Hill carried to the Senate a debatable title as the "favorite son of a pivotal state." He had a clear-cut tariff policy which was practically that pursued by the Underwood Democrats in 1911. Said *The World*, describing it:

> If the House passes a bill to put binding-twine upon the free list; another to do the same for the hoop-iron with which farmers bind their hay and cotton; others to free from tax wool, iron ores, tin-plate, and other raw materials of manufacture; others to remove the compensatory duties placed upon woolen fabrics and other manufactured articles, as an offset to the duties on raw materials, the Senate will meditate a long time before assuming the risk of denying to the people these concrete measures of relief.

It seemed in a man so near greatness an amazing blunder when Senator Hill, desiring to profit by conditions so promising of Democratic success, planned early in 1892 to call the state convention on Washington's Birthday, and at that unprecedented date to select New York's delegates to the Chicago convention. *The World* warned him in emphatic language, "Don't!" "We understand," it said, "that this day has been definitely decided upon by yourself and your friends after most careful consideration. We do not expect that you will change it. But we do say plainly and emphatically that you ought to do so."

Two weeks before the snap convention *The World* again warned Hill of what was to happen: "Don't overlook forty-three other States while seizing your own." A month after the convention it reminded him that the result of his active personal campaign had "revived Mr. Cleveland as a sentimental possibility in the face of Mr. Hill's unanimous State Committee, unanimous State Convention, unanimous delegation, the apparent unanimity

of nearly all Democratic politicians and office-holders in
New York, and the seeming impossibility that Mr. Cleveland can carry the State under such extraordinary circumstances." But Mr. Hill was far from being disquieted.
He mismeasured political forces by counting delegates and
estimating combinations of leaders.

In fact, he played *The World's* cards. The newspaper
regarded Cleveland as the logical candidate on a tariff-
reform platform, but doubted how the country would
view his chances in New York with his party divided and
his prestige broken by 1888. Hill's act convinced the
country that, if such desperate measures were necessary
to oppose a rival, that rival's strength must be formidable.
Also, it inspired doubts whether Hill himself was of
Presidential stature. In the end *The World* was able
to pronounce him "an impossible candidate." And
where in February, taking stock of the Democratic material, it had enumerated Gov. Horace Boies of Iowa,
Gov. Robert E. Pattison of Pennsylvania, Senator John
M. Palmer of Illinois, Senator John G. Carlisle of Kentucky, Chief Justice Melville W. Fuller, Senator Arthur
P. Gorman of Maryland, Gov. William E. Russell of
Massachusetts, Gov. Isaac P. Gray of Delaware, and
Gov. Leon Abbett of New Jersey as Presidential material, by June 10th it could announce that "the great
majority of the Democrats of the Union" seemed to prefer Mr. Cleveland. A month before the convention,
which assembled unusually late in July, it assured the
country that Mr. Cleveland "can carry it [New York] if
any Democrat can. He is stronger in this State than any
other man who is named." And the next day:

If the Convention shall have the courage of its preference
and nominate Mr. Cleveland, The World believes that he will
have the largest vote ever cast for a Democratic candidate in
this State.

We said this in 1884, and the election sustained our opinion. We did not say it in 1888 because the circumstances did not warrant it. We say it now to reassure any with whom doubt may linger at Chicago.

Cleveland can win.

Owing to ill health, Mr. Pulitzer was not in the country, but his position was well understood; and he had in charge of the editorial page the late William Henry Merrill, a man fully capable of impressing it upon the Democracy in Chicago that the candidate favored by the seventy-two delegates of New York, voting under the unit rule, was not the choice of the voters. How anxiously the paper was watched in Chicago, and what use the Cleveland men made of its smashing blows, is an inseparable part of the story of that brief and, on the surface, eventless gathering.

The paramount service *The World* rendered Mr. Cleveland in 1884 was in compelling his success at the polls by a narrow margin. Its previous work in convincing the convention that New York, like General Bragg, "loved him most for the enemies he had made" was secondary.

In 1892 the conditions were reversed. Perhaps any strong Democratic ticket would have won. The transcendant service rendered that year by *The World* was its heartening of Cleveland sentiment in the nominating body. The convention could not ignore such assurances as this, coming on the eve of its assembling from the columns of the great independent Democratic spokesman of the rank and file:

Mr. Cleveland is not a new and untried man. He was President for four years. He was under the searchlight during a second campaign. He has been before the public, in letter or speech, many times since his defeat. The people know him—his faults as well as his virtues. If they want him, why shouldn't they have him?

Are seventy-two delegates, elected last winter under snap rules, more sure to know the strength of a candidate than seven hundred delegates chosen at proper times, in proper ways, and assembled in June?

Democracy should be Democratic. . . .

To say that Mr. Cleveland would not be a strong candidate is to say that the Democracy does not prize honesty, sincerity, and courage. It is to say that the cause of tariff reform and honest and economical government, which triumphed greatly in the elections of 1890 and again last year, is not strong enough to elect its most conspicuous champion. Can a party that is afraid of its principles win? Does it deserve to win?

The World believes that the Democracy is strong enough to elect its first choice for President and that its first choice is stronger than any other would be.

Hill's snap convention failed of its purpose. He received but forty-two votes in the convention besides the seventy-two from New York. In that manner began *The World's* disagreement with Mr. Hill that lasted, with one brief truce, to the end of his career.

Just previous to the national convention had come one of the instances where the absence of Mr. Pulitzer affected the conduct of the paper in a crisis.

In the strike of the Carnegie workmen at Homestead, Pennsylvania, the country had an example of the "benefits to American labor" of the McKinley bill, and *The World* proceeded to improve it:

Under the McKinley Act the people are paying taxes of nearly $20,000,000 and a much larger sum in bounties to Carnegie, Phipps & Co., and their fellows, for the alleged purpose of benefiting the wage-earners. And yet there is war at the Homestead works, and the employers have enlisted Pinkerton Hessians and fortified their property in order that they may pour scalding water on their discharged workmen if an attack is made upon them.—*July 1st.*

Is it right that a private detective agency shall maintain a standing army, a thing forbidden even to the several States of the Union? Is it well that a body of armed mercenaries shall be held thus at the service of whomsoever has money with which to hire them?—*July 2d.*

If force must be used to sustain the beneficiaries of protection in reducing wages and breaking down labor organizations it is better that it should be the citizen soldiery of the State, for the workmen will not resist them.—*July 11th.*

There was nothing incendiary in this, nothing untrue. Provocation to plain speech was never greater. But a note that readers had learned to look for in *The World's* columns was lacking.

The World had never from its first day been a sensational paper. It had sought by every means to arrest attention, and it had been labeled sensational by rivals for surpassing them in initiative, originality, and success. But it had never played for popularity by muddling a question of morals.

Now in its editorial treatment of the Homestead crisis, taken with the presentation of the news, there was sensationalism. Here was a grave condition in which the supreme claims of order were to be enforced at all hazards upon workmen maddened by the blood of their seven dead, upon employers resolved to refuse compromise. Was *The World* to neglect the teaching that the public interest was paramount to private war?

Between July 11th and July 12th something happened in *The World* editorial rooms. The leading article of July 12th bears evidence of Mr. Pulitzer's personal touch. This was the burden of it:

There is but one thing for the locked-out men to do. They must submit to the law. They must keep the peace. Their quarrel is with their employers. They must not make it a quarrel with organized society. It is a protest against wage reduction. It must not be made a revolt against law and order. They must not resist the authority of the State. They must not make war upon the community.

There was no retraction of what had been said. The helmsman had nodded; the ship had veered. She was set right again, and went on. *The World* did not cease to score Mr. Frick for preferring to "appeal to Pinkerton rather than to the lawful officers of his State." It did not cease to hold up the lesson of this failure of the McKinley law to make protected working-men prosperous and contented. But it did not again forget to uphold the general interest in peace.

This is what had happened:

Mr. Pulitzer was in Paris, ill and suffering, when the Homestead trouble broke. His first thought was for *The World.* When day by day the accounts in the London journals grew more grave he had quotations from his paper sent to him by cable. At receipt of them he was horrified and incensed. Emotional by nature, strong in his sympathies with working-men, harassed by his inability more closely to direct his papers, he suffered one of the worst crises of his long illness.

One of *The World* editors who was with him tried to reassure him by saying that the trouble was perhaps exaggerated.

"There have been as many men killed and wounded in this labor war as in many a South American revolution," he said; and the wires grew hot with orders which reversed the editorial policy of *The World.* Some phrases from his cablegrams appear in the article just quoted.

Against men who blundered, as in this case, Mr. Pulitzer commonly cherished no resentment. He preferred a man who erred strongly, taking his own line in an emergency, to an irresolute one. Lack of courage in assuming responsibility was the fault he could not forgive.

The early part of 1892 was a busy time for *The World*. Late in 1891 a row had occurred in the drinking-houses of Valparaiso between United States navy men and Chilians, in which one of the former was killed and several were hurt. The Administration on October 26th made a demand upon Chili for reparation. By the new year the situation was acute. President Harrison was inclined to see a political asset in a vigorous attitude. Mr. Blaine, though he had erred in sending the fiery Patrick Egan as Minister to Chili, sought to compose the difficulty. So *The World* had again to speak of him as "the mitigation of this administration." To the talk of war preparations it opposed a cool common sense:

Preparations for what? For war with Chili. Indeed! And why?
Because, forsooth, a few United States sailors and a few Valparaiso policemen could not agree upon a fitting color for the town. We said red. They said blue. The result was a compromise on blue. It was their town.

When late in January the pacific bearing of Chili promised a prompt settlement of the dispute *The World* found in Mr. Blaine's "interference" the protest of reason against a policy of bluster, leading to needless and dishonorable war. "The sober judgment and the enlightened patriotism of the country" were behind Mr. Blaine, and would welcome such "interference" to save us from "the calamity of war and the shame of arrogant wrong-doing."

There was even then the coal conspiracy to rob New York, and *The World* in 1892 fought it as it did later. The Cœur d'Alene strike in the West and the railroad strikes in Buffalo, to which Governor Flower sent militia, kept the people's temper at boiling-point. In March an attempt was made by Boss Croker of Tammany to take from the west side of Central Park a strip of land for a "speedway," such a semi-private race-course for trotting-horse owners as now disfigures the western bank of the Harlem. A bill providing for this vandalism was rail-roaded through the Legislature and signed by Governor Flower. *The World,* focusing an instant storm of public anger upon the job, compelled a repeal.

With late summer came a cholera scare, the latest of any consequence in New York. Possibilities of trouble were shown in Hamburg, where eighty-five hundred people died. In New York *The World* took the occasion to secure some improvement in local sanitation. Governor Flower bought a landing-station upon Fire Island to quarantine arrivals by steamship. The embattled farmers and oystermen of Long Island gathered with pitchforks, fowling-guns, and clubs to prevent American citizens from stepping on the soil of their own country, and there was an exhibition of silly panic which it is not pleasant to remember.

But the chief interest of 1892 was its political revolution. In June, 1891, two events had put an end to Blaine's hopes for the Presidency. The first was his own recurring illness, which drove him to a long rest at Bar Harbor. The second was President Harrison's "swinging round the circle" with a series of public addresses which revealed him as one of the ablest men of his party and strengthened his following. On January 7th Mr. Blaine had again withdrawn his name from consideration as a candidate, but his friends refused to consider his declination final, and, with a devotion comparable to that of the Stalwart three hundred and six for Grant in 1880, Platt, Quay, and others carried the fight to the Minneapolis convention, where 182½ votes were cast for Blaine and 182 for the permanent chairman, that more favored man of destiny, William McKinley. But Harrison was an easy winner. Blaine had resigned from the cabinet on June 4th. Thus closed his public activities.

On the heels of the McKinley bill had come financial troubles. Between the signing of the bill in October, 1890, and July 20, 1892, four hundred strikes against wage reductions were listed by *The World*. To make its position clear for the campaign the Democratic House passed bills putting wool, binding-twine, and cotton ties on the free list, and these had been killed in the Republican Senate. The silver question had been by tacit consent relegated to the rear when Great Britain consented to an international conference upon bimetallism, which later adjourned without result. Extravagance had been notorious in the effort to spend the surplus without reducing taxation. Green B. Raum, who as Pension Commissioner had succeeded to Corporal Tanner and his cry of "God help the surplus!" had proved almost as "generous to the veterans." He estimated the pension expenditure for 1892 at one hundred and eighty million dollars, a sum never reached until 1913.

No one who followed Mr. Cleveland's second successful campaign for the Presidency is likely to forget the fight *The World* made for him. It had confidence in his success, as it had not had in 1888. It had four years of growth in strength and concentration. On June 12th it summarized the grounds of the contest:

The next President must be a Democrat. No more Force bills.

The next President must be a Democrat. No perpetual war taxes.

The next President must be a Democrat. No more billion-dollarism.

The next President must be a Democrat. No more Wanamakerism in the Cabinet or Woodses on the bench.

The next President must be a Democrat. No everlasting tariff for monopolies only.

The next President must be a Democrat. No more bounties or subsidies to favored classes.

The next President must be a Democrat. No more minority rule.

Throughout the campaign *The World* continued to insist upon its text. It early pointed out that Cleveland's chances of winning electors in the West were by no means chimerical. To advertise this fact, rather than for the financial aid it rendered, it began the collection of a Western campaign fund. This undertaking gave the chance for pointing some contrasts:

The Western Democratic Campaign Fund is not a Wanamaker fund. [Alluding to the money raised by Mr. Wanamaker in 1888, for which he was rewarded with a place in Harrison's Cabinet.]

It does not represent the campaign blackmail levied on favored plutocrats to perpetuate plutocratic legislation.

It is not an exaction wrung from office-holders in violation of the Civil Service law.

It does not appeal to the instincts of greed to swell the resources of venality.

It will not place in the hands of Quays and Dudleys the means of thwarting the will of the people.

And there was this further contrast—publicity. The people knew how much money *The World* raised, and for what. They did not know, they do not yet know, how much was raised by the Quays and the Dudleys. The activity of vote-buyers in the campaign was reserved for the closing smash of many an editorial, like this of October 2d:

The Republican record includes:
A squandered surplus of $100,000,000.
A worse than war tariff.
Increased taxes.
The multiplication of monopolies.
The menace of a Force bill.
Inflation with 65-cent dollars.
State-stealing and seat-grabbing.
The protection of Republican rascals.

7

A carnival of spoils.

Renomination by office-holders.

As a fitting climax the record is crowned with a bold attempt to carry the election by bribery and fraud.

Much use was made in the campaign of a tabulation of the strikes entered into since the passage of the McKinley bill—strikes against reductions of wages in many cases. No more forceful description of the genesis of the McKinley bill could well be made than that of Charles J. Harrah, a Pennsylvania steel-maker, who wrote toward the close of the campaign:

This tariff belongs to us; we bought it, we paid for it, and it is ours; we did not put up our money to increase the price of labor, to increase wages, and therefore we have not done it; we put up the money to buy the legislation we wanted, and we got it. It is ours; we bought it and paid for it, and that is the whole story.

Mr. Harrah's "We bought it and paid for it" was sarcastic and repentant. In 1888 he had been for Harrison; in 1892 he was for Cleveland. On November 3d he published in *The World* a letter worthy of preservation as an early recognition of how the nation-wide movement toward the trustification of industry received from the McKinley bill its tremendous impetus:

The results of the enactment of the measure were soon felt. Over-protection begat over-production. Plants were built and started that the natural laws of trade and commerce did not call into existence, and the men who had been foolishly entering into these new enterprises in the hope of speedily realizing large fortunes were threatened with bankruptcy. It became apparent to them that something had to be done in order to save their investment.

There were three courses for them to pursue. The first one, and the one which was most eminently successful, was that adopted by the syndicate which bought up the sugar refineries and, by closing down those that were most expensive to operate, restricted the production, curtailed expenses, and was able to regulate the prices of production in such a manner that enormous fortunes were soon made for its members at the expense of the public in general.

Mr. Harrah had given ten thousand dollars to the Harrison fund in 1888, and was disquieted at the uses to which money had been put. There were evidences in the new campaign of the desperation to which the buyers of the previous victory had been reduced. One such was amusing. *The World* offered a prize of five hundred dollars for the best Cleveland campaign song. It was won by a clerk in a government office, but his name could not be given. *The World* explained: "He would like the reward, but declines the fame. He holds office under the Republicans, and he thinks he cannot afford to wear the laurel crown." So the prize had to be paid privately through a well-known bank president.

The place taken in 1888 by "Blocks-of-Five" Dudley was filled in 1892 by a new figure in the limelight, Chairman Hackett, of the executive committee of the Republican National Committee, who sent to every postmaster in New York a confidential letter asking the names of "from eight to twelve of the most active, earnest, discreet, and trustworthy young Republicans of each town." "Discretion and ability to keep a secret" were insisted upon in another passage. Day after day *The World* reprinted this damning document, with comment drawn from the history of past corruption.

In the end the election turned upon public hatred of the McKinley bill, upon labor troubles which gave the lie to its promises of fostering the working-man, and upon manifold evidences of corruption. As *The World* summarized it after election "The corruption fund brought out the conscience vote."

And what a victory! A popular plurality of 382,956 was rolled up. Mr. Cleveland would have had sixty electoral majority even if New York had gone Republican, which it failed to do by the margin of 45,518. New Jersey and Connecticut, Indiana and Illinois, Wisconsin and California went for Cleveland, and he drew five district electoral votes from Michigan. One ludicrous result of the poll was "poetic justice in the gain of a Senator from Wyoming by the Democrats." This state was hustled into the Union to confirm the Republican grip upon the Senate. Now an unexpected Senator from Wyoming gave the Democrats the forty-four votes they needed to control the Upper House.

And so there came again to the Presidency the man of whom at the beginning of the campaign *The World* had said:

The secret of such a career is surely worth finding out. And it lies on the surface of the life-story told in The World to-day. Mr. Cleveland was never regarded as a man of exceptional ability before he was called to high place. But when the voters of New York made him Governor he accepted public office as a public trust, with a sincerity of mind rarely equaled. In office he put aside those considerations of policy which customarily govern even the most high-minded statesmen, and discharged every duty with sole reference to his convictions of right. He did many things that were sure to cost him votes in any subsequent candidacy he might enter upon. He did them with a sense of duty and with a courage and devotion truly admirable. He made mistakes, too, but they were mistakes of a sincere mind.

Without retracting one word of this tribute *The World* was forced to offer to Mr. Cleveland within the next four years, in issues of vital importance, as strong opposition as he or any President ever received. Yet it was to retain its own high appreciation of Mr. Cleveland's qualities and his gratitude and friendship to the end of his great career.

VIII

REACTION

1893–1895

A Period of Disaster—The Panic of 1893 and Its Political Consequences—Hawaii, and the Beginnings of Imperialism—A Bought Embassy—The Betrayal of the Wilson Bill—John Y. McKane's Downfall in Gravesend—Hill Runs for Governor Again and Is Beaten—The Pullman Strike—Cleveland Sends Soldiers—Republicans Sweep the Country in 1894—The China-Japanese War—The Income Tax Declared Unconstitutional—Theodore Roosevelt, Police Commissioner, and the Short-Lived Reform in New York Under Mayor Strong.

THE second term of Grover Cleveland as President covers a period upon which few thoughtful Americans can look back without regret. It was a time when people, pricked by petty annoyances, nurtured giant wrongs for fresh growth; when angered by causes they attacked consequences; when in the chase of economic heresy they delayed for almost twoscore years the initiative of reforms.

The advance-guard of the panic of 1893 was the Baring failure at Christmas, 1890. The trouble was well under way before Harrison left the White House. It was hastened by the failure of the Cordage Trust, an ordinary crime of swollen capitalization which attracted attention because it was managed by men prominent in New York society. The worst of the storm was spent while the McKinley tariff was still in force. It was much intensified by the financial recklessness of the Silver Purchase Act, a Republican measure. Yet the beneficiaries of high protection succeeded in making many believe it a

Democratic panic.   The labor troubles of 1893–95 heightened discontent.   Both parties coquetted with financial repudiation, and the party to which the country looked for federal reforms contracted with it a fatal mésalliance. A long record of defeat was to be the result.

At the end of 1892 Mr. Blaine's plans for the acquisition of Hawaii matured; and, though he was no longer in the State Department, there was upon the spot a friend and neighbor to represent the United States along Blaine lines.   Said *The World* February 10, 1893:

As early as November 24th the *Kennebec Journal*, of Maine, of which our Minister Stevens at Honolulu is editor, contained an article foreshadowing the recent revolution in Hawaii.

When the revolution occurred it happened, "by the merest accident in the world," that the man-of-war *Boston* was in the harbor.   It also happened that as soon as the revolutionists thought proper to act our Minister Stevens stood ready to "recognize the provisional government," and the commander of the *Boston* was ready to land, and did land, several hundred marines and sailors, "armed cap-a-pie," who paraded the streets and "preserved order."

The World's criticism of the Blaine tactics in Hawaii is an early instance of its hostility to imperialism.   It exposed and denounced the plot to complete a hurried annexation before Mr. Cleveland came into the White House, and sustained the new President in recalling the treaty with the provisional government and sending a "paramount commissioner," James H. Blount.   Blount erred through overzeal, and was replaced.   In the end the provisional government formed by the white residents of Honolulu was left in control until times more favorable to their project.   *The World* opposed Mr. Cleveland's plan to turn the government over to Queen Liliuokalani and leave the white residents at the mercy of native revenge—procedure which was checked by the Turpie resolution. But it as strongly opposed annexation, for reasons which apply to later times and larger islands. Hawaii was of little use to us. It would be difficult to prevent it from falling into an enemy's hands. Its people were alien. There were few residents upon whom citizenship could be conferred. Its government would be "a hard problem and a cause of scandals without end."

The World was disappointed in Mr. Cleveland's Attorney-General, Richard Olney. The exploitation of the people through the McKinley bill by the Sugar Trust, and its notoriously watered capitalization, made it a conspicuous mark for government attack under the Antitrust law; but Mr. Olney, though in some other cases he set about testing the Sherman Act, hesitated to attack the Sugar Trust. He even expressed after his retirement from office a guarded opinion that the law might be unconstitutional. A strike in June, 1893, among the ill-paid foreign workmen of the Havemeyer sugar-houses in Brooklyn gave opportunity for a sharp contrast of two kinds of lawlessness:

Mr. Havemeyer's firemen and boilermen work under inhuman conditions for twelve hours in twenty-four.

They very respectfully asked him to reduce their hours in consideration of the cruel and dangerous conditions.

Mr. Havemeyer refused to heed the demand of humanity, lest all the other refineries in the Sugar Trust should be compelled to conform to a rule of justice which costs money.

Then he sent for the police, in order that the trust might have the strong protection of the law for its pecuniary interests, although there was no menace or suggestion of violence.

But how admirable was Mr. Havemeyer's assurance in thus invoking the law quite as any law-abiding citizen might! He knows that this Sugar Trust of his is a lawless, criminal conspiracy, denounced as such by both Federal and State statute. He knows that its very existence is a crime, and that the only reason those who maintain it were not long ago brought to trial for their offense is that there has been an era of inefficiency and neglect in the Attorney-General's office, during which only those criminals who wear shabby clothes and have no social position have been prosecuted.

The next time a green-goods gang gets into difficulty, by all means let its manager send for the police.

It was in these disappointing years that *The World* began its long campaign to end the floggings inflicted by Superintendent Z. R. Brockway in the Elmira Reformatory, where in five years 19,497 blows were struck; not until Theodore Roosevelt became Governor, however, was Brockway ousted. *The World* urged rapid transit with its well-remembered insistence upon "Fifteen Minutes to Harlem," and pushed the consolidation of New York in the face of the bitter opposition of the McLaughlin Ring and of many Brooklyn property-owners. Its disclosures of the relations of the police to vice and crime forced the Lexow investigation which produced great, if temporary, benefits. It urged to passage the tenement-house law, which it has since defended against the greed that seeks to destroy it by amendment so that houses and human lives may be cheaper.

An instance of the influence of a newspaper in compelling a high type of diplomatic appointments was the Van Alen case, which in its time made some noise.

James J. Van Alen was a very wealthy man, a son-in-law of Mrs. Astor, a resident of Newport, undistinguished in public affairs, in which he had taken no part until the 1892 campaign, when he gave a large sum to the Cleveland fund with the understanding that he was to "have something." He chose the ministry to Rome, and was appointed. The selection was no worse than that of William Waldorf Astor for the same post by Arthur in 1882 or of Morton as Minister to Paris by Garfield. However, *The World* denounced it as "an affront to all patriotic citizens." It called attention to Van Alen's lack of "public service or prominence earned." It brought out the fact that he gave a large sum to the Democratic National Committee in expectation of appointment—"a fact which he has himself repeatedly stated with a frankness more ingenuous than diplomatic." Mr. Van Alen was confirmed by the Senate which was soon afterward to reject New York appointments of higher grade on lower motives, but, disgusted by the storm that had been raised, he soon resigned the post.

The country was now ripe for tariff legislation, and Mr. Cleveland called a special session of Congress August 7, 1893, for that purpose. The House, which chose Charles F. Crisp as Speaker and William L. Wilson as Chairman of the Ways and Means Committee, did its work promptly and well. With the provisions of the Wilson bill *The World* was well satisfied. "It is a higher tariff than the Morrill tariff of 1862. It is nearly as high as the tariff of 1883. It is a less average reduction of a 50-per-cent. tariff than the Republican Tariff Commission of 1882 recommended in a 40-per-cent. tariff." It was, in short, a compromise such as *The World* had urged between the extreme positions of theoretical free trade and confiscatory taxation; such a tariff as moderate men still desire.

This "reconstructive, not destructive" bill the Senate proceeded to destroy by amendment, greatly increasing protection. Senators Gorman of Maryland, Smith of New Jersey, Brice of Ohio, and others, all representatives of highly protected interests, accomplished this ruin. With them were associated Senator Hill, who opposed the income-tax feature of the bill, and Senator Edward Murphy, of Troy, who represented collars and cuffs, and who had been elected Senator against *The World's* protests for his services as a collector of campaign funds.

A long deadlock ensued. *The World*, seeing how the political tide was running against the party, advised that "When the Democrats of the House are satisfied that it is 'the Senate bill or nothing' they should agree to the Senate bill and end the contest."

This view was taken. The conference bill was passed upon Gorman lines, and President Cleveland contemptuously allowed it to become a law without his signature. Though he branded its treatment in the Senate as "party perfidy and dishonor," and wrote to Representative Catchings, of Mississippi, that the "livery of Democratic reform has been stolen and worn in the service of Republican protection," he considered it far better than the McKinley Act. *The World* also found it "a vast improvement in most particulars upon the McKinley law," and vainly hoped it would "give the country temporary peace at least."

In the thick of the tariff fight occurred the campaign of 1893, an off-year, but distinguished in New York State by an exhibition of independence which showed how *The World's* doctrine of revolt against bossism had gained in ten years. In winning his own senatorship and providing an echo in Edward Murphy, Hill had stepped down from his vantage as state leader, and had formed with Boss Richard Croker of New York, Boss Hugh McLaughlin of Brooklyn, and Boss William F. Sheehan of Buffalo a "big-four" combination. One of its fruits was the nomination in 1893 of Isaac H. Maynard as Judge of the Court of Appeals.

Maynard had been guilty of a political trick for the benefit of his party machine which the bosses thought worthy of reward, but which the State Bar Association pointed out was frowned upon by the penal code. *The World* made a hot campaign against Maynard and saw him beaten by one hundred and one thousand votes. Everything favored the revolution. The Legislature had made a bad record. Murphy's election had disgusted the people. At Sheehan's behest "ripper" bills had been passed to enhance his power over Buffalo which so angered the people that his ticket was beaten by twelve thousand votes and the bills had to be repealed. And just before election the famous war of John Y. McKane, of Gravesend, against the courts turned Brooklyn from a Democratic to a Republican city, replaced Boody by Schieren as Mayor, and affected many votes elsewhere.

Gravesend had been laid out by Lady Deborah Moody, a royal grantee of early days, with radiating streets and farm lines to facilitate access and defense against Indians. Four central blocks contained the church, the school, the fold for cattle at night, and the houses of the forty farmers, each of whom could go upon his own land from the inclosing village road. Traces of the Moody street-plan are still visible about the site of the town-hall where McKane, builder by profession, Sunday-school superintendent, austere, and careful of speech, pursued his career of crime.

Coney Island had been reserved by Lady Deborah as common lands, but the town officials were not prevented from alienating it, and the sale and lease of these lands provided the means of political debauchment, while semi-nomadic stable-boys, barkeepers, and other handy fellows furnished McKane's guerrillas. All the election districts voted in the town-hall, Lady Deborah's concentric plan favoring this convenience. In 1890 Gravesend had 8,414 inhabitants. It cast in 1892 3,286 votes. In 1893 it registered 6,218 names — a warning of fraud which stirred reformers to action. In this campaign William J. Gaynor, then a young attorney of Brooklyn, was conspicuous. Of him *The World* said, on November 21st: "Mr. Gaynor, of Brooklyn, goes to work in the right way. He has procured a copy of the registration lists of Gravesend. He has employed men to inspect every doubtful case, and in every instance of apparent false registration he will ask the Supreme Court to cancel it." What happened to the men from Brooklyn is thus told in a *World* editorial:

> John Y. McKane and his heelers have taken the law into their own hands and done what they pleased with it. They have defied the peremptory writs of the Supreme Court. They have seized peaceable citizens, engaged in executing a court order, taken their property from their persons, and lodged them in jail.
>
> A judicial officer under McKane's control has refused bail for these men as if they were accused of murder, and locked them up with as high-handed a disregard of law as any agent of the Russian Third Section ever showed.

Yet so silly was the Democratic ring that even after the election, when McKane was under sentence of thirty days and under eleven indictments which were to land him in Sing Sing, the board of supervisors elected him president. The district attorney, James W. Ridgway, having no stomach for trying McKane, Governor Flower named the late Edward M. Shepard and George C. Reynolds as special deputies of the Attorney-General.

Far out of proportion to the size of his district McKane made political history. In comment upon him and the fall of Maynard *The World* summed up its philosophy: "Discipline is as necessary to parties as to individuals. The Democratic leaders of New York invited it. It is to be hoped that they will profit by it."

For 1894 Democratic prospects were unfavorable. "No party," as *The World* pointed out, "has ever won on a general revision of the tariff, taking effect shortly before the election. The country feels the evil effects of uncertainty without time to get the good results of the change."

Yet Senator Hill took this unpromising occasion to tempt fate by running again for Governor. Admiration was compelled by his courage in facing such chances of defeat. *The World* sought to be fair to Senator Hill.

"He has had," it said, "eight years' experience as Governor, and, whatever his methods, he made surprisingly few serious mistakes in that office. When Hill was Governor he was the master of the lesser bosses, not their tool, as Flower has been. There were no extravagant or corrupt appropriations, no Huckleberry jobs [referring to the street-railway franchises in the Bronx region] or Sheehanized encroachments on local self-government under his rule. Though a strict and not overscrupulous partisan, his administration was clean."

Never were circumstances more untoward for a party. In July of that terrible year the great railroad strike, originating in Pullman, Illinois, had paralyzed the transportation service of the country, blocked commerce, and threatened wholesale destruction of property. The passage of the mails was interrupted, and the President called out federal troops to guard communications so that they might be moved. This act won for him the hatred of many labor-union men and is still remembered with bitterness. An incident of the strike of lasting importance was the arrest and imprisonment of Eugene V. Debs for violation of an injunction of a federal court, forbidding him to interfere with interstate traffic. This was the real beginning of the "government by injunction" issue and, more remotely, of the movement to exempt labor-unions and combinations of farmers and planters from the enforcement of the Anti-trust Act. It made Mr. Debs the candidate of the Socialist party for President in four successive elections from 1900 to 1912.

For Mr. Cleveland's resolute courage in this anxious time *The World* had only praise, as when on July 9th it said:

The World appeals to the reason of the working-men. It asks them what just cause of offense it is to them that the Federal and State troops are employed to sustain the law, to guard property against destruction, to protect commerce and the mails?

Whom are the troops opposing? Whom are they "oppressing?"

Somebody is preventing interstate commerce. Somebody is hindering the transit of mails. Somebody is destroying property. Somebody is assaulting and killing the officers of the law.

These men the troops are called upon to deal with. If there are no strikers among the rioters no strikers will be killed or wounded when the soldiers shoot.

The soldiers are citizens. They seek to oppress no one. They compel no man to work against his will. They seek only to protect men in their natural, necessary, and inalienable right to work.

What grievance is there for honest laborers in this?

The panic and a currency famine in 1893; strikes that called for federal troops in 1894; Tammany relapsed into corruption; Coxey's army marching on Washington to demand living conditions for poor men; other armies of unemployed not much less ragged, freighted thither in special trains by Republican committees to annoy the Administration; a new tariff law that pleased neither friend nor foe—here were conditions more unfavorable to the party in power than had existed since the Civil War. What chance was there of Democratic success?

To meet Hill, victorious veteran of a dozen battles, man of personal reputation untainted, master of arts political, the Republicans nominated Levi P. Morton. *The World* supported Hill. He was, upon the record, a better candidate than Morton. The party had suffered by his absence from Albany. But he had earned the hostility of the Cleveland wing of the party, first, in being elected Governor in 1888 when Cleveland failed to carry the state, which to many argued treachery; again in the Maynard nomination; more recently in engineering the refusal of the Senate to confirm the successive nominations of William B. Hornblower and Wheeler H. Peckham to the Supreme Court bench because they had opposed

Maynard and because Mr. Hill had resented the President's failure to consult him upon the appointments as a breach of "Senatorial courtesy."

In the local field *The World* fought an unrepentant Tammany; and the appalling discoveries of the Lexow committee investigating police conditions furnished the issue. Warned of hard going, Tammany sought to run Nathan Straus for Mayor, and upon his refusal again nominated Hugh Grant. The Republicans, fusing with disgusted Democrats, named William L. Strong, whom *The World* supported.

The result of the 1894 election was an almost unparalleled Democratic disaster. Hill, the invulnerable, was beaten by one hundred and fifty-six thousand votes by Morton. The country emphatically repudiated the tariff policy of the administration and rejected the Wilson bill. Mr. Wilson himself, its author, was not to sit in the House of Representatives; he was beaten in his own district, as the author of the McKinley bill had been in Ohio in 1890. A Democratic majority of eighty in the House of Representatives was replaced by a Republican majority of nearly one hundred and forty, outnumbering the Democrats nearly two to one. In the Senate the Republicans, with the tariff Populists, had a safe majority. But for a Presidential veto the path was clear for their repeal of the Wilson bill and for the enactment of a new high-tariff measure. They could claim with justice that they, and not the President, had the mandate of the people.

One gratifying result of the election was the success of Mr. Strong in New York, an early and emphatic notice to bosses that the citizens of the metropolis would assert their independence at the polls. Mayor Strong's term is remembered gratefully for some reforms, especially for an improvement in the personnel of the police magistrates under a new appointive law passed after the Lexow report, and for the appointment as Street Cleaning Commissioner of George E. Waring, Jr., a competent civil engineer, whose management of that previously neglected service astounded New York by its efficiency and set new standards for the future.

The World had come through the panic years with its material success unimpaired and its circulation greatly augmented, but upon the spectacle of ruined Democratic hopes it gazed with sorrow, and upon the new menace of silver agitation it turned with instant appreciation of a national danger. The only hope of staving off disaster was delay until financial conditions should improve. To this end *The World* favored another international monetary conference, as Arthur Balfour, the new British Premier, was a bimetallist. It was not averse to the coinage of silver at a true ratio with gold if all the nations were agreed—an impossible condition. It was not averse to any proposal that should avert or postpone the calamity of the United States undertaking alone to buy all the silver in the world at more than its value.

The outbreak of the China-Japan war in the closing months of 1894 gave *The World* an opportunity to enforce its doctrine of international peace. It was quick to recognize (March 11, 1895) that "This war has added another to the great powers on land and sea. There is reason to hope that it has also added another to the great progressive, intellectual, and achieving nations, alert to push humanity forward," and its sympathy with Japan when robbed of the fruits of its victory by the greed of Russia was pronounced.

From the first week of its new management *The World*, practically alone among journals of consequence in the East, had advocated the income tax. Its triumph in securing the income-tax provisions in the Wilson law was short-lived. In the spring of 1895 the tax came before the Supreme Court. The stumbling-block was the con-

stitutional provision against direct taxation except when
apportioned among the states according to population;
and Joseph H. Choate in opposing the law made skilful
use of this argument. *The World* showed that the direct-
tax clause "was adopted solely as a part of the compromise with slavery for the sake of securing the union of
the States. All the conditions it was intended to meet
have passed utterly away," and argued that "It is time
to free the country from the mortmain grasp of the old
dead slavery issue." It protested against the plea that
New York and Pennsylvania would pay more than their
share of the new tax. Was it not right that they should
pay, when the corporate wealth of the nation was so
largely concentrated in these states? Thus it traversed
in advance the lines that Senator Root followed in 1910
when repelling the idea that New York should object to
paying a tax on wealth because some New York men
were wealthy.

A decision by eight judges declared a portion of the law
invalid in so far as it imposed a tax upon the income from
real estate, which was held to be a direct tax. The
court was divided and inconclusive as to the constitu-
tionality of further sections. Because of this inconclusive
result, and because Associate Justice Jackson was ill and
absent, the case was again heard by the full bench, and,
by five voices to four, decision was rendered on May 20th
that "the tax imposed by sections 27 to 37, inclusive,
of the act of 1894, so far as it falls on the income of real
estate and of personal property, being a direct tax within
the meaning of the Constitution, . . . all those sections
constituting an entire scheme of taxation are necessarily
invalid."

The manner of the rendering of the decision was most
unfortunate. Justice Jackson, as anticipated, sustained
the law. Justice Harlan delivered the minority opinion
with a fervor of eloquence not often heard in the Supreme

8

Court chamber, characterizing the view of the majority as a "disaster to the country." But in the interval between the two decisions Justice Shiras had changed his opinion. This shifted vote of a single man decided the action of the government upon the income tax for almost twenty years. Nothing in recent times has done so much to weaken respect for the courts as did this disastrous outcome. Practically all the Eastern newspapers rejoiced in the decision. *The World* in deploring the result had some difficulty in showing respect for the high courts of the country:

The overthrow of the income tax is the triumph of selfishness over patriotism. It is another victory of greed over need. Great and rich corporations, by hiring the ablest lawyers in the land and fighting against a petty tax upon superfluity as other men have fought for their liberties and their lives, have secured the exemption of wealth from paying its just share toward the support of the Government that protects it.

In accomplishing this they have obtained from the Supreme Court a reversal of its decisions for thirty years past. More than that, they have persuaded one of the judges to reconsider and reverse his own opinion of a month ago.

No dictum or decision of any court can make wrong right. And it is not right that the entire cost of the Federal Government shall rest upon consumption. It is not right that wealth shall pay no more than poverty toward the support of the national administration. . . .

The decision leaves it doubtful if any income tax can stand before the court as it is now constituted that is not apportioned among the States in accordance with an obsolete provision as to population which was adopted as one of the compromises with slavery.

Such a law would be too unequal to be considered. But a way will be found—and the jubilant plutocrats and smiling tax-dodgers may as well prepare for it—a way will be found to revoke what Justice Brown well calls this "surrender of the taxing power to the moneyed class." This country will not,

again in the indignant words of the dissenting judge, consent
to "the submergence of the liberties of the people in a sordid
despotism of wealth."

Twenty years after the great victory of 1892 *The
World*, replying to Henry Watterson's dispraise of Grover
Cleveland's moderate policy upon the tariff, compressed
into a piquant paragraph a description of the calamity
that struck the Democratic party, and with it and through
it the country, in that disheartening time:

Marse Henry holds up his hands in horror at our reference
to Grover Cleveland's letter of acceptance in 1892, and screams
that because of it "the whole ship's crew of us went to hell
in a hand-basket." Something of that sort took place, although
we are not so certain about the vehicle, but the editor of the
Courier-Journal is quite mistaken as to the causes. If the
Democrats in 1893 had made an honest, intelligent downward
revision of the McKinley Act the country would have sustained
them. But they jobbed it, they were trapped in a disgusting
Sugar Trust scandal, their own President refused to sign their
tariff bill because of its "party perfidy and dishonor," their
income-tax provision was upset by the Supreme Court, the
Cleveland administration had a deficit to deal with, crops were
bad, the silver issue bedeviled the whole economic situation,
the secret bond sales made a bad matter infinitely worse—
and that is why "the whole ship's crew of us" landed where
we did.

An income-tax-amendment resolution, passed by a
Republican Congress with Democratic help and urged
by a Republican President, is now ratified by the states.
The country is awake to the redress of tariff excesses as
one means of halting the increase in the cost of living.
It is resolute in its determination to deal with the problems
raised by the trusts. *The World's* battle has not been
without result.

One regrettable result of the Lexow investigation had

been the passage of a bi-partisan or, more accurately, bi-boss police bill.   Mayor Strong drafted Theodore Roosevelt from the Civil Service Commission and placed him upon the police board, with which he ran away.   Setting out with the purpose of enforcing the excise law, he began a series of Harun-al-Rashid raids, which made him the terror not more of evil-doers than of peaceable pinochle-players in saloon back rooms.   If the city could have voted upon the Sunday laws there is no doubt how it would have voted then or later.   The law was retained because to the city boss it was a source of illegitimate profit through the sale of privileges to break it, while upon the strength of it the sympathetic country boss could appeal to no-license men within the party.   Said *The World*, therefore, to Theodore Roosevelt, president of the Police Board of New York City:

When you say that you seek by the obnoxious enforcement of this law to secure its repeal, are you not indulging in self-deception?   You know that the people who are wronged and oppressed by your proceedings have no power to repeal the law. You know that those who have such power are in no way annoyed by your nagging and exasperating activity in preventing the hard-working laborer from getting a pitcher of beer for his Sunday dinner.

Your course advertises yourself, Mr. Roosevelt, as effectively as if you were a brand of soap.   But does it do any good? Is it wise?   Does it commend "reform" to have the innocent annoyed in its name while crime runs riot and criminals go free?

In spite of all disadvantages *The World* was not without hope that the Democrats might reclaim the state in November, 1895.   "The Legislature," it said, "is extravagant, corrupt, subservient.   It has surrendered to one boss, while the Democrats had four or more.   Hunger for spoils dominates everything."   Platt was for the moment a worse boss than the state had seen since Tweed, dominating his party, in league with corrupt finance, ever ready to "deal" with Tammany. But his time was not come. The state went Republican again that year by ninety thousand. Hard times were still pressing upon the party in power as they had done in the débâcle of 1894. In New York City Tammany won a series of local offices of small importance chiefly upon the issue of Roosevelt and beer. The better administration Strong was giving the city went for naught. "The reactionary result was provoked by the pig-headed folly of the President of the Police Board." Reform defeated reforms.

IX

1895

The Romance of a Young Explorer—Schomburgk's Line—Disputed Venezuelan Boundary Becomes Disquieting in 1895—Grover Cleveland's Message Threatening Great Britain—War Measures Passed by Congress—The Belligerent American Press—"The World's" Opposition—Its Christmas Messages of Good-Will from Abroad—Mr. Olney and Senator Lodge as Jingoes—How the Trouble Was Settled—Presentation of an Address to Mr. Pulitzer in England—His Eloquent Response.

ROBERT SCHOMBURGK, a youth of twenty-four years, landed in Virginia in 1828 as supercargo of a flock of merino sheep.

The son of a Saxon clergyman, he had been trained to commerce, but took a livelier interest in science and philanthropy. After hours in the Richmond counting-house where he found brief employment he scoured the neighborhood for botanical specimens. At the local slave-mart he learned to hold slavery in deep detestation.

The following year found Schomburgk at St. Thomas, West Indies. At Anegada Island one day he saw through the clear water the sharks nuzzling out from the 'tween-decks of a slaver on the reefs the bodies of negroes from Africa who had gone down with her. The sight stirred him deeply, and he spent three months in charting reefs and currents; once nearly killed by a wrecker with whose trade he was interfering.

The charts, sent to the Royal Geographical Society in London, and some notes upon plants and fishes, won

Schomburgk in 1835 the command of an exploring expedition in British Guiana. He found the famous urari poison, *Strichnos Toxifera, Schomb.*, and "Schomburgk's four-cornered fish"; he found also, at the falls of the Berbice, a great water-lily which he later named after the young queen, the Victoria Regia.

What was sixty years later to make Sir Robert Schomburgk's name a war-cry was the map in the account of his travels published in London, May, 1840. This showed the boundary line between Venezuela and British Guiana, as claimed by the latter, running up the Amaruru, or Amacuro, River and its small branch, the Cuyuni, to the eighth parallel, and thence across country to Brazil. The line claimed by Venezuela, as mapped by Schomburgk, followed the Maroco and Essequibo rivers. But Schomburgk's map was quite inaccurate as to natural details.

Venezuela drew title from the Spanish conquest; British Guiana succeeded to Holland's. Neither old nor new owners had fixed the boundary. British Guiana had freed her slaves in 1838, but the slave-trade still flourished; and, as it was Schomburgk's dream to see free British colonies in America fostered to offset the slave-holding United States, he urged the survey of the Guiana boundary by a joint commission and energetic colonization. The British cabinet thought it better to map the boundary first and consult Venezuela afterward, and sent Schomburgk in 1841 to survey the line, which was found for physical reasons impossible.

Venezuela never accepted the Schomburgk line. In April, 1895, Venezuelan authorities arrested two British inspectors of police for acting on Venezuelan soil in the valley of the Cuyuwini or greater Cuyuni River, a branch of the Essequibo. The men were released under British pressure. Friction increased between the big and the little power. President Crespo begged the American Administration to help Venezuela; Minister Andrade in Washington cited the Monroe doctrine against British aggression, and the Venezuelan question became pressing, but no one looked for serious trouble.

Then came Grover Cleveland's famous message on December 18, 1895, espousing the Venezuelan cause, asking for an American commission to "determine the true divisional line," and proclaiming that the threatening attitude of Great Britain toward a South American state was a menace to the "peace and safety" of the United States and to "the integrity of our free institutions."

The British had a poor case. The Salisbury claim of 1890 went far beyond the Schomburgk line, which had been practically accepted by the Aberdeen ministry, and took in the entire watershed of the greater Cuyuni River. Even the original Schomburgk line crossed the Cuyuni twenty miles west of the Dutch boundary fort, to which the English had succeeded. But the difference was certainly not worth fighting about.

Eighteen years after the event it is hard to realize that the two English-speaking nations were at the verge of war over a bit of equatorial back country where white men cannot live. It was a time of much agitation over Irish Home Rule, and Irish sympathizers in the United States burned to seize every occasion for "twisting the lion's tail." American jingoes cried for war. The jingoes of England refused to be outshrieked; moderate men feared that war was inevitable, and hostile preparations were pushed.

The House of Representatives passed by unanimous vote the Hitt resolution authorizing a boundary commission and appropriating one hundred thousand dollars for its expenses. Although a commission in whose doings Great Britain was not consulted was as preposterous as had been the mapping of the Schomburgk line without consulting Venezuela, the shrewd lawyers of the Senate made no effort to stem the tide of jingoism. Prevented for one day by the objection of Senator Allen, of Nebraska, from proceeding to the second reading of the Hitt resolution, the Senate passed it unanimously on Saturday, the 22d of December. Mr. Cleveland signed it the same day.

All that week ruled indescribable tumult. The President's message was read in schools. Old soldiers proffered their services. In Wall Street, in spite of a panic that sent quotations tumbling from ten to twenty-five points and caused the failure of several firms, the war sentiment was so unanimous that Charles Stewart Smith could not secure ten signatures to call a Chamber of Commerce meeting to deprecate the reign of unreason.

Almost without conspicuous exception the American press upheld Mr. Cleveland in having used the language of threat. *The Sun* branded as "an alien or a traitor" "any American citizen, whether inside or outside of Congress, who hesitates at this conjuncture to uphold the President of the United States." "Not an hour should be lost," it said, "in making ready for any duty that may come upon the country." On the day following the Cleveland message *The Sun* thus urged the making of allies:

It will be the fault of our State Department—and we do not believe that Mr. Richard Olney will omit any precaution at this crisis—if such an understanding is not betimes arrived at with the Court of St. Petersburg and the French Republic as will assure to us the co-operation of the French and Russian navies in the event of war. It should be the aim of American diplomacy to see to it that of the naval battles, which the British government no doubt imagines would be confined to American waters, some at least should be fought in the British Channel and the Irish Sea.

The Sun was not alone in inviting war. Apropos the pacific efforts of Mr. Smith and others, *The New York Times* said:

Under the teaching of these bloodless Philistines, these patriots of the ticker, if they were heeded, American civilization would degenerate to the level of the Digger Indians, who eat dirt all their lives and appear to like it. We should become a nation of hucksters, flabby in spirit, flabby in muscle, flabby in principle, and devoid of honor, for it is always a characteristic of the weak and cowardly to try to make up by craft and trickery for their defect of noble qualities.

The *Tribune* said that:

The message will not be welcome to the peace-at-any-price cuckoos who have been clamoring that the Monroe doctrine is a myth, and that we have no business to meddle with affairs between Great Britain and Venezuela.

To the chorus of war provocatives *The Evening Post* opposed a corrective common sense; The *Herald* urged "the desirability of international arbitration."

Taking vigorously the side of peace in the controversy, *The World* said in its article, "No Cause of War," on December 21st:

The President justified his proposed enforcement of what he mistakenly regarded as the Monroe doctrine on the ground that it is "important to our peace and safety as a nation, and is essential to the integrity of our free institutions and the tranquil maintenance of our distinctive form of government."

Is this true? Does any possible divisional line between Venezuela and British Guiana hold a menace to "our peace and safety as a nation"? Is the integrity of Venezuela "essential to the integrity of our free institutions?" Does the determination of a boundary line in South America threaten "the tranquil maintenance of our distinctive form of government"?

Merely to ask these questions is to expose the utterly and preposterously inadequate basis of the war-threat which the President has fulminated. It is an insult to the understanding of an intelligent American school-child. There is not a hothead among all the jingoes who does not know that England is more likely to become a republic than the United States are to revert to monarchism. The entire trend of government for the past fifty years has been toward democracy. Witness republican France, Mexico and Brazil. Note the evolution of republics from the warring despotisms of Central and South America. Observe the working of the leaven of democracy in England, and even in Germany. . . .

The reasons urged for the forcible application of a false Monroe doctrine in the Venezuela case therefore fall to pieces at a touch. There is no substance to them. There is no menace in the boundary line. It is not our frontier. It is none of our business. To make it such without cause, and to raise the specter of war over a false sentiment and a false conception, is something more than "a grave blunder." If persisted in it will be a colossal crime.

From the appeal of common sense to the appeal of common sentiment was a quick transition. In its Sunday editorial review of the relapse into barbarism *The World* said, under the head-line "Peace on Earth":

During this week the American people are to celebrate their annual social and fraternal holiday. . . . From rich to poor we have all agreed that its appropriate motto shall be that of the original heralds of its good tidings, "Peace on earth, good will to men." . . .

When we are doing our best to lighten some hearts with merriment and wipe away some tears with charity, what have the two representative Christian nations of the world been doing? The blood of innocence cries out from the stones of Armenia, the races of Madagascar have been falling in heaps before the rapid-fire guns of conquest, and the Christian missionaries in Turkey and China are huddling in vain for protection round the doors of the embassies.

In this sad crisis of humanity the two nations who have made Christmas both a memorial and a mockery, whose moral agreement alone would have quenched fanaticism and stayed rapine, have been set by the ears over a remote and unimportant boundary line, and fill the air with threats of war. It had been believed that peace on earth has its promise and its hopes in America, but the voice of fratricidal hatred has disturbed the faith. Even ministers of religion and eminent dignitaries of the Church have carried human hero-worship so far as to forget the mission of their Master, and have joined in the clamor for war.

Before the Sunday World again appears we shall have taken down our wreaths; the holly and the mistletoe will have gone with the voices of the merry-making children. But we shall retain our hopes. The white doves, unseen, will be fluttering somewhere. There have been too many Christmases past for brothers at this late day to set about killing each other without provocation. . . . Rancor and revenge have come and gone, but they will not dampen the desire of men for peace on earth.

But it was upon Christmas eve and Christmas day, one week after the reading of the Cleveland message in Congress, that *The World* made for peace an appeal that will long be memorable. For the entire week it had been weighting the wires that bound the two nations together with messages whose fruit was then set forth.

The Prince of Wales, later King Edward VII., and the Duke of York, now King George V., authorized this despatch:

SANDRINGHAM, *December 24, 1895.*

MR. PULITZER,
    New York *World*, New York.

Sir Francis Knollys is desired by the Prince of Wales and the Duke of York to thank Mr. Pulitzer for his cablegram.

They earnestly trust, and cannot but believe, the present crisis will be arranged in a manner satisfactory to both countries, and will be succeeded by the same warm feeling of friendship which has existed between them for so many years.

Lord Salisbury's representative in the foreign office, while not prejudicing Great Britain's case by admissions, thus indicated the temper of that Conservative statesman:

LONDON, *December 22, 1895.*

J. PULITZER,
    The World, New York.

While fully reciprocating your friendly sentiments, it is impossible for the Foreign Secretary to take the course you suggest [respecting arbitration].   E. BARRINGTON,
                                                            Foreign Office.

From Hawarden, December 21st, William E. Gladstone, former Prime Minister, while stating that he "dared not interfere," cabled the famous phrase: "Only common sense is necessary."

Another former Prime Minister, Lord Rosebery, was not restrained from a more extended response. Wiring from Edinburgh three days before Christmas, he said:

EDINBURGH, *December 23, 1895.*

JOSEPH PULITZER,
World Office, New York.

I can only reply that I absolutely disbelieve in the possibility of war between the United States and Great Britain on such an issue as this, for it would be the greatest crime on record.

History would have to relate that the two mighty nations of the Anglo-Saxon race, at a time when they appeared to be about to overshadow the world in best interests of Christianity and civilization, preferred to cut each other's throats about a frontier squabble in a small South American republic.

The proposition only requires to be stated to demonstrate its absurdity. All that is wanted is a level head and cool common sense in our governments.

I congratulate you on the good work that your paper appears to be doing in this direction.

The great churchmen of England and Ireland, in the despatches that follow, remembered the injunction laid upon Christians to live at peace one with another:

LONDON, *December 24, 1895.*

The World, PULITZER,
New York.

With all my heart I pray to God to avert from this country and the United States the crime and disaster of war between them, and I hold it to be the bounden duty of every man in both countries to avoid all provocative language and do all that he conscientiously can to promote peace.

F., London,
(*Bishop of London*).

LONDON, *December 23, 1895.*

NEW YORK *World,*
            New York.

Our common humanity and our Christianity would sternly condemn a fratricidal war. Every Christian patriot on both sides of the Atlantic must employ every effort to avert a curse that would strike us all alike.

We are too closely bound to America by blood, respect, and affection for her people to tolerate the idea of bloodshed.

Let us all remember the words "Blessed are the peacemakers, for they shall be called the children of God."

HERBERT CARDINAL VAUGHAN,
Archbishop of Westminster.

DUBLIN, *December 23, 1895.*

NEW YORK *World,*
            New York.

Wholly unaware of merits of case. Can only express abhorrence of war in general.

It will be deplorable if wise precedent of 1871 [the Alabama claims arbitration] cannot be followed.

ARCHBISHOP, Dublin,
            (Archbishop Walsh).

MANCHESTER, *December 23, 1895.*

PULITZER,
      World, New York.

The possibility of a war with America fills most of us with a feeling of horror. It would be to all intents and purposes a civil war, and could not fail to arouse passions and create enmities which many years would fail to allay.

This would be all the more unfortunate because of late years the feeling in England for America and Americans has been one of continually increasing, and even fraternal interest and admiration.

We cannot see what there is in the present dispute to create such deep irritation as we hear of, and we are sure that if for such a cause war is allowed to arise between brethren before every legitimate means of conciliation is exhausted those who precipitate the contest on either side will have committed a crime against civilization.

May God avert so great a crime and calamity!

J., .MANCHESTER,
            (Bishop of Manchester).

December 26, 1895.

PULITZER,

World Office, New York.

Earnestly hope peaceful solution may be found; every circumstance contributes to render war between the two countries a dreadful calamity. CARDINAL LOGUE (of Ireland).

ARMAGH, *December 23, 1895.*

JOSEPH PULITZER,

The World, New York.

War [between] England [and] America unnatural, strife between mother and daughter, the leaders in [the] progress [of] Christianity and civilization, who will continue so with [the] blessing of peace.

ARCHBISHOP (of Armagh).

DUBLIN, *December 23, 1895.*

World, New York.

I am fully assured that every member of the Church of Ireland most earnestly deprecates anything that could imperil peace or cause disunion between us and our American brethren.

LORD PLUNKETT,

Archbishop of Dublin.

LIVERPOOL, *December 23, 1895.*

The World, JOSEPH PULITZER,

New York.

American excitement very sorrowful and surprising in England. No feeling here but peaceful and brotherly.

Much prayer going up. BISHOP OF LIVERPOOL.

CHESTER, *December 23, 1895.*

JOSEPH PULITZER,

New York *World.*

Every generous and Christian heart in England, and not least in kindly Chester, is wholly with you in your high appeal to the more deliberate judgment of your great and understanding people.

God speed you in your patriotic endeavor.

BISHOP OF CHESTER.

The late Henry Labouchere cabled with refreshing coolness:

So far as I am concerned, would prefer Venezuela and Guiana consigned to bottom of sea [rather] than war with United States.

[It is] thought here United States [will] insist on being the arbitratist in frontier dispute. If distinctly understood, proposal is that an unbiased arbitrator be appointed to delimit frontier. Am certain public opinion would insist on our government accepting this solution. Most desirable public men in America should explain.

Especial interest attaches to the cablegram of John Redmond in view of his prominence as a leader in the Home Rule cause:

The World,   DUBLIN, *December 23, 1895.*
      New York.

You ask for expression of opinion on war crisis from me as representative of British thought. In this, as in all other matters, I can speak only as a representative of Irish opinion.

If war results from reassertion of Monroe doctrine, Irish national sentiment will be solid on side of America.

With Home Rule rejected, Ireland can have no feeling of friendliness toward Great Britain.   JOHN E. REDMOND, M. P.

The World's editorial comment upon this exhibition of pacific sentiment drove home the lesson:

No one can question the sincerity or the manliness of these utterances. They have the added merit that under the provocation of a threat against the nation which they represent their authors do not reply in kind. Some of them suggest arbitration as the proper solution of the difficulty. There could not be a happier or more timely suggestion. . . . Arbitration is the right and reasonable policy. Lord Salisbury approved the principle and applauded the practice. But he objected that no suitable arbitrator of the present dispute could be found, and he diplomatically—which does not necessarily mean finally—objected to including a certain part of the disputed territory to any agreement to arbitrate. But with public opinion in both countries favoring arbitration as a thousand times preferable to war in such a petty dispute as this, no government can afford to stand out against it. . . .

In what manner could the President so gracefully and fittingly inaugurate the glad holiday season as by sending to the English public the words of his great predecessor in office, "Let us have peace"?

The author of the main portion of the President's Venezuela message was Richard Olney, Secretary of State. The message was "the result of the false assumptions and unwarranted deductions contained in Secretary Olney's 'note' communicated through Mr. Bayard [then our Ambassador to England] to Lord Salisbury." His note was thus handled by *The World* on December 27th:

1. First of all, Mr. Olney falsely assumes that this Venezuela boundary dispute is the kind of thing contemplated in the Monroe doctrine. It is inconceivable that a lawyer of Mr. Olney's astuteness should be honestly mistaken upon such a point and in so egregious a way.

2. Mr. Olney says, very offensively, "The United States is to-day practically sovereign on this continent, and its fiat is law."

This is obviously untrue. The "fiat" of the United States is not law in Canada or in British Columbia; it is certainly not law in Chili or in Mexico or in Brazil. Our Government is sovereign within its own borders, but it is neither actually nor practically sovereign anywhere else on earth. . . .

3. As if to make the insolence of the foregoing assertion more offensive, Mr. Olney explains to the British Government that our "practical sovereignty" and the influence of our "fiat" are due, not chiefly to our exalted character as a nation, but to our ability to "lick all creation." It is, he says, "because, in addition to all other grounds its infinite resources, combined with its isolated position, render it master of the situation and practically invulnerable, as against any or all other powers." This is a boast 'which the General of the Army has flatly contradicted in his latest official report. So far from being "invulnerable," Gen. Miles says we are in a defenseless condition as regards our seacoast. So far from being "master of the situation," we should have to trust to luck in any foreign war.
9

So far from being ready to fight "any or all other powers," we are unready to fight any power, if readiness implies a proper equipment.

Mr. Olney was not an antagonist without resource. He "dragged down from the ancient armory of the law" as still "in full force and unrepealed" section 5335 of the Revised Statutes of the United States. This statute, passed January 30, 1799, sets forth:

> Any citizen of the United States who, without the permission or authority of the Government . . . carries on any verbal correspondence or intercourse with any foreign government, with an intent to influence the conduct of any foreign government in relation to any controversy with the United States, . . . shall be punished by a fine of not more than $5,000 and by imprisonment during a term not less than six months, nor more than three years.

On January 7, 1896, Senator Lodge, of Massachusetts, quoted this section with approval in the Senate, bringing from *The World* an amused rejoinder:

> This is undoubtedly law. It is on the statute books. It is section 5335. It is reinforced by section 2113, of the same era, which forbids corresponding with foreign governments to incite the Indians to raids on the settlers. . . . The World pleads guilty in advance to having, "without the permission or authority" of Mr. Cleveland or Mr. Olney, carried on intercourse by cable with Lord Salisbury, the Prince of Wales and Duke of York, the Rothschilds and other foreign dignitaries.
> The statute cited is aged, obsolete, moldy, moth-eaten, dust-covered, and was forgotten until resuscitated by the zeal and watchfulness of Secretary Olney. It is true, furthermore, that the more modern laws, notably the anti-trust laws and anti-monopoly laws, are not enforced. But this does not relieve the ex-Attorney-General from enforcing the law to which he has called attention through the newspapers. It is really time to make an example of presumptuous editors who dare to interfere to break the force and repair the damage of an imitation jingo policy with its disturbing threat of war.

The ironical article closed with a loftier defiance: "The World will not descend into the dungeon and put out its million-candle-power torch of liberty and intelligence without a struggle." When, years later, an eminent friend of Mr. Lodge was to imitate him in invoking an obsolete statute to silence *The World* in a matter of political conscience it was to fight him to the last ditch in the same spirit and win another notable triumph.

"Only common sense" was, as it proved, necessary. The men who after reflection desired peace were in a majority in both countries. What was needed was a voice.

That there was nothing to fight about was shown in the sequel. When negotiation succeeded to threats interest in the Venezuelan question lapsed. Why should it not? The claims of the two countries differed by sixty-three thousand square miles; but it is doubtful if there were a hundred white men in the disputed territory. In all British Guiana in Schomburgk's day were four thousand whites. There are less than five thousand now, aside from the Portuguese drawn thither by the nearness of Brazil; and in 1908, in this pestilential region for a bit of which Britain and America were seventeen years ago at the point of war, deaths exceeded births by thirteen per cent.

It is doubtful if one man in a hundred in either country remembers what became of the controversy. With the dawning of the new year the work of clearing up the misunderstanding went forward. Direct relations between Venezuela and Great Britain having been broken off, the United States continued to act in behalf of the former state. On June 6, 1897, an arbitration treaty between Great Britain and Venezuela was ratified. Venezuela chose as her representatives upon a boundary commission Chief Justice Fuller, of the United States Supreme Court, and Associate Justice Brewer; Great Britain, Lord

Herschel and Justice Collins; and the four agreed upon Professor Martens, the Russian peace advocate, as a fifth. On October 3, 1899, the "modified Schomburgk line" was unanimously adopted. Again it was found impossible to follow in the field a line laid down from imperfect maps, and in 1902 the little that was left of the dispute was referred to the King of Italy, who in 1904 fixed the present line.

There are those who think that Grover Cleveland's Venezuela message was a masterpiece of statecraft, that it "put the country on the map" where diplomats forever docket the shifting war strength of the world and scheme for preponderant combinations. So a war lord may reason, eager not to be overlooked in any division of the spoil of weak nations, but what have such considerations to do with a peaceable republic, remote from the battlegrounds of the Old World and committed by wise founders to avoid entangling alliances and occasions of warfare?

Had *The World* cast its influence upon the side of war in December, 1895, a conflict might still have been averted. But no one who has studied the incident will fail to rejoice that the margin by which that calamity was avoided was widened by the courage and the eloquence of one American newspaper.

For *The World* and its proprietor there came some months later a reminder of the part they had taken in the controversy. The presentation of an address of thanks to Joseph Pulitzer by the peace societies of Great Britain is here told in the Associated Press despatch under date of London, June 5, 1896:

LONDON, June 5: A remarkable tribute was paid to an American journalist and to American journalism at Moray Lodge this afternoon.

Representatives of all the leading peace and arbitration societies in the United Kingdom, others in sympathy with the movement, and a number of leading American and English personages assembled on the occasion of the presentation of an address of thanks to Mr. Joseph

Pulitzer, proprietor of the New York *World*, for his efforts in behalf of good feeling between the United States and Great Britain.

In addition to delegates from these societies the company included Cardinal Vaughan, Sir Lewis Morris, the Hon. Rev. Carr Glynn, Sir James Reckitt, Sir Robert Head Cook, editor of the *Daily News*, and Mr. Henry Watterson, editor of *The Louisville Courier-Journal.*

The deputation was introduced by Passmore Edwards, and included delegates from the Peace Society, the International Arbitration and Peace Association, the International Arbitration League, the Peace Committee of the Society of Friends, and the Dublin Peace Society.

The engrossed address, on vellum, presented to Mr. Pulitzer, which was read, says:

"We desire, on behalf of all who wish to see knit, even more firmly, the ties of history and kinship between the two great branches of the English-speaking race, to proffer our hearty thanks for the prompt efforts made by you and the great journal you direct toward that noble object, and to congratulate you on the immense and gratifying success resulting from that beneficent exemplification of the marvelous facilities of modern journalism in the dark days of last December.

"Your prompt intervention evoked from the best, wisest, and most influential persons of the day so united and emphatic a protest that the counsels of moderation and sanity were enabled to exert their rightful sway over true public sentiment."

The address . . . dwells upon the desire of both nations for permanent arbitration and closes with a renewed tribute to Mr. Pulitzer and *The World.*

The reading of the address was much applauded, and a number of speeches followed.

Cardinal Vaughan said:

"I desire to bear testimony to the great services you, sir, have rendered in the cause of peace between two great peoples of a common language and tradition; the two great nations in which the democratic spirit most rapidly develops. Fears have been expressed that a democracy would be unable to bear up in a time of political excitement and stress. But it was seen how a great journalist, directing a great journal, representing the popular mind, was able to seize the moment when trouble threatened, and by a timely warning, by the use of common sense, by an appeal to humanity and morality, which reside in both, was able to calm the public mind and create in both nations a feeling that peace must prevail. Your great efforts were widely appreciated. But your task is far from complete. You, with us, must desire and must work for a permanent tribunal. It has been my happiness and privilege to be here and to add my tribute of respect."

Sir Robert Head Cook, editor of the *Daily News*, then spoke of the services rendered to the profession of journalism by Mr. Pulitzer's action.

After more speeches touching his efforts, Mr. Pulitzer stepped forward to reply, and was greeted with loud applause. He said:

"I am deeply touched, but am, unfortunately, an invalid, and under a doctor's orders, and I ask permission that my response be read by a young American friend—my son."

Ralph Pulitzer then read his father's reply, as follows:

"THE REIGN OF REASON VS. THE REIGN OF FORCE

"I am deeply sensible of the great compliment of your presence. Yet I feel that you come to do honor to a principle, and not to a person. It is a natural desire with men of earnest conviction to find expression for that conviction.

"I know of no purely moral sentiment that has been advanced in England since the abolition of slavery that appeals so strongly to the mind and heart as this idea of substituting civilized methods of peace and reason for barbarism and needless war.

"It is encouraging to feel that there are men in the world like those constituting your various peace and arbitration organizations; men who, putting aside their own interest and pleasure, and neglecting their own comfort and their own affairs, labor for the public good and a high ideal. We beyond the Atlantic have watched with admiration your devoted enthusiasm, often under discouragement and not seldom in the face of misapprehension. I congratulate you upon the fruit of your labors in the progress of this sentiment which I have observed during my present visit.

"In America there is not—or, at least, recently there was not—a single organized society such as yours. But this is not because the American people are opposed to the principle you represent. Just the reverse. It is because all of the people in the United States, regardless of parties and sections, are in favor of arbitration and, as it were, form one national arbitration society, which has grown from a membership of seven million that it had when arbitration was provided for in the Treaty of Ghent to seventy million to-day. It is growing at the rate of over a million a year, and will number over a a hundred millions in twenty years.

"True Americanism means arbitration. If the great Republic across the sea stands for anything it stands for the reign of reason as opposed to the reign of force; for argument, peaceful discussion, and lawful adjustment as opposed to passion and war.

"America is proud of the fact that arbitration is an American idea.

"Even our jingoes all were and are for arbitration, and the dark cloud that recently passed over America was only made possible by an unfortunate refusal of arbitration.

"It was a noble idea that stirred the American people, even though that idea was based upon a mistaken conception of fact. The spirit of protest was called out by a natural sympathy with the under dog, as we say—with the weak against the strong—and not by any personal feeling for Venezuela, with which country Americans have hardly anything in common. It was produced by the regard of our people for the very appearance of justice, though the substance itself were not there, and by their determination to protect American ideas against foreign intrusion, even outside our boundary line.

"In the mind of every American the cherished Monroe doctrine stands almost side by side with the Constitution and the Declaration of Independence, and if, from their great devotion to that doctrine—which in an impulsive enthusiasm they thought was involved—Americans espoused the Venezuelan cause, is that not more creditable to them than if they had acted from mere personal sympathy?

"If the New York *World* has been to any degree helpful in this Venezuelan affair, your warm words of appreciation are welcome, and are an encouragement to all members of my profession on both sides of the Atlantic who have fearlessly discharged their duty under great difficulties. For it is not pleasant both to criticize the government and offend the people in free countries, where popular opinion is always the force behind the government. Where that opinion is subject to impulses, often from an excess of enthusiasm, the responsibility of the press becomes most grave.

"*It is a duty to interpret the right, to expose the wrong, to teach the moral, to advocate the true and oppose the false, constantly and conscientiously, judicially and fearlessly.*

"*Without sacrificing conscience to the natural desire of plaudits and popularity, it must attack error, whether emanating from the Cabinet or from the people themselves.*

"*It must do its duty against that false and perverted patriotism called jingoism.*

"True patriotism, true Americanism mean love of and pride in country. But we love our great Republic, not because it has seventy millions of people, not because of its vast area and exhaustless resources, not even because of its wonderful progress. We love her because her corner-stone is enlightened intelligence, and her foundations are freedom, equality, public morality, national honor, tolerance, and, above all, justice.

"Jingoism is not confined to any one country, but is found in England as well as in America, in Germany as well as in France, in Russia as well as in Japan. Jingoism is an appeal to national vanity, national prejudices, or national animosities.

"Every day there rests upon the conscientious press the responsibility of combating these prejudices and of teaching lessons of enlightenment.

"*Arbitration, as I have said, is an American idea. The very first treaty of peace into which the United States entered, the treaty with England in 1783, provided that any dispute that might arise under it should be settled by arbitration.* The second treaty of peace, the Treaty of Ghent, made in 1814, also contained an arbitration clause, which was the means of settling several acute disputes that otherwise might have reopened the smarting wounds of war.

"Three times since the war of 1812 peace was threatened more darkly than in the Venezuela incident. The first occasion was the dispute as to the northeastern boundary, which came to a crisis in 1828. War seemed inevitable, but the arrangements for arbitration gave time for passion to cool and for reason to have a fair hearing, and the crisis ended in a compromise. Then there were the difficulties arising from the Trent affair and the Alabama claims.

"In the Trent affair war was averted because both nations listened to reason. In the affair of the Alabama claims the Treaty of Washington was made in 1871, providing for the Geneva Arbitration Tribunal.

"The force of the idea of arbitration in America is well illustrated by the settlement of the Canadian fisheries dispute in 1878. The Arbitration Commission decided in favor of England. After the decision was announced it was discovered that the award was based on false evidence. But America honorably insisted upon abiding by the decision of the commission and paid the award of $5,000,000 to our Canadian friends—a gigantic sum for a few fish.

"In the eighty years since the Treaty of Ghent America has an unbroken record for arbitration. Only a short time ago, in 1890, both Houses of the American Congress joined in a resolution authorizing the President to negotiate with the powers to the end that differences and disputes which cannot be adjusted by diplomatic agency may be referred to arbitration. In all, the United States have taken part in twelve great arbitrations. Ten of these were arbitrations of disputes with Great Britain. Also, we have acted as arbiters in six international disputes.

"In no case have the United States ever refused arbitration. In no case have they made war, except for independence and self-preservation. Those facts go far toward assuring peace as an outcome of the Venezuela case.

"But the chief danger was passed when England recognized the American Commission now sitting at Washington. That was really the first step toward arbitration.

"When England accepted our commission, when she made a courteous and tactful offer of facilities, she insured a peaceful settlement of the question. She might have refused to recognize the commission. She not only did recognize it, but she also submitted her claim and case to it with all the evidence in her possession.

"You may feel assured that the decision of the American Commission, composed of four judges and scholars, will be as fair and judicial as would be the result reached by any four of your own judges. The American Commission, gentlemen, will justify both the moderation and the confidence of the British Government.

"The outcome will be peace; peace with a better understanding, with friendlier good will, with kindlier feeling.

"But I hope and believe that both nations will provide against the recurrence of such a crisis.

"If you will vigorously carry on your campaign of education you can make it most improbable that any government will refuse to arbitrate such trifling disputes again.

"*But as to the future danger, let us trust that there will be either a treaty or a tribunal making it impossible for the two nations to go to war about any issue that does not involve the national existence.*

"Civilization means that disputes and differences, whether individual or international, shall be settled by reason or by some judicial process, and not by force. Civilization is no more possible without peace than permanent peace is possible without arbitration. Yet it does not mean peace at any price.

"There are certain issues that are not arbitrable. War against a cruel despotism or slavery Americans regard as not only just, but as inevitable.

"They believe in the French Revolution. They naturally sympathize with the uprising of any people against despotism, whether in Greece or Hungary or Poland in the past, or in Cuba to-day.

"I cannot help feeling that you, as Englishmen, share with the Americans at least in some of these sympathies. I have always held it one of England's greatest glories, almost equal to her matchless literature, almost equal to her genius for conquest, colonization and government in the remotest parts of the globe, unsurpassed since the days of the Romans, that for a century she has been for all Europe the strong place of refuge for political offenders.

"She, with Switzerland, has been practically the only European asylum for liberty-loving revolutionists and political exiles. She has protected all alike, whether anarchist or monarchist, whether rebel or pretender to a throne. And since England has shown this devotion to political freedom, Englishmen will understand a similar spirit in America.

"However we may differ on many questions, we have common sympathies for liberty and humanity, just as we have a common language.

"*We speak, we read, we think, we feel, we hope, we love, we pray— aye, we dream—in the same language. The twentieth century is dawning. Let us dream that it will realize our ideals and the higher destiny of mankind.*

"*Let us dream not of hideous war and butchery, of barbarism and darkness, but of enlightenment, progress and peace.*"

X

THE BOND RING

1896

*Two Splendid Journalistic Exploits in Three Weeks—Vast Profit of the
Morgan Syndicate on the February, 1895, Bond Sale—Failure to Protect
the Government from the "Endless Chain" of Gold Depletion—"The
World's" Offer of $1,000,000 for Bonds—Its Telegrams to Bankers
Throughout the Country Produce Hundreds of Millions of Offers for
the Securities at Open Sale—The Ring Defeated—Immense Success of the
Offered Bonds—How Republicanism Was Driven to Become the Sound-
Money Party—Dilemma of the Democratic Press.*

NOT until the appearance of Mr. Cleveland's message,
on December 18, 1895, did the Venezuela crisis become
acute.

Within the next twenty days *The World* had not only
powerfully aided the cause of peace and friendship with
Great Britain, but had halted another of Mr. Cleveland's
blunders and had saved to the federal Treasury millions
of dollars.

The calendar threw the service to the nation in the
Venezuela matter into 1895 and the breaking of the Bond
Ring into 1896, but both these exploits were crowded
into three splendid weeks.

The Bond Ring, the silver craze, the tariff struggle, and
the financial panic of 1893–97 were interrelated. The
Treasury surplus had disappeared, partly dissipated by
Republican extravagance, partly because of the reduction
of importation and the curtailing of private expenditure
during the panic, more directly because of the failure
of revenue through the decision of the Supreme Court

annulling the income tax. But Congress in 1895, with
the House heavily Republican, the Republicans in the
Senate slightly overbalanced by Democrats and Populists, and with both parties warring over silver, was in
no mood for sane finance.

The World had a simple plan for replenishing the
Treasury. It was to put another dollar a barrel of internal-revenue tax on beer and to levy some slight stamp
taxes such as those imposed during the Spanish war.
But neither party was disposed to do away with the
deficit. To both it seemed useful. The Republicans
employed it as an excuse for increasing tariff exactions
under the guise of a revenue measure. The Populists and
the silver Democrats, now in control of their party, almost
welcomed any calamity which could emphasize a demand
for radical cures.

In February, 1895, to maintain the failing reserve, the
Treasury had privately sold bonds at a low price to a
syndicate headed by J. P. Morgan, which undertook to
import part of the gold for the purchase. The syndicate
was also to "protect" the government by some mysterious
method which failed to operate; the drain of gold from the
Treasury continued, and an "endless chain" of with-
drawals worked in favor of new bond issues. As early
as August 15, 1895, *The World* warned Mr. Cleveland and
Secretary Carlisle:

> In any event the Government should not again be caught
> napping. If there shall be necessity for selling bonds they
> should be sold in time and in the open market at something
> like their real value. The Government should not again allow
> itself to be "cornered." It should not again sell bonds to a
> syndicate for 104½ which the people are eager to take at
> 120 or more.

The Morgan participants' undertaking to protect the
government reserves was impossible in the face of inade-

quate revenues and a vast outstanding mass of convertible greenbacks; it was also against their interests as merchants seeking another opportunity to buy the obligations of the nation. "The men," said *The World*, "who undertook to protect the reserve in return for many millions of profit on bonds worth 120 which they got at 104½ will have no interest after October 1st except to deplete the reserve as rapidly as possible and thus compel another deal." On December 26th, immediately after the publication of the Christmas messages on Venezuela from British public men, *The World* turned to its fight with the Treasury. Congress, not the President, it said, should judge what should be done. "And especially there should be no further costly dickers with a bond syndicate, even under the pretense now put forth at Washington that the underwriting of a syndicate is necessary to make sure of a sufficient bond subscription."

No public notice was given that the Treasury was preparing for another bond issue, but evidence lay upon the surface of affairs in Washington. Chronicling the fact, *The World* said:

It certainly should not be another bond "deal" like that which discredited the nation last February. The credit of the country is immeasurably greater now than it was in the sixties, the seventies or the eighties. Yet on a small loan of sixty odd millions it sold its 4-per-cents to a syndicate at a price which was suggestive of a greatly impaired credit. . . . The country wants no more of that sort of thing.

By telegrams to banks and financial houses in every part of the country *The World* secured an immense mass of testimony that there would be no lack of subscriptions to a popular loan. Proof accumulated that the government was not "at the mercy of one individual."

On January 3, 1896, in connection with a mass of telegrams and other offers and pledges of capital for the pur-

chase of bonds, *The World* played its trump card in the
following editorial, one of those that have made history:

To you, Mr. Cleveland, The World appeals. It asks you to
save the country from the mischief, the wrong and the scandal
of the pending bond deal. You only have power even yet to
veto it. If it is consummated its memory will be a colossal
scandal, and you will bear the blame.

The needless waste of ten or fifteen millions in this transaction
is not the only or even the chief objection to it. It involves
something of immeasurably greater worth than any number
of millions. It involves popular confidence in the integrity of
the Government, that faith of the people in their rulers which
is the life-blood of free institutions.

You have not asked advice of the party leaders in Congress
or out. The only person whose counsel you have taken is
the bond-broker who has millions to make by inducing you to
take his advice. His lawyer, who was formerly your partner,
is in Washington to help his secret deal.

James T. Woodward, President of the Hanover Bank, has
also been in Washington, and he is publicly known to have
accumulated $4,000,000 in gold in expectation of the exorbitant
profit of this deal.

Mr. Stillman, of the National City Bank, who has also been
at the capital to help on the dicker, has a hoard of $8,000,000
in gold to invest in the speculation.

Secrecy of negotiation under such circumstances awakens,
unjustly, suspicions against the honor of the Government itself.
These suspicions are more threatening to the stability of our
institutions than the enmity of any foreign foe could be. The
most damaging thing that could happen to the Republic is
the lodgment of conviction in the people's mind that ours has
become a Government by Syndicates for Syndicates.

Trust the people, Mr. Cleveland! You can get all the gold
you need in Europe at 1 per cent., or less, premium. You can
get it in our own country without paying any premium at all.
An issue of $50,000,000 in bonds, ample for present needs,
would be subscribed by the public many times over at 3 per
cent., or on a 3-per-cent. basis.

So sure are we of this that The World now offers to head the list with a subscription of *one million dollars* on its own account. It will take that amount, and it will promptly find and furnish the gold with which to pay for the bonds. The whole country will respond with like alacrity. Europe will clamor for them. Trust the People, Mr. Cleveland,

And smash the Ring!

The World recalled the war-time spirit which had made subscription for government bonds a patriotic service. "The millions involved as a loss to the people are as nothing," it pointed out, "compared with the calamity of disgust. Better a hundred millions lost, or a thousand, than that the people of the Republic shall doubt the integrity of the Government and learn to believe that money has taken the place of manhood as the controlling force in the nation."

Late in the evening of January 5th the President and Secretary Carlisle yielded. The private bargain was abandoned. A public bond sale was decided upon. As *The World* said in promptly acknowledging the President's act, Mr. Cleveland had "preserved the public credit and maintained the national credit."

Two strong New York banks in the Bond Ring withdrew on January 9th. When the bonds were bid for in early February the entire issue of $100,000,000—larger than had been contemplated—was oversubscribed nearly six times. "The organizer of the syndicate," as was chronicled, "bid over $6,000,000 more for the $100,000,000 of bonds than he negotiated to get them for in December." *The World's* own bid was $114, the highest received except for small amounts. The price of the new issue soon rose; two weeks later a bidder offered $114.50 for $5,000,000 of "lapsed-bid" bonds, but under a ruling of the Treasury these were awarded to the Morgan syndicate for $110.6877.

Despite this splendid success for the method of trusting the people, Mr. Cleveland could never see the blunder of the secret negotiations with Mr. Morgan. In an account published May 7, 1904, of the bond transactions of his administration he defended the Morgan-Belmont contract on the ground that it "required of them such labor, risk and expense as perhaps entitled them to a favorable bargain." "I shall always recall with satisfaction and self-congratulation," he added, "my collusion with them at a time when our country sorely needed their aid."

The World's response to this challenge, afterward published in pamphlet form, was a history of the "Great Bond Conspiracy." In this it showed that the value of United States bonds at the time of the February secret bargain was higher than that shown by any other government security in the world save only British consols; that under the February contract $60,000,000 in bonds were sold to the syndicate for $65,112,743 and immediately sold by it to the public for $73,418,575; that the terms of the contract were arranged by Morgan's lawyer after a four-hour conference between Morgan and the President in the White House; that in all the war-time period of 1861-65, when the nation was assailed and Europe looked hopefully for its dissolution, less commission was paid upon more than two billions of bonds than the Morgan syndicate cleared in this one secret bargain; that the operation of the "endless chain" drew from the Treasury $31,907,221 in gold in December, 1894, and $45,117,738 in January, 1895; that, according to Mr. Cleveland's story of the White House conference, "He [Mr. Morgan] suddenly asked me why we did not buy $100,000,000 in gold at a fixed price and pay for it in bonds under section 3700 of the Revised Statutes"; that, according to the same account, "the position of Mr. Morgan was that they were abundantly able not only to furnish the gold we needed, but to protect us in the manner indicated against its immediate loss" by bond speculators depleting the Treasury of gold in exchange for cur-

rency; that the price arranged for the issue was $104.49,
though the bonds when issued rose to $119 1-8 within five
days; that the syndicate broke its promise to obtain one-
half the gold abroad, the total net gold imports for five
months being only $15,000,000; that the new syndicate
which *The World* smashed in January, 1896, was a "blind
pool" invited by a private circular on December 31st;
that Congress debated gravely *The World's* exposure of
the deal and its offer to take $1,000,000 of the bonds on a
3-per-cent. basis; that only six Senators out of fifty-four
voted against an investigation of secret bond deals; that
in smashing the ring *The World* sent out 10,370 telegrams,
prepaying answers; that the 5,300 replies broke the
Western Union record of messages in one day forwarded
to any person or corporation; that as a result of the
offers *The World* was able to pledge over $235,000,000 in
gold for the bonds; and that under its day-by-day urgings
the sale became so successful that more than half a
billion dollars were offered at rates averaging nearly
$112 instead of $104.49.

There were no more secret bond bargains. The system
was broken. On February 6th, the day after the bond
sale, *The World* said:

The public loan is bid for nearly six times over. The credit
of the Government is maintained. The financial independence
of the Government is successfully demonstrated. The confidence, the resources and the patriotism of the people are splen-
didly vindicated. That which The World predicted and proclaimed has come to pass. The false assumptions of a scheming
syndicate and the baseless claims of its servants and sympathizers are overthrown. It is indeed a "famous victory."

Hard upon the heels of the Venezuela flurry and the
breaking of the Bond Ring *The World* was called upon to
face a difficult political dilemma. By the middle of
February the hopelessness of avoiding a fight upon the
10

silver issue became apparent.   The House had passed for election purposes a tariff bill which the Senate tabled by a decisive vote.   The Senate, in turn, had passed a free-silver bill to which the House gave a quietus.

On February 25th and 26th the silver Republican Senators bolted their party, giving notice "with two demonstrations of their ability to carry out their purpose, that they will not permit even the consideration of any tariff legislation until their demand for free silver coinage at the ratio of sixteen to one is granted."

In consequence of this state of affairs in Washington *The World* predicted the nomination of William McKinley by the Republicans:

The bosses are already beaten.   Quay, Platt, Clarkson, Manley, Reed and the rest are still planning and bargaining and arranging trades, but the masses of the Republican party have taken the matter out of their hands, and in spite of them McKinley will be nominated—not improbably on the first ballot—perhaps even by acclamation.

The bosses are beaten, and we are glad of it:

1. Because it is always well for the people to beat the bosses.

2. Because McKinley is the only Republican candidate who represents a principle in national politics, the only one whose candidacy will mean what the party means, the only one whose candidacy will be an honest reflection of the party's principles and purposes.

3. Because he is the most vulnerable of all possible Republican candidates.   His nomination will put directly in issue the only principle or policy on which his party really has any conviction, and the people of the country are so well informed respecting that policy and so hostile to it that a campaign against him will be a fight in the open, with better hope of success than any fight under cover of equivocations could offer.

Breaking a precedent, the national convention of the party out of power was first to be held.   This gave precedence in initiative to one of the most remarkable men that have arisen in American politics. Writing at a later date, when Mark Alonzo Hanna's achievement was known of all men, *The World* described his methods, and forecast the dangers inherent in the new standards he set for party management:

Mr. Hanna has managed McKinley's campaign from the first precisely as he would manage any other business enterprise. There are men who make a business of politics. Mark Hanna has made politics a business. If he were to undertake the work of combining forty-five iron foundries in a trust he would pursue substantially the same methods that he has employed in consolidating into an irresistible mass the McKinley strength in forty-five States. The same tactics that he adopted in breaking down the Sailors' Union on the great lakes he has displayed in crushing the bosses' combination against McKinley. . . .

It is impossible to conceive of the Democrats or the Whigs of forty or fifty years ago submitting the direction of the Presidential nomination and the phrasing of the platform to the "management" of a rich iron contractor who had never held an office, made a speech, written a line, or contributed a political idea toward the government of the country.

Is Hanna more than a passing episode? Has the new style of management in national politics come to stay? Are the multi-millionaires who have substituted monopoly for competition in business to apply their method and their money directly to politics, acting in person instead of through agents, as heretofore?

New York had a candidate for the Republican nomination, Levi P. Morton. It had had a more amazing one when, eight years earlier, it had cast its votes and those of recruits from other states for Chauncey M. Depew. A man of another stamp was pressed by New England delegates in Thomas B. Reed—"Czar Reed" of the Speakership quarrel, a big, broad-gauge man of fine brain and mordant humor, a tariff Republican of the old school, but no puppet of trusts. Morton was, as *The World* phrased it, "merely a courtesy candidate." For the rest, it again remarked on March 25th that "McKinley and Reed are the only real candidates, and McKinley will be nominated on the first ballot."

The World was an independent Democratic paper. It had given many proofs of its independence, but in national affairs it desired the success of the party from which alone a sane tariff might be expected. So late as the meeting of the Republican national convention it still hoped against hope that Democracy might be saved from free silver as by a miracle of grace and win a national triumph under the banners of tariff reform and honest money. If that were impossible, the best it could hope was that both parties would compromise upon silver to tempt back alienated votes and retain the wavering, and that delay until the panic should be past might save the situation.

For once, therefore, it departed from its rule of desiring the candidates and platforms of both parties to be on as high a level as possible, and rejoiced in McKinley's own shakiness upon the silver issue. Shaky he was, probably confused as to the right, certainly cautious of offending silver voters. As recently as the 27th of October, 1890, he had made this formal profession of faith: "I am in favor of the use of all the silver product of the United States for money as circulating medium. I would have silver and gold alike."

Hanna caused to be inserted in the Ohio Republican platform a "straddle" resolution, approved by McKinley, demanding "the use of both gold and silver as standard money" under restrictions "to be determined by legislation" if international consent could not be had. This was supposed to blaze the path the greater convention would tread in June, but before that month Democratic state conventions in the West had adopted such an

extreme attitude upon silver as to make it unlikely that
a straddle resolution would hold many ardent silverites.
In the reverse direction Eastern Republican and Democratic conventions alike were taking pronounced stand
for honest money.   The breach was widening; the parties
were realigning upon the new issue.

Whatever lingering doubts Hanna may have had were
dispelled, when the convention met, by Platt and others
from the East; and when McKinley was named for President upon the first ballot a platform had already been
adopted pledging the party "unreservedly for sound
money" and specifying its opposition "to the free coinage
of silver except by international agreement with the
leading commercial nations of the world."

What would Democracy do?

It was a question bristling with difficulties.   *The
World's* proprietor in 1884 had seen the chief Democratic
paper in New York dragged down in three months from
its high place for opposing the candidate of its party in
a national election, vacating the leadership which *The
World* occupied.   That was the material side of the
problem.   There was also the paramount study of public
benefit.   Democracy meant, or should mean, tariff
reform.   It meant, or should mean, the purifying of
election machinery from corruption.   Except in the city
of New York the men in control of the Democratic party
were more favorable than their adversaries to the reforms
The World had at heart.   Democracy held its briefs for
equal opportunity and the downfall of privilege.   Its
name spelled progress.   Was all this pressing, vital work
of reform, of which a constitutional tariff was only the
beginning, to be indefinitely postponed?   Were the trusts
and monopolies to gain out of a new lease of life the
opportunity for fresh exactions, while the Democratic
Quixote was tilting at windmills?

To such a question there could be but one answer.

"Come what may, the first duty of The World is to fight and slay the dragon.   To save the public credit, the public honor, the public fame—that is the instant need.   Later there will be opportunities to promote the reforms for which the Democracy in its pure estate has the mandate and of which democracy has need."

XI

FREE SILVER

1896

*Fiat Money in Previous Elections—Demonetization, "The Crime of '73"—
Fall in Value of Silver Due to Increased Production — The Quantity
Theory of Money—Why a Third Term for Cleveland Was Impossible—
Republican Party Hesitant Upon Silver Until the Eve of the Convention—
The Ohio McKinley Straddle—William J. Bryan's "Cross of Gold" Speech
and His Nomination—"The World's" Good-Natured Campaign—Rising
Price of Wheat Confutes the Silver Argument—Senator Platt and the
Tammany Victory of 1897.*

WAS there danger that free silver might prevail?

By all rules of political analogy, yes. The alarm of
business men in the summer of 1896 was justified.

It needed no long memory to recall what had happened
in previous periods of shrinking prosperity through opposition to the resumption of specie payment. In 1878 a
Greenback ticket received 55,000 votes in Texas and
39,448 in Indiana. In 1880 Gen. James B. Weaver,
Greenback candidate for President, had 307,306 votes, and
a Fusion Greenback Governor of Maine was elected.
In 1882 a Greenback candidate for Governor of Kansas
polled 20,989 votes. A Democratic-Greenback Fusion
movement carried Michigan three of the first five years
of that decade. In 1892 General Weaver had 22 electoral
votes and 1,041,028 popular votes on a People's party
ticket.

These movements, which won the suffrages of hundreds
of thousands of honest men, contemplated "fiat money."
The name was not with their partisans a reproach. They

could see little difference between the government die-mark on a coin and its stamp on a paper promise to pay.

Free silver made a higher intellectual appeal. The silver dollar was a historic fact. The "crime of 1873" had demonetized silver only to the extent of forbidding the coinage of dollars which had not in fact been coined because silver had been too dear. But until 1873 the silver dollar had been legal. After that year, because of the very rapid increase in silver production, the market price fell rapidly. Under the Bland-Allison Act coinage was resumed in 1878 at the rate of two million dollars a month. In 1890 the sound-money men in Congress, to head off free coinage, agreed to the Sherman compromise which committed the Treasury to buy four million five hundred thousand ounces of silver bullion a month. Only under pressure of the 1893 panic and by Mr. Cleveland's "patriotic unscrupulousness" in the use of patronage was this purchase act finally repealed.

In July, 1893, *The World* thus stated the history of the case:

The coinage law of 1792 authorized the unrestricted coinage of gold and silver at the ratio of 1 to 15. The ratio was changed by the acts of 1834 and 1837 to 1 to 16. Silver was demonetized in 1873 because it was dearer than gold. . . .

In 1792, when the United States fixed the ratio of 1 to 15, an ounce of gold was worth 15.17 ounces of silver—more than the legal ratio. In 1834 the true ratio was 1 to 15.73—less than the legal ratio of 1 to 16; in 1837 it was 1 to 15.83.

The ratio kept changing, but all the time a silver dollar was worth more than a gold dollar. . . . In 1873, when silver was demonetized, it was still too dear for the established ratio, the true ratio being 1 to 15.92. The next year it was 1 to 16.17, and the silver dollar was cheaper than gold. In 1878 what is falsely called the Bland law was passed, but the price of silver continued to fall, the true ratio in 1879 being 1 to 18.40. The act of 1890, known as the Sherman act, did not arrest the downward progress of silver. In 1891 the true ratio was 1 to 20.92, and now it is 1 to nearly 22.

It was the contention of the free-silver men that we should coin silver bullion at any man's call at the ratio of sixteen to one. This would have meant a new inflation, a new era of wild speculation, a new gold premium. That it would have meant a partial remission of debts was understood and approved by the silver men. They argued that men who had borrowed money previous to 1879 were burdened by the resumption of specie payments with a heavier debt, measured in commodities, than they had assumed. This hardship was a natural sequel to the war, to vast borrowings, to inflation, and to the recovery. Many who would have admitted this held that in demonetizing silver, in "walking upon one leg," we were burdening debtors and creating a gold famine by overuse of the dearer metal. They attributed solely to demonetization the sensational fall in the price of silver poured from the Bonanza mines.

Defenders of the gold standard trod dangerous ground when they assailed the quantity theory of money, on which the silver men relied: the theory that prices rise and fall in inverse proportion to the money in circulation. Denounced, then, by most American statesmen and nearly every American economist, this theory is now generally accepted; gold and credit inflation is laden with much of the blame for the high cost of living. In *The Purchasing Power of Money* Professor Irving Fisher, of Yale, has sought to reduce to a mathematical formula the relation of circulating medium and instruments of credit to prices. Indeed, the present tendency seems to be to load upon inflation too great a share of the effect of many and complex causes.

Prices of products had fallen after the demonetization of silver; the peasants of Germany and France were as well aware of that fact as the farmers of the United States. Self-interest and local feeling raised the silver agitation to boiling-point in the West, where wheat was grown and silver mined. Governor Waite of Colorado, an honest man and executive whom the East pictured as a monster, had said the people would "ride in blood to their horses' bridles" rather than submit to Wall Street dictation on silver. In some Western states to doubt the wisdom of free coinage was to be a marked man.

Had there been a fair chance of securing through the Republican organization laws to check corruption and a tariff not too predatory *The World* would have been ready to follow McKinley with less misgiving. As it was, its efforts were bent upon seeking to delay the crisis. In its anxiety to strengthen the sound-money cause it had coquetted with the third term, and had said that "There is nothing either in the Constitution or in history to forbid a third term for any President."

But Cleveland had split his party. It was not alone because he would have represented the sound-money faction that Democrats would have none of him. Nemesis was upon his trail, as she is wont to be with those who do wrong that right may follow. In toling Congress with patronage to halt silver coinage Cleveland had waked the spirit of faction. However praiseworthy his motives, his patronage bargains had roused in every state the anger of powerful anti-administration groups who in many cases cared less for free silver than they did for rebuking the President. Mr. Cleveland had done his work but he had closed his own political career.

So when in June the Republican platform gave notice that the party would no longer, in Chairman Carter's phrase, "plow round the silver stump" nothing could stem the inflation onslaught at Chicago. The Sound-money Democrats had the National Committee, and when the convention met on July 7th nominated Senator

Hill of New York for chairman. The convention by 556 to 349 rejected Hill and chose Senator Daniel of Virginia. By 628 to 301 it adopted a platform declaring for "free and unlimited coinage of both silver and gold" at sixteen to one without waiting for the "consent of any other nation."

Another plank criticized the decision of the Supreme Court on the income tax. Another denounced "arbitrary interference by federal authorities in local affairs," a rebuke to President Cleveland for sending soldiers to Chicago during the Pullman strike. Another decried national-bank currency.

In the debate upon this platform a picturesque incident occurred that was to give to the cause of free silver, which had already so many elements of strength, one of the great public leaders of American history.

William Jennings Bryan, a member of Congress, 1891–96, and in 1896 an editor in Omaha, was one year past the age of thirty-five, which an American President must have attained, when the Democratic convention met in Chicago. He was a member of a contested delegation representing the silver men in Nebraska, and his delegation was admitted by the convention.

There are three or four speeches in American history which by phrase or circumstance have left an unusual impress upon the imagination. In the Virginia Legislature, and again in the Continental Congress, Patrick Henry uttered an unforgotten sentence. Half a sentence by John Adams lives in most men's memories. What Webster's reply to Hayne was many know in effect, though few can quote it. Lincoln's address at Gettysburg is an inspiration to patriotism. But has any other speech delivered upon New World soil ever had such an effect upon events as that of Mr. Bryan in the vast auditorium in Chicago during the debate upon the silver plank—that speech which closed, "You shall not

press down upon the brow of labor this crown of thorns;
you shall not crucify mankind upon a cross of gold"?

It may become legendary that the speech stampeded
the convention. This was not the case. No nomination
was made until the following day; even then five ballots
were necessary. But on the first ballot the hero of the
"cross of gold" was second only to Richard P. Bland, the
putative author of the silver bill of 1878. Votes were also
cast for Governor Pattison of Pennsylvania; Governor
Blackburn of Kentucky; Governor Boies, of Iowa;
John R. McLean, of Ohio; Claude Matthews; Benjamin
R. Tillman, of South Carolina; William E. Russell, of
Massachusetts; Governor Pennoyer of Oregon; and
David B. Hill. When after the fifth ballot Bryan lacked
twelve votes of a two-thirds majority the other silver
delegates swung to him and the nomination was made.
In the search for a wealthy man as running-mate John
R. McLean led for four ballots, but the choice fell upon
Arthur Sewall, of Maine.

The Silver party, now of small consequence, nominated
Bryan and Sewall; the Populists, Bryan and Thomas E.
Watson, of Georgia.

With the glamour of his sudden upspring, his spotless
reputation, his youth, his beauty, his earnestness, his
wonderful voice, his power of swaying assemblies, Mr.
Bryan was the strongest candidate the Silver Democracy
could have named.

The Gold Democrats met in Indianapolis on September
2d, adopted the name of the National Democratic party,
and, after the refusal of their nomination by General
Bragg, of Wisconsin, put Palmer and Buckner in the
field. In the choice *The World* was now forced to make it
was not alone, and deserves no especial credit among
Eastern Democratic journals. What did single it out in
effectiveness was the vigor and moderation of its campaign
and the numbers to whom its economic teachings brought

conviction. As Colonel A. K. McClure says in *Our Presidents and How We Make Them:*

A number of the leading newspapers of the country which had supported Cleveland in his three contests repudiated the Chicago platform and its candidate, and they stood in the forefront of American journalism. . . . Not one of them ever had conference or communication with the McKinley leaders, or received or proposed any terms for their support, or ever sought, accepted, or desired favors from the McKinley administration. Some of them suffered pecuniary sacrifice, but they performed a heroic duty, and it was the inspiration they gave to the conservative Democratic sentiment of the country that made McKinley President by an overwhelming majority.

In reviewing the campaign of *The World* one is struck by its good nature. It did not bandy epithets. It did not say the silver leaders were scoundrels or brand six million voters as thieves. It conducted a campaign of education, and it foresaw the rout that would follow. "The World has warned Democrats," it said, "that the adoption of the free-silver heresy would be suicide." But "parties may commit suicide for a year, for two or four years. The duration of the suspended animation of the Democratic party will depend in some measure upon its canvass, but more upon the spirit in which it shall accept the discipline of defeat." Chiding later a too zealous ally, it describes a better plan for the contest, the plan that would leave fewest wounds and soonest lead back to union:

[The Silverites'] outbreak is a craze, a species of hysteria, but there may be lunacy and hysteria displayed in abusing them, as our contemporary is demonstrating by example.

Let us trust the people. Let us reason with them and teach them. There remain over a hundred days before election.

In its educational campaign the most straightforward methods were used by *The World*. Such was the "Shorter Silver Catechism," in method as follows:

Q. What silver-standard countries have free coinage? *A.* Not one. There is not in all the world a mint open to the free coinage of silver at any ratio.

Q. Does not Mexico coin all silver brought to her mints? *A.* Yes; but she charges $4.41 for each one hundred coins, and the coinage is at 16.51 to 1, so that she recoins European silver at a cost to the holder of about 10 per cent., and American silver at a cost of 7 per cent. [Mexico is now practically on a gold basis.]

Q. Does not India coin free silver? *A.* No. The mint was closed three years ago.

Q. Does not Japan coin free? *A.* No. The mint closed some years ago. It coins subsidiary silver on Government account, as all mints do.

Perhaps *The World* deserved some gratitude from Republicans who were almost by accident the directors of the honest-money fight. It asked nothing except upon public grounds. It demanded of these leaders, "Do they lack the discretion or the power to keep Hanna, with his money-bags, his fat-friers, and his professional corruptionists, out of sight?" It urged Mr. McKinley to take an advanced stand upon the trust question, to make more endurable his necessary election. It rebuked him when he spoke of Matt Quay as "that distinguished leader and unrivaled Republican organizer whose devotion to Republicanism has never wavered."

Odd as the fact may appear now, Mr. McKinley and Mark Hanna had planned to make the campaign chiefly upon the tariff. They had so thoroughly assimilated the lesson of the Democratic defeat of 1894 that they did not at first realize how much more potent an issue fate had thrust into their reluctant hands. Mr. Bryan put the country under an obligation, he performed a public service quite other than he intended, when he made the silver issue prominent and thus opened the way for its decisive settlement. Tariff reformer as he was, in his

first speech in the "enemy's country" of New York he
made no reference to the tariff but insisted upon the issue
of free coinage.   In August *The World* told him:

You can be elected if you will give sound reasons convincing
the country that you stand for law and order, and that there
is no occasion to fear precipitate, radical, and wholly experi-
mental action upon the currency as the result of your success,
and at the same time pledge yourself to enforce the anti-trust
laws, to secure their amendment wherein they are deficient,
and to use all the power of the executive office to protect the
people from the injustice and wrongs from which they now
suffer.

Mr. Bryan could see little but the silver question. *The
World* labored to get him upon firmer fighting-ground
with the tariff and the trusts.   It reminded him that there
were in New York 1,732,382 depositors in savings-
banks, or 130,000 more than its voters at the last Presidential election, and asked how they would like the
"free - silver attitude toward their savings."   It applauded John Boyd Thacher when, nominated for Governor by the Democratic state convention, he refused to
run as a candidate of a repudiation party; but it advised
him that he could make his protest stronger by staying on
the ticket and "standing by his honest repudiation of the
repudiators of Democracy."

Six weeks before election it seemed any man's race.
Republican victories in Maine and Vermont in the early
elections gave the sound-money men assurances of success.
But a circumstance more potent for victory was a gradual
lightening of the commercial skies with growing prices
for produce.   The most telling proof of this was thus
noted on October 18th: "A month ago wheat was worth
sixty-four cents in New York.   Yesterday it was worth
eighty-two cents."   Silver continued to decline.   Wheat
in a month had advanced twenty-eight per cent.; far off

and faint the hard-pressed farmer began to see glimmering daylight.

Mr. Bryan received the greatest vote ever cast for a Democrat. Six and a half million men supported him to the last; yet McKinley's majority was more than six hundred thousand votes at the polls and ninety-five in the electoral college. What the victory involved, what their dilemma had meant to independent Democrats, *The World* thus recounted:

It was a terrible choice for Democrats. On one side the regular ticket of their party, on a platform undemocratic in almost every plank, and dangerous and dishonest in many, but representing a recognition of some very real grievances and wrongs of the people. On the other side was a candidate embodying in an odious degree the policy of protection for bounties and a tariff for trusts, and of reckless extravagance in the public expenditures. But feeling that the honor and credit of the nation, the independence of its judiciary, and the supremacy of the national authority were issues of vital importance, lifting the contest far above the plane of party contention, these patriotic Democrats threw their votes on the side of their country.

To this thought *The World* often returned. On November 19th it noted that Carl Schurz and William L. Wilson had on the same day "felt it incumbent upon them to deliver to the country the same strenuous message of counsel and warning." They had warned the people that "behind the late outbreak of Populism there was a cause deeper than any reckless whim, more earnest than a mere desire for change." There were "real wrongs, real grievances, real oppressions to be righted."

It was in part because of this sympathetic treatment of the issues that *The World* could say of its own course, "never before in a Presidential campaign had the leading newspaper of either party declined to support the ticket and platform presented by the politicians, not only without loss of power and prestige, but actually with a gain in both."

But only at fearful public cost had silver been defeated. Mark Hanna's campaign of debauchery had passed all limits. What Senator Thomas C. Platt much later called "moral obligations" had been assumed toward illegal corporations that hampered the government for years. In New York Frank Black rode into office upon the shoulders of McKinley, a bright, shrewd man with a cynical conception of public morals, who as Governor angered the state by naming Lou Payn, "a notorious, confessed and branded lobbyist," as superintendent of insurance, and by announcing that the civil-service law would "work better with less starch," but who was dropped by Platt after a single term.

With a Republican administration the plans of Blaine and Harrison for the annexation of Hawaii were revived, and *The World* found itself in 1897 engaged in a desperate fight against "leprosy and loot." "Do we really need to go fifty-six hundred miles away for another rotten borough?" it asked. "Have we not difficulties enough in assimilating our immense immigration from every quarter of the globe without taking in the mongrel population of this remote island in the Pacific?"

The annexation movement justified criticism. The sugar barons were interested in getting inside the tariff barriers against their plantations in the islands. John Sherman was placed in the State Department with President McKinley's law partner, William R. Day, as his assistant secretary and the real power. Sherman was won over to annexation by the pretense that Japan, not then Russia's conqueror or a naval power, was about to seize the group. Senator Hoar, "who has the courage to refuse to dishonor himself at the bidding of the leprous Administration Hawaiian Ring," introduced a protest

11

against annexation signed by 21,869 native Hawaiians. The traders and missionaries' sons who made up the provisional government, of which Sanford B. Dole was president, had no notion of a republican form of government, and admitted less than four thousand men to the vote. Yet it was in vain for *The World* to protest in the words of Jefferson to Madison that "nothing should ever be accepted which would require a navy to defend it," or to denounce the obliquity of a republic ruling other men without those other men's consent. Before annexation came to a decision in Congress we were in the midst of the Spanish war, opposition would have been quixotic, and the job went through almost without protest.

The enactment of a new tariff of excessive protection was another blow the country sustained by the surrender of Democracy to free silver. The election of 1896 had of course retained the House of Representatives in full control of the Republicans; it had given them just short of a majority in the Senate, but enough of the considerable third-party contingent—Populists and independent silver men—were in sympathy with their tariff views to make their course clear. A tariff bill had been practically framed by the Republican Ways and Means Committee before the administration was changed on March 4, 1897, and at the special session which soon assembled for the purpose the Dingley bill was passed.

"Of course," said *The World*, "there is the rational way out—namely, to let the tariff alone and raise the needed extra revenue by imposing additional taxes on beer, and some revenue imposts upon bank-checks, title-deeds and like agencies for the transfer of wealth"—exactly what was done the following year. But, "elected to power by the aid of Democratic votes for the sole purpose of conserving the financial integrity of the nation," Congress devoted itself to "the framing of a tariff for robbery chiefly." Yet *The World* foresaw the success of the

undertaking, even with a narrowly divided Senate.   Here
was one of the remaining disservices which the silver
agitation in its decadence could do the country:

> Even with the vote of the Sugar Democrat, McEnery, the
> Republicans are in a minority of one.
> Why, then, will [the Dingley bill] pass the Senate?
> First—Because some of the Silver party and Populist oppo-
> nents of the bill believe that by letting the Republicans alone
> they will make political capital for "16 to 1" in 1898 and 1900.
> Second—Because the direct personal agents of the Silver
> Trust are voting for the bill.   These agents hold the balance
> of power.   They make opposition useless.
> These 'two reasons for the coming carnival of plunder are at
> bottom one—silver.

If the monopolists who swung the Republican party
were prompt to take their fees in the Dingley bill it was
left to one of their agents, Senator Platt of New York,
to work a mischief to the metropolis which gave *The
World* the opportunity for the hardest hitting it had done
in a political campaign since 1892.

The Act of Consolidation of Greater New York, which
owed much to *The World's* advocacy and which both
Boss Platt and Boss Croker had delayed as long as they
dared, had passed; the charter was enacted early in 1897,
and the first election was to take place in November.
Brooklyn and old New York had Republican mayors.
Assuming that the party, with the prestige of its enmity
to free silver, would hold its advantage, the Republican
Legislature had arranged for the new Mayor a four-
year term and wide powers.   Fusion with independent
Democrats was expected, and it was supposed that the
Republican machine would accept Seth Low, a Republican
who had been Mayor of Brooklyn for two terms and was
now president of Columbia University.

There were two reasons—one of them a real reason—

why Platt was not enthusiastic about Mr. Low.   The real
reason was that he could not control him.   Another
plausible reason was that in 1884 Mr. Low had been
unwilling to share in the Blaine campaign.   He had said
that the Mayor of Brooklyn had no vote, and that Seth
Low would vote as he pleased.   He did vote for Blaine
and Logan, but he was not sufficiently convinced of the
wisdom of Blaine's election to take part in the campaign.
Now, with the citizens' organizations uniting upon Low,
this ancient grievance was made an excuse for separate
Republican action.   Low was nominated; Mr. Platt
preferred defeat with a "straight" candidate to victory
with Low, and his convention put up Judge Tracy, a law
partner of Platt's son.

For Tammany, victory with three candidates would be
easy.   This was Croker's position: "The man I name
must be, first, a man who voted for Bryan last year.
He must be a member of Tammany Hall—a regular
member of that organization.   He must be a regular
machine man, and, what is more, a man whom I control."
Nevertheless, *The World*, true to its rule of neglecting no
faintest hope of serving the city, begged Croker to name
a "Democratic Low," a "reformer who has done things,"
the man who helped send McKane to prison, Judge
Gaynor, instead of "a mere puppet of the boss."

One result of the convention was amusing.   *The World*
had offered a prize for any person who could name in
advance Croker's candidate for Mayor.   The day after
the Tammany city convention it said: "This reward has
not been earned by anybody.   Among the multitudinous
responses, in which almost every possible Tammany
candidate was named, there was not one which held the
name of Judge Robert A. Van Wyck."   Judge Van
Wyck was to this extent acceptable—he was unknown.
He was not conspicuous enough to have made enemies.
But whatever his personal qualities, he would sit in

the Mayor's chair as the representative of Richard Croker.

A seething rage took possession of *The World*. After years of struggle a great idealistic plan had been carried. A city, the second in the world and destined to be first, had been set up in the new continent. A liberal charter had been provided. The eyes of the world were upon it. And now a Republican boss and a Democratic boss were conspiring to turn over this great experiment in self-government to be smirched and well-nigh ruined! Here was no call for courtesy of phrase. The wrath of *The World* flamed in a series of appeals to the people to put away the shame that threatened.

One little hope there was, and that faded. There were in the field, besides Low, Tracy, and Van Wyck, two other candidates: Mayor "Big Pat" Gleason of Long Island City, a picturesque character who would draw local support, and Henry George. Mr. George entered the campaign to aid Low and to save the city. He overtaxed his strength and on the eve of election died. To him *The World* paid sincere tribute:

He died as he lived. He died a hero's death. He died as he would have wished to die—on the battle-field, spending his last strength in a blow at the enemies of the people.

Liberty has lost a friend. Democracy has lost a leader!

Henry George's son, then thirty-five years old, was nominated to succeed his father. But Democrats by the thousand who had been held by Henry George went back to Tammany. The great city was put in Boss Croker's hands to sink to a depth only less abysmal than that remembered filth of Tweedism which had given the classic measure of municipal degradation.

Van Wyck had 233,997 votes; Low, 151,540, on a Citizens' Union ticket; Tracy, 101,863; George, 21,693.

In the city which had given McKinley more than sixty thousand majority the previous year the candidate of his party was a weak third. In the state which had given McKinley 268,000 majority the candidate of his party for judge of the Court of Appeals was beaten by more than sixty thousand. Small comfort was there, in this evidence of the wrath of the independent voter, for New York, thrown under the wheels of juggernaut.

XII

A WAR FOR AN IDEAL

1898–1899

What Caused the War with Spain—"The World" as a Military Critic— The Firm Friendship of Britain in the Crisis—First News of the Battle of Manila—The Arrival of "The Man on Horseback"—Theodore Roosevelt and Boss Platt —Forcing the Franchise Tax—Ramapo and Rapid Transit —Great Britain and the Boer War—President Kruger's Appeal to "The World"—Prompt Protests Against Imperialism.

IN slavery days Southern politicians had cast longing eyes upon Cuba for the reason that they forced the Mexican war, to strengthen the political power of the slave states. Cuba, with its immense sugar plantations, was the last considerable stronghold of slavery in the New World. The Spanish authorities had ruled the island brutally, corruptly, and in disregard of native public sentiment, so that filibustering expeditions from the United States, often winked at by the government, were welcomed. In Buchanan's administration the Ostend Manifesto, announced in London, Paris, and Madrid by American ministers, stated that if Spain would not sell Cuba the United States would seize it—a policy that might have been carried out but for anticipated protests by other nations.

When in 1895 a new rebellion broke out and when the Spanish authorities fought it by concentrado there was no longer any question of the slavery interest. There was simply a feeling that it was time for Spain to leave the continent. The war desire grew gradually for years;

with the blowing up of the *Maine,* it burst into sudden flame.

Captain-General Campos as early as November 1, 1895, had cabled his government that "if this war is not brought to a speedy termination by granting home rule to Cuba the United States will surely give aid to the insurgents and espouse their cause sooner or later." By the beginning of 1896 Congress was discussing the recognition of belligerent rights and offering Spain our "friendly offices" for the composing of the trouble. In February, 1897, *The World* was asking questions like these:

How long is the peasantry of Spain to be drafted away to Cuba, to die miserably in a hopeless war, that Spanish nobles and Spanish officers may get medals and honors?

How long shall old men and women and children be murdered by the score, the innocent victims of Spanish rage against the patriot armies they cannot conquer?

How long shall American citizens, arbitrarily arrested while on peaceful and legitimate errands, be immured in foul Spanish prisons without trial?

How long shall the navy of the United States be used as the sea-police of barbarous Spain?

Little need be allowed for the rhetoric of passion in this indictment; it was true. Spain's policy in the New World was medieval, and the task of repressing overt acts of American sympathy was becoming more and more difficult. What "reconcentration" meant *The World* explained on May 16, 1897:

The President sent a message to Congress yesterday asking for $50,000 with which to relieve or remove starving American citizens [in Cuba]. The message is thoroughly unsatisfactory. So is the form of relief proposed. These American citizens own plantations or work upon plantations of others. On these plantations there is plenty of food. But the military despot who rules Cuba will not let these Americans live upon the plantations. They are starving, not of any necessity, but solely by Weyler's abhorrent command. He has compelled them to leave their homes and go to the towns, where they have no bread-winning employment. . . .

A resolute attitude on our part is all the excuse Spain needs for recalling the butcher Weyler and abandoning the inhuman purpose of making one of the fairest regions of the earth a depopulated desert, and calling that peace.

The blowing up of the *Maine* removed the last hope of settlement by negotiation. Even then *The World* affected to believe that war was not inevitable, but in Spain it was becoming as hard to restrain public anger at the "Yankee pigs" as it was in our own country to hold back the hotheads who wished Weyler driven into the sea.

Now was seen the wisdom of *The World* and those who with it had protested against warlike passion in the Venezuela crisis. The British were openly sympathetic with us at Manila. The continent of Europe was strongly against us. The French ambassador, M. Jules Cambon, and the German ambassador, Baron von Holleben, concerted in Washington a plan to involve Great Britain in an expression of this enmity. An identical despatch signed by the representatives of five continental powers, advising a joint European remonstrance against the war, was submitted to Lord Pauncefote, and he was induced to sign and present it by methods which may be left in dispute. It has even been charged that the despatch was "doctored." Lord Salisbury ignored the paper when it was forwarded to him. Four years later sensational Berlin cablegrams, supposedly inspired, revealed Lord Pauncefote's part in the transaction, and accused Great Britain of unfriendly action; neither Washington nor London was moved by the publication, and Von Holleben was recalled. Such friendship as that of Salisbury was worth much in 1898.

No apologies for *The World's* urgency that Cuba be freed

by force will be necessary if that contest answered its description of a holy war:

Is war always a crime? Are all wars unholy?
History answers the question. The Declaration of Independence was a declaration of war, but it was not a crime. The war of the Revolution was not unholy.
War waged by an alien power to perpetuate its despotism over a subject race is always unholy.
War waged in behalf of freedom, of self-government, of law and order, of humanity, to end oppression, misrule, plunder and savagery, is a holy war in itself. It is doubly justified if it is free from the taint of selfishness, the greed of acquisition, the lust of power.

War was declared April 23d. Almost at once Admiral Dewey, in command of the Asiatic squadron, sailed for Manila. It was known that a battle must have taken place there, probably on May 1st. For six days the wildest rumors prevailed, but with Manila cut off from cable communication no authentic news was possible. Upon this tense period of waiting there broke, on the morning of May 7th, this despatch exclusively printed in *The World*, which gave the world its first information:

HONGKONG, *May 7th.*
I have just arrived here on the United States revenue cutter *Hugh McCulloch*, with my report of the great American triumph at Manila.
The entire Spanish fleet of eleven vessels was destroyed.
Three hundred Spaniards were killed and four hundred wounded.
Our loss was none killed and but six slightly wounded.
Not one of the American ships was injured.
E. W. HARDEN,
(*World's* Staff Correspondent.)

This initial triumph of the war was speedily followed by other victories. The army was necessarily slow in attacking Cuba in force, but the navy began at once patrolling the waters about the ever-faithful isle, to which, in spite of silly fears of raids by Spanish ships along our Atlantic coast, it was reasonable to suppose Cervera's squadron of ships from Spain would be sent. On May 19th the Cervera squadron arrived in Santiago de Cuba and was almost at once bottled up.   Lieutenant Hobson and a detachment of plucky naval volunteers sunk the *Merrimac* in the fairway, which did not completely block the channel, but the Atlantic fleet of Admiral Sampson kept constant guard.   General Shafter's army, assembled at Tampa and embarked at Key West, Florida, arrived at Daiquiri, Cuba, on June 20–22 and was almost immediately involved in actions at Las Guasimas and at El Caney on the outskirts of Santiago.   On July 1–2 the Spanish works at El Caney and San Juan were carried with relatively heavy losses and on the following day Cervera's ships, attempting to escape from the harbor, were beached or sunk in a running fight.   Santiago was surrendered two weeks later.   A little later still General Miles took Porto Rico almost without opposition; and on August 13th, the day after the peace protocol was signed and armistice proclaimed, Manila surrendered to the American Pacific expedition with assistance from native revolutionists.

Thus ended, except for long-drawn-out campaigns with the Filipino insurgents, a war in which the navy had distinguished itself from first to last.   The voyage of the *Oregon* from our Pacific coast right around South America in time to take part in the destruction of Cervera's fleet was one of the most striking proofs of efficiency in that service.   Quite otherwise were the conditions in the War Department, where unreadiness and incompetency deprived the administration of all the political advantage it might have expected to gain by the campaign.   The Secretary of War, Gen. Russell A. Alger, was over-weighted by his sudden responsibility. Bad beef was foisted upon soldiers by army contractors. Military camps were laid out with such disregard of sanitary precautions that commands that never went to Cuba almost rivaled the death-rate of those that did. Returning soldiers were placed in rest-camps not much better. The military experts of the world were amazed by the appearance during the Santiago campaign of a "round robin" signed by many officers of volunteer troops, including Colonel Roosevelt, protesting against the quality of food furnished to the soldiers and intimating that for sanitary reasons and lack of commissariat it might be necessary to abandon positions which the valor of the army had won.

The World had not shone in military criticism, which was rather out of its field. For a time it joined in shouting "On to Cadiz," and advocating an attack upon Spain, but after the fall of Santiago it recovered its poise and realized that the war had lasted long enough. Henceforward it favored an early peace. In exposing the beef scandals it led the way and did much good work.

The political campaign of 1898 began as the protocol of peace was signed. Boss Platt, more concerned to retain his hold on the state government than he had been to keep Croker out of power in New York City, looked for a "war hero" who could not be held responsible for the blunders of the administration. There was one such man in New York, practically only one, Colonel Roosevelt of the Rough Riders, fresh from the front, an intense, ambitious man, familiar with political conditions in Albany and not unduly sensitive about being bossed. For the Roosevelt who has since thundered so fiercely against bosses gave out in September, 1898, an interview stating that if elected Governor he would "on all matters of importance consult Senator Platt as leader of the party."

Had *The World's* advice been heeded in 1898 the country might have been spared the picturesque, costly

career of this child of destiny.   It was an opportunity
for a strong Democratic candidate.   *The World* had such
a candidate, a man whom for years it had urged upon
attention for Mayor or for Governor.   On September 16th
it said:

Judge Gaynor certainly possesses many qualities desirable
in a candidate.   There can be no doubt in any mind as to what
the man who sent McKane to prison would do to the Canal
Ring if he were elected Governor.   No Force bill would receive
his approval.   No corporations with interests inimical to the
public interest could either buy or dictate legislation if Gaynor
were Governor.   He is as brave as Roosevelt, and is superior
as a stump-speaker.   No boss could control him.   He has
shown himself to be a reformer who reforms evils.

Had Gaynor been a candidate against Colonel Roosevelt the man on horseback would have been left to his
pen and his study.   Judge Gaynor was not then, nor on
the other occasions mentioned, desirous of the nomination.   He would not have been accepted in any case by
Boss Croker, whose influence secured the selection of
Mayor Van Wyck's brother, Judge Augustus Van Wyck,
of Brooklyn.   It was a nomination to justify the often-
repeated question, "Must a boss be an ass?"   Voters
feared that Judge Van Wyck might be as servile to
bossism in Albany as his brother in New York.   To make
matters worse, Croker denied a renomination to Supreme
Court Justice Daly, and thus heightened the revolt.

The World was not unfriendly to Colonel Roosevelt,
with his newly won laurels as a popular soldier, but it
saw in him an accepted agent of Boss Platt; and upon
the Platt machine rather than upon Roosevelt personally
it trained its batteries.   There was plenty of ammunition:
the new series of canal scandals, which showed the machine in an unfavorable light; the Force bill, passed to
hamper free elections in New York; imperialism and

Republican extravagance. It was a losing battle. But with all the advantages of a war candidate, with an antagonist so weak as Van Wyck, and with the Daly issue to help in the metropolis, Colonel Roosevelt won only by eighteen thousand plurality. Almost any popular candidate would have beaten him. Judge Gaynor could have won by a tremendous margin. So fortune serves her favorites. Elsewhere in the country there were decided Democratic gains in spite of a successful war. The temporary relegation of the silver issue to the rear had made them possible.

Immediately after the election of Roosevelt as Governor of New York pressure was renewed upon the 1899 Legislature for a law taxing franchises, a project initiated by *The World*. The bill was drawn by Lawson Purdy and Senator John Ford, now a Supreme Court justice, from a draft sent by *The World*. Governor Roosevelt suggested a commission to investigate taxation, but by mass-meetings and other means of voicing public sentiment it was made plain that delay would score against the party responsible. Boss Platt did not favor the act. Boss Croker, who testified before the Mazet Committee that he was "working for his own pocket all the time," looked with disfavor upon taxing the corporations that had bought franchises. But publicity was too powerful for the old-time partnership, and on April 29th *The World* was able to announce its triumph:

The passage by the Assembly of the Ford bill taxing franchises, by the strong vote of 104 to 38, completes a notable victory for justice through publicity.

On the 11th of January last The World took up the question of unequal assessments and unjust taxation in this city. It showed that over $6,000,000,000 of personal property assessed for taxation escaped through "swearing off." It revealed the enormous value of the franchises of street-using corporations and the ridiculously small amount paid by these corporations for their privileges. . . .

From that day to this not an issue of The World has appeared without an array of facts, arguments and appeals bearing on this question. More than 350 columns of this matter have been printed in The World during its fight for just taxation.

In addition to this The World procured and sent to the Legislature a petition for the Ford bill, containing the names of 20,000 property-owners and rent-payers. . . . And finally, when the measure was to all appearances dead in the hostile hands of the Assembly Rules Committee, The World organized and sent, at its own expense by special train to Albany, a committee of one hundred citizens to make a last demand upon the Assembly for action on the bill. The revived hope of its friends dated from that demonstration.

The relief to overburdened taxpayers from this measure of justice will be perceptible and welcome. It will reduce by $15,000,000 the burden upon the present taxpayers of this city. It will increase the bond-issuing capacity of the city $100,000,000. But greater than this is the demonstration that when the people will do so they still rule.

Governor Roosevelt had found in the bill what he described as faults and called the Legislature in special session to remedy them. In the opinion of Senator Ford the Roosevelt changes weakened the law, but it has continued to serve a useful purpose in the economy of the state, after having been held valid by the United States Supreme Court.

In the same month *The World* defeated a long-pending plot of water-right and water-option owners to exploit the city through a contract to provide water from the Ramapo River for a sum which, it was supposed, would mount to two hundred million dollars. A water system half public-owned and half privately controlled was preposterous. Yet in the low moral state of the city government the project would probably have succeeded had not *The World* enjoined the Board of Public Improvements, called mass-meetings, and roused public sentiment. A good part of the battle was in a telling phrase; as "The

Great Chartered Ramapo Robbery" the scheme became notorious; and with the aid of Comptroller Bird S. Coler it was killed.

Similar services were rendered to rapid transit. A tablet in City Hall Park shows where the first subway was begun by Mayor Van Wyck's throwing out a spadeful of earth; it does not tell how Van Wyck's administration followed the Tammany traditions of hostility to the measure, even to the point of securing an opinion from Corporation Counsel Whalen, a Croker appointee, that the city's debt limit was exhausted and it could not issue rapid-transit bonds. *The World* with its rallying cry of "Fifteen Minutes to Harlem" had powerfully aided in arousing public sentiment in favor of quicker transit until it would not be denied. The beginning of the first public-built and public-owned subway in New York was an event of great importance. The magnitude of the work would alone have made its inception memorable. The original subway cost $35,000,000 to construct; with improvements and extensions, including that to Brooklyn under the East River, it had cost $55,000,000 before arrangements were made to complete and supplement it.

The cause of international peace, which *The World* had so powerfully aided, again interested it in 1899. The summoning of the first Hague Conference by "the ruler of the most backward of the peoples commonly called civilized," the Czar of Russia, was scoffed at by the statesmen of Europe. They saw in it the idealism of a dreamy monarch; or with Kipling, warning Britain against the truce of the "bear that walks like a man," they saw danger to themselves. That the American representatives went to the conference in a more hopeful spirit was in part due to the long support of *The World*.

Britain was just then in greater need of warning against the aggression of the bear than against the fate of Adam-

Zad. She was in the full course of the provocative steps which, beginning with the Jameson raid, were to bring on the Boer War in the interest of a few cosmopolitan mine-owners and of Joseph Chamberlain's schemes of colonial empire. *The World* threw open its columns to President "Oom Paul" Kruger of the Transvaal. His statement was summarized editorially:

President Kruger says that the crisis is due to two main causes:

First—"A certain section of British residents, to whom the existence of the Republic, embracing the most flourishing parts of South Africa, is a standing eyesore, and who are suffering from the prevailing jingo mania."

Second—"The mining capitalists, who, not content with having the best mining laws in the world, wish also to have complete control of legislation and administration."

The object, he says, is as clear as are the causes:

"The destruction of the Republic and the complete control of the richest mines in the world."

There is a dignified and profoundly touching pathos in "Oom Paul's" conclusion:

"Though we have no such powerful friend as you proved to be to Venezuela and other republics, we have strong faith that the cause of freedom and republicanism will triumph in the end."

A month later President Kruger, the President of the Orange Free State, and the Premier of Cape Colony joined in protests through *The World* against the impending war. Its columns were used to secure signatures to petitions which begged President McKinley to offer the friendly services of the United States in reconciling Great Britain and the two republics. To these petitions the President replied through a cabinet minister as summarized by *The World:*

First—The United States, having been the recipient of moral support from England during the war with Spain, will do nothing distasteful to England.

12

Second—While the sympathies of the President and his Cabinet are, to a certain extent, with the Boers, yet their love for England is stronger and outweighs their friendliness for the Krugerites.

Third—The President will not intervene, believing, as he does, that intervention might enable some foreign power to take a hand in the Philippine war.

"'Love of England,'" replied *The World* to President McKinley, "you are right; we are under moral obligations to England and her moral support last year. Deepen that obligation! Show for England that higher friendship, that higher love, which is not inconsistent with your duty as a civilized man and as the representative of the great republic—love of peace, love of justice, love of the American principle of arbitration!"

Against the first suggestion that the United States should retain the Philippines *The World* was in revolt. Upon the trial balloons sent up by the Administration to test public opinion upon "benevolent assimilation" it trained its artillery. It characterized the proposed treaty as coming from "the inner temple of Mammon," as an attempt to extend markets with monopoly by the war power, instead of inviting trade by tariff concessions; and to the suggestion that we should "pay Spain forty million dollars indemnity [twenty million dollars in the treaty as signed] for the destruction of her fleet" by Dewey it answered that "destiny" was a hifalutin name for bunco. The spirit of many editorial protests against holding subject races without constitutional guarantees is shown in the following article of November 3, 1898:

The Great Republic has won a position as a world-power, a world-influence, by means of a war, not for "criminal aggression," but for humanity and liberty alone.

How shall she begin to use the power? . . .

There is a demand that the first step shall be the establish-

ment of a military despotism over remote and forever alien
Malay millions.

But is there not a worthier, a more fitting way of first making
ourselves felt in the world's politics?

"Vampire empire" will drain the blood of our young men
sent out as garrisons. It will degrade us to the level of war-
makers for "criminal aggression." It will rob us of our un-
sullied character as the friends of liberty, the advocates of
government only with the consent of the governed.

Would it not be nobler, wiser, to keep to the course of humanity and civilized progress? Would it not be better to continue
to define our international responsibilities as George Washington defined them when he wrote, "give to mankind the
magnanimous and too novel example of a people always guided
by an exalted justice and benevolence"?

No imperialism. No indemnity to Spain. No permanent
war taxes. No annex of despotism. No shoulder-strap
satrapies. No infusion of Malay hordes into the Republic.
No plutocracy at home. No autocracy abroad.

Yet the country was not displeased with the tinsel
of its new toy. In the 1899 elections imperialism was not
directly involved, as no members of Congress were elected
except to fill vacancies; but the verdict of the states,
though indirect, was emphatic. Mr. Bryan represented
anti - imperialism, but he also continued to represent
free silver, which, though dead as an issue, could be
galvanized by skilful political foes into horrendous signs
of renewed vitality. After the November elections *The
World* was constrained to say:

The elections mean a victory for imperialism in a majority
of the States voting. There is neither honesty nor profit in
denying this. They mean also a triumph for McKinley—but
a triumph that was made easy by Mr. Bryan and his friends
in thrusting again to the front at the beginning of the campaign
the futile and fatal fallacy of free silver and the thrice-con-
demned Chicago platform.

Yet the blunder was to be repeated.

XIII

Mr. Bryan's Tactical Error—He Assists the Spanish Treaty and Acquisition of the Philippines—Republican Platform Determined by the Results of the War—Reciprocity Yields to the Theory of Markets Won and Held by Military Power—Theodore Roosevelt for Vice-President—The Free-Silver Issue Insisted Upon by Mr. Bryan—Devery and the New York Police Department—Governor Odell Rescues the City by Favoring Fusion—The Shepard-Low Campaign.

MR. BRYAN saw that imperialism was an inescapable issue. But at the crisis which decided American policy he was smitten with vacillation of purpose or errancy of judgment which robbed his influence of its due effect.

That he felt the peril of the shifting national course he showed in December, 1898. "Heretofore," said he, "greed has perverted the government and used its instrumental interference for private gain; but now the very foundation principles of our government are assaulted." And, adapting Lincoln's phrase, "this nation cannot endure half republic and half colony, half free and half vassal."

How, then, did he justify his action only two months later? The Treaty of Paris, ceding the Philippines, was submitted to the Senate early in 1899 and debated four weeks. Enlightened public sentiment was unfavorable. *The World* and other journals of influence protested. The majority of the American Peace Commissioners in Paris had opposed the Philippine cession until instructed by

President McKinley to insist upon it.   One reason for his course was gratitude to Great Britain and a wish to oblige her by keeping the islands out of unfriendly hands.   But jingoism was already keen among the war enthusiasts in the two military services and in business interests which thrive on war contracts.

Whatever the reasons for the cession, the treaty containing it nearly failed of ratification, receiving in the Senate only one vote to spare.   The veteran Republican Senators, Hoar of Massachusetts and Hale of Maine, both voted against the innovation.   But for Mr. Bryan's advice the seventeen Democrats and Populists who supported the treaty could not have been mustered.   "I believe," said he, when taxed with inconsistency, "that we are now in a better position to wage a successful war against imperialism than we would have been had the treaty been rejected."   "You thought," commented *The World*, "a great wrong should be done that you might fight the great wrong after it was accomplished."

The World had no idea of such an error of postponement. It fought the Treaty of Paris in the making and in the ratification and did not cease the fight even when it was ratified.   Unanswerable were its arguments—unless the Declaration of Independence was a mistake.   The native inhabitants "possessed the right to govern themselves or to give their consent to being governed, which is included in the natural and unalienable right of all men to life, liberty and the pursuit of happiness."   Telling use was made of the treaty made by Mr. McKinley with the Sultan of Sulu—"recognition of the Sultan's complete independence and even sovereignty under the protection of the United States"; the "subsidies to himself, his harem keepers, etc., recognition of and protection to slavery and bigamy."

But whatever Mr. Bryan's error in 1899 in causing the Treaty of Paris to be ratified with Democratic aid, he did sincerely believe that ruling the Philippines outside of the Constitution was wrong; he held to that belief, and remained a power on the side of justice to our island wards and to our own traditions. "We should not only give the Filipino independence," he said, later, but "we should protect him from his enemies. We should establish a government and then tell him that it is his, and then we should tell the world 'Hands off.'" In a speech in Keokuk in October, 1899, Mr. Bryan swept away in a sentence the whole defense of McKinley's war of subjugation. "Must we keep these islands because Dewey sank a Spanish fleet?" he asked. "Schley sank one, and we promise to free Cuba."

Because of such utterances and because silver was no longer a danger *The World* viewed Mr. Bryan's nomination in 1900 with less misgiving than in 1896. It was apparent long before the convention met that there would be little chance of naming another man. *The World* had hoped to find such a man in Admiral Dewey. Perhaps a war hero might wrest the country from the Republicans. Unwilling in the fall of 1899 to announce himself a candidate, the admiral permitted the use of his name on April 3, 1900. "What citizen would refuse," he said, "the highest honor in the gift of the nation?" Mournfully *The World* admitted that "Admiral Dewey is perhaps for the first time in his life too late. Last October opportunity sought him in vain. Now he seeks it in vain."

The Republican platform was written in advance by the name of the President and the result of the war. Reciprocity was dead. A favoring tariff had been refused to Porto Rico by Congress, though that island was an integral part of the nation "Mondays, Wednesdays, and Fridays." Washington was dreaming of trade in Asia. Of these sinister facts in the Republican outlook *The World* said:

Reciprocity was a valuable idea, because it proposed more and more widely to open to us, to our superior skill in production, the markets of the civilized world. . . .

The Republican policy of to-day is a complete reversal of the sagacious plans of the Republican leader and party of a dozen years ago.

The McKinleys and Hannas invite our producers to turn their whole attention to the meager markets of barbaric and semi-barbaric peoples, to the "gorgeous East"—gorgeous in poetry and romance, but squalid and poor in reality.

The World opposed the nomination of a third ticket by the Gold Democrats. "Four years ago," it said, "free silver was the dominant issue in the campaign. This year, though it may be talked about in certain sections, it will not be an issue at all because the money question is settled for at least four years to come by an unchangeable Republican majority in the Senate." It begged all Democrats to concentrate their attention upon the more pressing danger:

A country with subject possessions secured by conquest and governed by force is not a republic. And where plutocracy rules, democracy becomes merely a name without force or effect.

It is for these reasons that a third ticket this year is not only uncalled for, but would be even more farcical than it was in 1896. Mr. Bryan, who, as The World said two months ago, will be renominated by acclamation, represents the American and, therefore, the democratic side of these living, burning, dominating issues. He is for this reason entitled to and will receive the support of The World and of all who believe with us that "the only issue worth considering in this campaign is the preservation of the Republic, the maintenance of the Constitution and a return to the principles of the Declaration of Independence."

The death of Vice-President Hobart made it necessary for the Republican national convention to select a new candidate for his office—the only real business of the gathering. Naturally, the energetic Governor of New York was discussed. Mr. Roosevelt had refused to be considered, but "the 'irrevocable' was revoked. 'Vowing he would ne'er consent,' he consented." Platt had "desired and schemed for this result in order to get Roosevelt out of the Governor's chair." Yet *The World* saw in the disposition of the delegates to select Mr. Roosevelt, "in spite of the sinister support of the bosses, the undisguised hostility of the corporations in this State and the opposition of Hanna, a fine tribute to his character, his high purpose and real achievements in public life."

The Democratic convention, meeting in Kansas City July 4th, adopted one plank to which *The World* could take no exception: "The burning issue of imperialism, growing out of the Spanish war, involves the very exis- tence of the Republic and the destruction of our free in- stitutions. *We regard it as the paramount issue of the campaign.*"

But a party cannot always determine upon what issue it will fight its battles. Issues are thrust upon it by cir- cumstances, by dumb chance, by an accusing past. Mr. Bryan, with his genius for defeat, did not trust to anything less certain than deliberate intent to provide himself with a losing cause. To the Gold Democrats who besought him to make it possible for them to rejoin the party his answer was a telegram, printed the day the convention met:

If by any chance the Committee on Resolutions decides to report a platform in which there is not a silver plank, there must be a minority report and a fight on the floor of the convention. I will come to Kansas City on the fastest train available, make a fight for free silver on the floor of the convention, and then decline to take the nomination if the convention omits the ratio. This is final.

This unwelcome action and the adoption of a free-silver plank did not deter *The World* from Bryan's support, though it felt that support to be hopeless. During the campaign Mr. Bryan devoted much attention to the new issue of the far-away islands—so much that *The World* described him as "The New Bryan." It said on September 26th:

It is not necessary to agree with Mr. Bryan—and we certainly do not agree with him on his financial theories—in order to do him the simple justice of admitting that he is a far different man from what he was four years ago; more dignified, more temperate, more respectful in every way of the conservative opinion of the country. . . .

Venerable and life-long Republican statesmen, like George S. Boutwell, over eighty years old, and Carl Schurz, seventy-two, have nothing in the world to gain by coming out for Mr. Bryan now, if they saw in him the same representative of dangerous political experiments as four years ago.

The result of the election was never in much doubt. Hope upon the one side, apprehension on the other, rose to no such heights as in 1896. Defeat was more crushing. Bryan's popular vote was 150,000 smaller; McKinley's 100,000 greater. The electoral college showed a plurality of 137. It was a heavy blow to anti-imperialism. For the time being, the country was committed to the continuance of that rule over the Philippines and their eight million people which an old-fashioned Republican, Senator Hoar, described as "pure, simple, undiluted, unchecked despotism."

Because of his services to the city in the Ramapo and other matters *The World* favored the nomination of Comptroller Coler for Governor in 1900, but the reasons which made him at that time a popular candidate made him also unpalatable to Tammany, and John B. Stanchfield, Mr. Hill's candidate, was placed in the field. It would have made little difference that year whom the party nominated. Seeing his opportunity to ride into office upon the backs of the sound-money men, Senator Platt named for Governor his deputy boss, Representative Benjamin B. Odell, Jr., a politician of more than ordinary shrewdness. Perhaps Odell nominated himself; he was already grasping the power from Platt's enfeebled hands.

Little as it liked Stanchfield, *The World* liked less Odell's nomination, which "raised the question clean-cut whether one man shall hold both the executive and the law-making power." As Platt's proxy, he had been the Legislature the previous winter; his election would mean "a practical subversion of popular government and the substitution of one-man rule pure and simple."

Weak candidate as he would have been under happier circumstances, Odell won, with McKinley's help, by one hundred and eleven thousand. He proved to be the ablest Governor New York had had for years. A fair vision of the Presidency shone before him, and he was keen to note how Cleveland had attained that office by disregard of bosses and service of the people.

If *The World's* efforts for national reform were made of no avail by the silver obsession; if in the state its desire for good government was unexpectedly aided by a man whom it had reasons for opposing, it triumphed greatly in the city of New York against the alliance between vice and politics which throve in the shelter of Tammany.

The Van Wyck administration had proved all that had been feared. The Police Department, under four commissioners—one Tammany man, one McLaughlin Democrat from Brooklyn, and two nominal Republicans, who were really assistant Tammanyites—was practically controlled by William S. Devery as chief. The Republican Legislature changed the charter, putting the chief and the Police Board out of office and substituting a single commissioner. Croker countered by making Devery deputy commissioner; for commissioner he selected Michael C. Murphy, a wizened atomy of a man performing the daily miracle of living with a closed œsophagus, which required feeding through a tube, a process that could not long keep him alive. Even with the best of intentions Murphy could be no more than a figurehead.

The tale of Van Wyck's unfitness did not stop with his surrender of the Police Department to Croker; he was willing also to receive personal profit from a trust that proposed to exploit the people by municipal favor. This was the famous Ice Trust; with Devery, it gave Van Wyck the title of "the Ice-Trust-Vice-Trust Mayor."

The Ice Trust was the creation of Charles W. Morse, of Bath, Maine, who has since served a term in a federal prison for banking offenses. Morse's idea was simplicity itself. Combining various ice companies, he planned to shut out competition by control of private and public docks at which independent dealers could land ice. In this he counted upon the co-operation of the Dock Board, in which Charles F. Murphy, afterward the Tammany boss, was the ruling spirit. On May 1, 1890, the trust notified domestic customers that ice would cost sixty cents a hundred pounds, and that no five-cent pieces would be sold. On May 23d *The World* announced that it had found in the armory of the law a weapon for the protection of the people against extortion, in section 1534 of the Greater New York charter, providing for the summary public examination of any city official or other person:

This provision of law was originally enacted in 1874 to remedy the difficulty that had then lately arisen in compelling the testimony of official and other persons concerned in the crimes of the Tweed Ring. Wisely incorporated in the consolidated city's charter, it is now invoked by The World to compel the disclosure, by public examination, of whatever "knowledge or information" the officials of the city and their unofficial partners have in their possession as to the Ice Trust and the dealings of the Dock Board therewith.

Justice Gaynor, on application made by The World under this section, has issued an order to Mayor Van Wyck, Mr. John F. Carroll, and the three members of the Dock Board—all of whom have so far refused to say one word as to their official or personal relations with the Ice Trust—and also to the President and Vice-President of the American Ice Company, to appear before him on Saturday next and submit to examination on oath on that intensely interesting subject.

Mayor Van Wyck admitted that through a ground-floor arrangement he had obtained 3,050 shares of preferred stock and 2,750 shares of common stock of the Ice Trust, although the city charter forbade such investment. Others who held stock were his brother, Augustus Van Wyck, defeated candidate for Governor in 1898; John F. Carroll; Richard Croker and members of his family; Dock Commissioners Murphy and J. Sergeant Cram; Hugh McLaughlin, of Brooklyn; Frank Black, Republican ex-Governor; Corporation Counsel Whalen; "Honest John" Daly, gambler; James A. Mahoney, the "King of the Poolrooms," and certain judges, some of whom had been investors in companies absorbed by the trust.

The World sent Governor Roosevelt a citizens' petition for the removal of Mayor Van Wyck. Though nothing directly came of this action, it aided in causing the trust to cut twenty cents a ton from the price of ice, and the issue thus raised was potent the following year in redeeming the city.

Nothing is farther from truth than the assumption that a political boss like Richard Croker must be a shrewd politician to gain and wield his power.

Croker had an iron will, great stubbornness, and poor judgment. His political acumen reached only so far as that, given a strong situation, a party plurality, or a magnetic candidate, he could load upon that element of strength a burden of jobbery or of unfit nominations, and possibly win.   But, as he was incapable of estimating the mental processes of the average citizen, he was constantly overloading his tickets.   He did that in 1898 when he nominated a second Van Wyck for Governor and denied a nomination to Judge Daly, and lost the state.   He did it in 1901, and lost the city and the county.   It was practically his last exploit.

There was a new power in the field, of which *The World* said in March, 1901—while McKinley was still living:

Gov. Odell has not merely "broken with the boss."   His move is far bolder, far more significant.   In asserting his independence he has struck for the leadership of his party.

Like Roosevelt, Odell is of lofty ambition.   Like Roosevelt two years ago, he wants a second term as Governor, and hopes for the Presidency afterward.   But his problem is the reverse of that which Roosevelt had to solve.   Roosevelt had a reputation as an independent, and to win he had to keep it and at the same time gain the favor of the machine.   He failed measurably in both directions.   Odell has a reputation as a machine and corporation man, and to win he must keep the favor of the machine, or himself secure control of it, and at the same time win the favor of the people by such measures as the corporation-tax laws and his policy of economy.

The rising star of Odell gave promise that the Republican machine would not this year be unfavorable to fusion against Tammany, while the Citizens' Union also, chastened by defeat and aghast at the consequences of disunion, was in a more reasonable frame of mind than in 1897.   The nomination of Seth Low could almost be taken for granted.   For safety's sake *The World* would have preferred a strong Democrat on the fusion side, but it was well pleased with Low.   It turned also to Croker, urging him to name a man of high type, so that the city would be safe, no matter who was chosen.   Croker, quite capable of adding the Low and Tracy vote of 1897 and subtracting Tammany's, realized that he must not try another Van Wyck. He nominated Edward M. Shepard, of whom *The World* said:

In accepting Edward M. Shepard as the Democratic nominee for Mayor, Mr. Croker is entitled to credit for acting on the suggestion made by The World, which nearly a month ago first named Mr. Shepard as one of the strongest candidates who could be nominated. No matter what his motive may be for yielding to The World's advice, even if it be no higher than the making a virtue of necessity, the fact that Mr. Croker has so yielded and has rendered the city a signal service by so doing deserves full and ungrudging acknowledgment.

Whatever the outcome of the election may be in other respects, the city is assured in advance that the Mayor's chair will be filled by a man, and not a puppet.

Shepard was an ideal candidate. He had been a municipal reformer all his life, had rendered distinguished public service. He was able. His speeches were fine and strong. Upon both sides, so far as the Mayoralty was concerned, the campaign was kept upon a high plane. *The World* asked only that Shepard pledge himself to the purification of the Police Department. Seth Low had said that if he were elected, "as soon as practicable after the first of January the official heads of Mr. Murphy and Mr. Devery will roll upon the ground." Would Mr. Shepard, *The World* asked, "define his position and purpose in equally plain terms?" There was something quixotic in the tenor of Mr. Shepard's reply to the crucial question of his campaign. It is thus summarized in *The World* editorial of October 14th:

He quoted Mr. Low's pledge . . . and admitted that "the temptation upon me to give it is strong," as "there is no doubt pre-election advantage in this pledge." But he refused to give it:

1. Upon the constitutional ground that the oath of office

requires the successful candidate to swear that he has "not made any promise to influence the giving or withholding of any vote." This provision, Mr. Shepard contends, was established in order that when an elected public servant of the people enters upon his duties "he shall do so subject to no personal pledge, promise or mortgage which will prevent his acting in office with an absolute freedom upon the facts as he shall find them to be, and upon his conscience."

2. He refused upon the ethical ground that "No man, whatever my present impression or opinion of him, and however strong my impression may be now, shall, by any promise I now give, be deprived of the right to submit to me as a sworn Mayor in office, ready with an unclosed mind to hear, his defense if he has one."

"For all the votes in Christendom," declared Mr. Shepard, "I will not preclude myself, if I become Mayor, from listening to any defense of any subordinate officer with a fair and intelligent mind and a resolute will."

Incongruous the spectacle of such a scrupulous candidate running upon a Croker platform and ticket! The incongruity was to receive visible illustration when Mr. Shepard, a man of slender physique, appeared upon the platform at Tammany Hall surrounded by men of splendid physique who had won their way to power in part by their muscular strength. Many a voter who saw the contrast wondered if Shepard could hold his own against such men if elected. *The World* pointed out inescapable comparisons:

Mr. Shepard has not only put himself upon the Tammany ticket and upon the Tammany platform praising and eulogizing the Van Wyck administration, but he has spoken in Tammany Hall itself.

This is "the same Mr. Shepard" who, four years ago, said that "the most burning and disgraceful blot upon the municipal history of this country is the career of Tammany Hall." . . .

We congratulate Mr. Croker upon his master stroke.

Probably Mr. Shepard could not have been elected at this time; against Low, and with so poor a ticket in support, he should not have been. Croker, who consoled himself for the need of a fine candidate for Mayor by nominating for minor offices men after his own heart, set the capstone to his folly by naming Mayor Van Wyck to be a Justice of the Supreme Court. Van Wyck had upon the platform the unique experience, for a Tammany candidate, of being hissed by audiences in Tammany strongholds, and was branded by the Bar Association as "conspicuously unfit." *The World*, while strongly supporting Low, urged Democrats who would not leave their party to vote for Shepard, in whose hands the Mayoralty would be safe, but at any rate to oppose all the creatures of Croker upon the ticket. Many thousands must have done this. Mr. Low's plurality was 31,000. Edward M. Grout, who ran upon the Fusion ticket for Comptroller against a weaker candidate than Shepard, had 46,000. Van Wyck received but 129,000 votes for Justice in New York County. This was 14,000 less than he had in the same county four years earlier for Mayor, even in a three-cornered fight. Where Tammany candidates were accustomed to get 25,000 to 30,000 plurality he ran 43,000 below the highest Fusion candidate.

By this magnificent victory *The World* was moved to some characteristic reflections:

Mr. Croker, who used to sneer at newspaper influence, now says: "I give full credit for the result of the election to the newspapers." Mr. Platt, whose modest habit it has been to attribute Republican triumphs to Divine Providence, on the day after the late election gave the credit of Tammany's overthrow to the newspapers. . . .

If newspaper power has developed so greatly and so largely in right directions and for the public welfare in a hundred years, what illimitable opportunities for growth and for good in the future open before it at the beginning of the twentieth century! More and more the saying of Constant becomes true: "The press is the mistress of intelligence, and intelligence is the mistress of the world."

There has never been occasion to regret the action of *The World* or the decision of the people in that campaign. The Low administration was not free from grave faults. But it resolutely set up service as its ideal. Unfortunately, an opportunity was soon to be given for New York to swing back into Tammany rule.

In 1897, when Strong was Mayor and New York temporarily in revolt against Tammany, the Legislature had fixed the Mayor's term in the city charter at four years. Croker reaped the benefit under Van Wyck. In a panic at the result the Legislature shortened the term to two years. Mayor Low was the first to be elected for the shorter term, and had barely time to get well under way with an administration of fine beginnings when he was ousted. Later the term was again made four years, and it so remains.

13

XIV

IN PRAISE OF ROOSEVELT

1902–1904

The Coal Strike and President Roosevelt's Energetic Action—Hill's Socialistic Platform in New York—Defeat by a Narrow Margin—The Rise of a New Power in Tammany Hall—Murphy's Skilful Campaign in 1903— George B. McClellan's Long Service as Mayor—Hugh McLaughlin's Last Fight—The Northern Securities Merger Smashed by the Supreme Court— Growing Power of the President—Some Early Misgivings.

A GREAT mistake would be his who should fancy that because *The World* has criticized many of Theodore Roosevelt's policies and activities it has been his never-satisfied detractor. No paper has been more emphatic in praising him. In its comments upon no other public man has it more often verified its denial that it was a party paper, or more often proved its "independence of bosses, machines, candidates and platforms."

The year 1902, when Mr. Roosevelt was fresh in the President's chair, furnished many opportunities for praise. *The World* was pleased with his appointment of Judge Oliver Wendell Holmes to the Supreme Court. In calling for more such appointments it showed the President how he could counter upon Mr. Bryan. If a justice like Mr. Shiras, who by shifting his vote on the income tax created an issue for Mr. Bryan, were to retire and if President Roosevelt were to appoint in his place another man of the type of Justice Holmes he would "add still more to the prestige of the Supreme Court among those very followers of Mr. Bryan who most distrusted it."

The victory of the people in the decision of Judge Thayer against the Northern Securities merger was hailed with satisfaction. Judge Thayer's decision is, *The World* said, "of the highest importance as a long step in the reaction against the hitherto triumphant march of monopoly and the passion for 'combining' anything and everything."

More emphatic was the commendation of Mr. Roosevelt for effecting a settlement of the coal strike which in the autumn of 1902 endangered the prosperity and even the lives of the people—for if by that fortune which waits upon "fools, drunkards and the United States of America" the ensuing winter had not been mild the calamity must have been appalling. *The World* branded the attitude of the employers in refusing arbitration as "unfair to the miners, injurious to the country and in contemptuous defiance of public opinion."

The object of the trust which Mr. Morgan had formed of the coal railroads was to break the miners' union. In this *The World* predicted failure. When Mr. Roosevelt compelled the operators to consent to an arbitration arrangement under which mining could be resumed *The World* gave him the heartiest praise. Work was not begun too soon. The need of coal was urgent. Schools and hospitals were with difficulty kept open. Shade trees were in some cases chopped down for firewood. Many dealers required physicians' prescriptions before yielding up the precious fuel at triple prices. In such conditions of public suffering, which continued long after mining was recommenced, the board of arbitrators, headed by Judge Gray, of Delaware, produced the sliding scale of wages which has since been the basis of agreements.

An echo of the coal strike in the politics of New York State once more illustrated how foolish is the politician who relies upon claptrap. The Governorship was again in question. *The World* recognized that upon his record

Mr. Odell would be a strong candidate; that "as a corporation - taxer, a reformer and a sensible, practical, independent executive—the most successful since Tilden, far more efficient than Roosevelt—he would certainly be re-elected could he stand isolated upon the record of his administration." But Odell, because of the forces he represented, could be beaten by a candidate of the highest type. *The World* mentioned, "not as candidates but as types," Edward M. Shepard, Judge Alton B. Parker, Justice Peckham, and Judge Gaynor. Why, with such wealth of material, Senator Hill selected Mr. Coler, already past his maximum strength, was a mystery soon forgotten in a greater blunder.

This was Mr. Hill's plank in the Democratic state platform declaring in the name of the followers of Thomas Jefferson that "We advocate the national ownership and operation of the anthracite-coal mines by the exercise of the right of eminent domain."

At the time this platform was adopted a coal-ownership plank may have seemed sharp politics. But President Roosevelt, who knew the political trade even better than Senator Hill, by compelling arbitration had taken the plank from under Hill and left him dangling in air. With the miners all at work again before election there was little excuse for the travesty of Democratic doctrine.

The World supported Coler while denouncing the Hill coal plank. Of this it said:

Whatever the principle is, it is not original, for the Populist national platform of 1896 . . . declared that "the Government should own and operate the railroads and telegraph," the former of which rank with coal as a national necessity; and the Social Democratic party in 1900 pushed this doctrine still further toward its logical end in demanding "the public ownership of all gold, silver, copper, lead, iron, coal and other mines, and all oil and gas wells."

But, passing by the paternity of the theory, how would it

work? If the anthracite mines are to be owned by the Federal Government and operated by Federal agents, who would select and control these agents? Who selects the Federal office-holders in Pennsylvania now? Is there one of them, from the highest to the lowest, who is not appointed by Matt Quay, the boss? Is there any doubt that he would, so long as the Republicans hold power, select and dominate every supervisor of Federal coal-mining and dragoon the votes of this great army of employees?

The national government could no more secure and operate the coal-mines in time to avert a coal famine than it could "cut up the moon under the 'right of eminent domain' and divide it among the people." The plank was not a menace; like the silver issue in 1900, it was a handicap. *The World* begged its readers not to vote, through Odell, for a second term of Roosevelt or for "a Republican Congress pledged not to disturb the monopoly-protecting tariff." It placed against Roosevelt's surrender to the tariff stand-patters McKinley's later view of the need of broadening our markets abroad. It quoted Charles M. Schwab's letter to H. C. Frick in 1899:

As to the future, even on low prices, I am most sanguine. I know positively that England cannot produce pig-iron at the actual cost for less than $11.50 per ton, even allowing no profit on raw materials, and cannot put pig-iron into a rail with their most efficient works for less than $7.50 a ton. This would make rails at net cost to them at $19. We can sell at this price and ship abroad so as to net us $16 at works for foreign business, nearly as good as home business has been. What is true of rails is equally true of other steel products. As a result of this we are going to control the steel business of the world.

You know we can make rails for less than $12 per ton, leaving a nice margin on foreign business.

The election result was a surprise; not that Odell was elected, but that, with the help of his own good record as

Governor, the coal plank in the Democratic platform, and the prestige of Roosevelt, he should be elected by only eight thousand votes. This narrow result proved that "if Judge Parker had been nominated and the socialistic coal-ownership plank omitted—as it would have been under his candidacy—the Democrats would have carried the State." Common sense in New York might not have been without effect in making still narrower the Republican majority of thirty in the new House of Representatives.

The World had as little success in seeking to stem the current that next year swept Tammany back into control in New York.

In retiring as boss of Tammany with an ample fortune, to become a sporting country gentleman in England, Richard Croker for a second time dropped the leadership with a string attached running to his own fist. Once before he had left John C. Sheehan in charge of Tammany, and a few months later had returned and driven him from control. Now, at the beginning of 1902, he had left the Hall in the hands of Lewis Nixon, who, finding that he could not so conduct Tammany as to make sponsorship tolerable, resigned. Of him *The World* said:

> By squarely recognizing this fact and retiring from a position which, as he says, he could not retain without losing his self-respect, he has done the people of Greater New York, as well as his party, a large service. He was not and, under existing conditions, could not be the real representative of the men who hold Tammany in their grip. . . . Mr. Nixon was misrepresentative of the men behind and around him. He goes, and gains in public respect by going. They remain, and the popular judgment of them remains also.

Croker, not willing or not in health to resume leadership, temporized after Nixon's retirement by setting up a triumvirate, composed of Daniel F. McMahon, Louis F. Haffen, and Charles F. Murphy—"a two-spot, a joke and a sport," as they were described by Chief of Police Devery, retired. Of these three men the "sport" played Napoleon to his Directorate. The campaign of 1903 was his first; it was tactically his best.

Mayor Low's administration was excellent, but hardly popular. For this many reasons were given, not always the right reasons or the only ones.

Twenty years before, when he was twice elected as a Republican mayor of Democratic Brooklyn, Mr. Low had done two fine things. He had drawn about him assistants of the best kind, and he had taken the people into his confidence. Perhaps both feats were easier in the smaller city. In the Brooklyn of 1881–85 Mr. Low had upon occasion hired the Clermont Avenue Rink, had invited the people to hear him, had stood before them without preliminary music or chairman, told them what policies he proposed, and—even if it were higher taxation for a neglected community—had carried conviction. In the larger city such an improvised town-meeting was impossible. Low's appointments were generally good, but they were weakest upon the firing-line.

Particularly was he unfortunate in the Police Department, where he placed Col. John N. Partridge, whom he had used in the same capacity in Brooklyn. Colonel Partridge was twenty years older, New York was many times a more difficult problem in 1902 than Brooklyn in 1882. Police administration was well-meaning but inefficient, and it was stained, without fault at its head, by a grave scandal when a witness against police graft, one McAuliffe, was beaten to death in a mysterious manner— the agents of his death being presumably policemen's clubs and the place possibly a police station. Toward the end of his term Mayor Low, under the prodding of *The World*, confided the Police Department to Gen. Francis Vinton Greene, a man of military experience, ability, and energy, who did much to improve its efficiency.

The World saw, however, that:

It has been the misfortune of most reform administrations to fail of re-election. Some of their appointments proved disappointments. Some elements in the fusion failed to get the share of offices they thought themselves entitled to. The "awful example" of boss rule and machine misgovernment was not before the voters to inspire them to action. Indifference succeeded enthusiasm, and "the cat came back."

William Travers Jerome, the Fusion district attorney, stated in August that Mayor Low could not be re-elected, not on account of anything he had "done or left undone" as Mayor, but because of the "unlovable personality of the man himself." "Egotism, self - complacency and constitutional timidity," he said, "are not the elements to make a leader." Unjust as the statement was, it was believed by many people. The administration had made more beginnings than it was able in so short a time to follow up. In Brooklyn a borough administration, still a standard of excellence, had been furnished by J. Edward Swanstrom as Borough President and William C. Redfield, later a Representative in Congress and Secretary of Commerce in President Wilson's Cabinet, as Commissioner of Public Works; but in that Low stronghold every shopkeeper whose encroaching sign had been removed from the sidewalk was in revolt against the law and its enforcers. There was, besides, the "swing" of a Democratic city.

Despite Mr. Jerome's warning Mayor Low was placed in nomination, and *The World* unhesitatingly commended the choice:

Besides being logical and courageous, the renomination of Mayor Low was deserved. He has come nearer to fulfilling the pledges upon which he was elected than any Mayor the city has had in fifty years. He has given New York a decent, honest, efficient and businesslike administration — "the best this city has ever had," in the words of Mr. Jerome, on August 5th. The talk of unpopularity can only be tested convincingly in the election.

The prospects were not unfavorable. But if the Fusion forces expected from the new leader of Tammany the blundering of Croker's later campaigns they were undeceived. Murphy named for Mayor George B. McClellan, treasurer of the Bridge Board, ex-president of the Board of Aldermen, and later a Representative in Congress, a man popular with his fellow-members, of excellent appearance and education, the son of the famous Union general who in 1864 had been the Democratic candidate for President against Abraham Lincoln. Of Mr. McClellan *The World* said:

The Tammany candidate's fair-sounding speech must be judged in the light of his indorsement two years ago of the shameless administration of the "unswerving and fearless Democrat, Robert A. Van Wyck," and his unblushing declaration then that "we have nothing for which to apologize"; not even for Devery and the "red lights," not even for the Ice Trust and the Vice Trust! Mayor Low did not state it too strongly in declaring in his Brooklyn speech that "the nomination this year of the man who said that is a challenge thrown in the face of the city by Tammany Hall."

But Murphy's crowning stroke was to draw from the Fusion ticket two Democratic city officials and candidates for re-election, Edward M. Grout, the Comptroller, and Charles V. Fornes, president of the Board of Aldermen, later a Representative. Both consented; Fusion was obliged to seek new candidates. Of Mr. Grout *The World* said:

[His] public self-degradation in attending the Tammany notification proceedings and pledging his support to the boss's puppet candidate for Mayor is lamentable to those who have felt confidence in his sincerity and his unselfish high purposes.

Hugh McLaughlin, the veteran boss of Brooklyn, was no snow-white lamb, but he had preserved a few prejudices—among them a dislike for protected vice. In state matters he had generally acted with the rural Democrats against Tammany. He believed in "Brooklyn autonomy," and did not wish the Tammany tiger to "cross the bridge." A picturesque figure was the taciturn old boss, sitting day by day in the back room of Kerrigan's auction-rooms, a dismantled church on Willoughby Street. McLaughlin was against Murphy with something of an old man's feeling toward an upstart. He faced a revolt within the Kings County organization, headed by Patrick H. McCarren, the "Tim Sullivan of Brooklyn," who "with all a gambler's desperation staked his political future" upon the indorsement of Grout and Fornes by the Democratic committee. McLaughlin, who expressed contempt for the two backsliders, held the committee against them. It was his last exploit; perhaps no finer feat of its kind was ever performed by a boss than this victorious stand of the old lion of Willoughby Street, whose "noble victory," useless as it proved, won *The World's* high commendation.

Into this hopeless campaign *The World* threw itself with as much vigor as it had done six years before. Every effort was made to stir the pride of the people in the fact that theirs was no mean city, and that for the first time in years they could look at its local government without a blush:

Carl Schurz, in his admirable letter in support of the Fusion ticket, said the "Low administration has given the world the comforting assurance that the perplexing problems of good municipal government in the large American cities can practically be solved." And yet now, he exclaims, with pardonable heat, "the Tammany freebooters ask us to put that municipal government again under their piratical control!"

This is the heart of the issue: Shall we keep on or turn back?

Will the friends of honest, decent, efficient, businesslike municipal government fight the battle through and secure firmly the fruits of victory in two years more of "the best administration New York ever had," or will they lose all that has been gained and dash the hopes of municipal reformers, not only here, but throughout the country?

The question was kept before the people whether Mr. McClellan, "this young protégé of the bosses, who had always 'done as he was told' and never shown a sign of political or personal independence, was likely to succeed, where Grant, Gilroy and even Hewitt failed." Short must be the memory of the man who could not remember how, six years earlier, when it was known that Van Wyck was elected Mayor, "New York streets witnessed such a saturnalia of diabolic rejoicing" as they had never seen before, and how every saloon and every dive was celebrating "the triumph of the combined and conspiring evil forces of the community." Did the people wish the repetition of that scene of rejoicing? If they did it was because they were led astray by the name of Democracy. To such readers there was an especial appeal:

The supporters of Mr. McClellan proclaim that his election would have a great influence upon the State and national elections next year.

The World admits it. It goes further, and declares its deliberate conviction that the success of the Tammany ticket on Tuesday next would *destroy any chance that the Democrats might otherwise have of electing a President in 1904.*

What are the lessons of history?

Why was Tilden nominated and elected in 1876 against the bitter opposition of John Kelly and the Tammany organization? Why was Cleveland nominated and elected in 1884 and again in 1892, in spite of the angry protest of Tammany Hall, voiced by Bourke Cockran and Richard Croker?

Was it not because the Democrats of the nation respected

and trusted Tilden and Cleveland "for the enemies they had made"? Was not Tammany hostility regarded as a certificate of merit?

In the election the Democrats of Brooklyn did admirably; they furnished only about one thousand of the sixty-two thousand plurality which made McClellan Mayor of New York for two years, with a re-election for four years in 1905—a longer period than any Mayor had held that office since Richard Varick of 1789. "The moral of this defeat," *The World* reflected when the figures were announced, "is plain to read: *The next Fusion candidate for Mayor must be a Democrat* if the anti-Tammany forces wish to carry the election. There are some prejudices and predilections that are proof against argument." This reasoning had much to do with *The World's* attitude six years later in favoring the election of William J. Gaynor, as a Democratic chief magistrate of a Democratic city.

Thousands of Democrats who proved Murphy's skill in nominating Mr. McClellan by voting for him in the expectation that he would be his own man, thousands who did not join the rejoicings in the death of reform, bewailed their action after the first of January, when McClellan appointed a cabinet named by the boss in a deal with the Sullivans, the lords of the lower East Side. Certain appointments credited to Mr. McClellan's own choice, as those for tenement commissioner, health commissioner, police commissioner, and others, drew less criticism, though these men were not in all cases able to control their departments. The five borough presidents elected at the same time were John F. Ahearn, Louis Haffen, Joseph Cassidy, Martin W. Littleton, and George Cromwell. Of these five men the three first named were on the lowest level of unfitness. And they were charter members of the Board of Estimate, through which New York is practically governed by commission.

This period of *The World's* editorial history closes as it began in praise of Roosevelt. The Northern Securities merger was an outgrowth of the semi-panic of 1901. A contest having arisen between two groups of stock-jobbers for the control of the Northern Pacific Railway, the price of its shares rose on 'Change to one thousand dollars each. Punters who had sold short were ruined if the day closed without relief. It came in a notification from Morgan interests that peace had been declared. The truce was followed by a treaty that united the Northern Pacific, the Great Northern, and the Burlington in a holding company, whose shares were divided in proportions which involved gross stock-watering. The death of competition and the substitution of a carrying monopoly in a group of great agricultural states was, however, paramount to this consideration. Because the agreement set up monopoly the Supreme Court, upholding Judge Thayer, ordered it dissolved and its stock-holdings redivided.

Ungrudging as was *The World's* praise of the energy of the Roosevelt administration in pushing the merger case, it could not be blind to the weapons the decision placed in the hands of the President. It said on March 15, 1904, the day after the announcement:

Politically, the effect of the decision can hardly be exaggerated. It will greatly strengthen President Roosevelt as a candidate. People will love him for the enemies he has made. Mr. Cleveland lost popularity among the Democratic masses by not enforcing this law. Mr. Roosevelt will gain by enforcing it. It cannot now be said that the Republican party is owned by the trusts. It cannot now be said that Mr. Roosevelt is controlled by them. His prospects of re-election were not small before; they are brighter to-day, and, barring some act of impetuous unwisdom on his part before November, brighter they will remain. But in the last analysis it is not the President who has triumphed. It is not the court. It is not the law.

It is the people—the plain people who elect Presidents and set up courts and through their representatives ordain the laws.

Inseparable from the possession of power is the possibility of its abuse. Discussing this consequence of the decision, *The World* said, on March 20th:

The power of the President even before the Supreme Court decision in the Northern Securities case was enormous beyond precedent.

He could make peace and war, frame treaties, with a Senate cowed into merely indorsing his acts, or form alliances with foreign powers. He was commander-in-chief of the army and navy and of the far larger army of over 200,000 civil appointees, holding the very means of subsistence at his pleasure or the pleasure of his subordinates. Powers and attributes gravitated to him as the nation grew, until he was in effect the most potent ruler on earth.

Now comes this new power over corporations, a power never dreamed of by the framers of the Constitution. He can unsheath a Damocles sword and, chief of a party as well as head of the people, can hang it over the head of the finance, the commerce and industry of the nation. . . .

From the foundation of the Government the President has been Executive. Through his control of the Attorney-General he can select cases for presentation to the court; he is therefore largely Judiciary. By executive order he commands the service pension at which Congress balked; he is therefore Legislature. He is Everything. He is Power. He is Patronage. He is Protection. He is Privilege. . . .

Whatever their past politics may have been, many newspaper organs of both parties are to-day all for State rights. They are seeking comfort in the fact that the decision was made by a single vote, forgetting that the income-tax decision was made and remade by one vote, that Mr. Hayes was made President by one vote—and the vote of a Supreme Court Justice.

They are vigorously imploring Congress to disenact that which it has enacted and to reopen for Plutocracy and Monopoly the golden way that led straight toward the Universal Trust.

Not more remarkable than the amazing futility of such a demand is its financial unwisdom. . . .

Against the new danger what means may avail? There are two remedies. One can be applied at once by public opinion. One is more slowly to be reached through legislation.

There should be specific statutes prohibiting the acceptance of campaign contributions from corporations. The infractions of such statutes should be heavily punishable as a criminal offense.

The term of the President should be six years, and he should be ineligible to succeed himself; thus there would be removed the temptation to use this great power for his personal ends.

And for the quicker remedy:

It is to be sought in steadfast resistance by the press and by the public to demagogues and agitators of the Bryan type, who, by appeals to passion and to prejudice, to poverty and to discontent, by misrepresentation and the abuse of the prosperous, by clamor and by false teaching, seek profit or place or power at the cost of the common weal.

The Presidential power over corporations was to be an issue in the coming election to an extent not fully discovered even in these forebodings.

XV

1904

How Parker Became a "Favorite Son"—High Finance and Practical Politics Take Possession of His Campaign—Parker's Gold Telegram to the St. Louis Convention—The Nomination of Judge Herrick for Governor—Cortelyou and the Republican Campaign Fund—The Famous "Ten Questions"—Judge Parker's Challenge—President Roosevelt's Unqualified Denial—His Re-election the "Triumph of Hope Over Experience."

ALTON B. PARKER was the only Democrat who carried New York State on a general ticket for sixteen years. In 1897, immediately following the first Bryan débâcle, Mr. Parker was chosen chief judge of the Court of Appeals by sixty thousand plurality on a state ticket. Men grew old and died, children matured to men and women before the feat was repeated by a Democrat. A monotony of defeat fell upon the party. It soon became a common thing for disheartened leaders, looking back over the record of disaster, to linger at the figures for 1897 and to see in Judge Parker an "availability."

Judge Parker owed his victory mainly to Senator Platt's nomination of a Republican candidate for Mayor of New York against Seth Low and to the division of the Low vote between Parker and his opponent. His personal strength, except in one or two rural counties, had nothing to do with his triumph. But if Judge Parker had been merely an accident the Democratic party would not have been considering him seven years later as a Moses to lead it out of bondage. He was a strong chief judge of the

highest court of New York, a court that had never fallen
into full control of either Tammany boss or Republican
machine.   He was broad in his views of public questions,
and his influence was liberal in decisions upon constitutional questions affecting the rights of working-men.

For two years Mr. Bryan had renewed in addresses
in every part of the country his fight for free silver—a
hopeless fight, but full of hope for the favorites of privilege.   *The World* protested against having this burden
tied about the neck of Democracy.   The fact that in 1903
most of the Democratic state conventions had dropped
the "body of death" from their platforms encouraged
it to hope that "sense, sanity and sagacity will rule the
National Convention this year and give the party at least
a fighting chance to win by deserving to win."

Of all candidates *The World* would have preferred
Mr. Cleveland.   He was the man whose name meant not
only victories, but the issues that had won victories, and
particularly the issue of the reform of the tariff.

But Mr. Cleveland, as in 1896, was impossible even if
he had not refused to be considered.   The Bryan elements
were still in full control of the party in the West, and,
while they might consent to the nomination of a candidate representing the other wing of the party, they
would have interposed to Cleveland's name an absolute
veto.   In the circumstances the legend of Parker's
strength in New York, aided by some deft preliminary
work by his supporters, made him the leading figure in the
field.

The World was not optimistic of the outcome.   Some
encouragement was afforded by the action of Governor
Odell in taking the chairmanship of the Republican State
Committee.

From the point of view of partisan advantage [said *The
World*] Democrats can afford to regard this deal with com-
14

placency. Gov. Odell is President Roosevelt's only rival as a
vote-reducer.   In 1896 McKinley carried New York by 268,469.
Two years later Roosevelt squeezed through on Croker's bull-
headed blundering by less than 18,000.   At his first election
as Governor, in 1900, Odell had a plurality of 111,000.   Two
years later he lost more than 100,000 of this, receiving only
8,803.   With these two majority-choppers united in "conducting
the campaign" the Democrats ought to be able to carry New
York by a rousing plurality.

But even the faint hope awakened by an adversary's
blunder was darkened by worse than blunders on the
other side.   In the pre-convention stage Mr. Parker was
silent upon the issues of the campaign.   *The World* urged
him to speak out, assuring him that the people were not
to be won in a still hunt.   His candidacy had fallen into
the hands of a combination of high finance, represented by
August Belmont and Thomas F. Ryan, and practical
politics, represented by William F. Sheehan, ex-boss of
Buffalo.   They doubtless counseled silence; and at the
New York convention in April they played politics by a
bid for Western support, against which *The World*
promptly protested:

1. The omission of a declaration in favor of the historic
Democratic principle of sound money seems to us a great
mistake.
2. The abandonment of the protest against the Philippine
acquisition and the general policy of imperial colonialism,
which was so justly and forcibly made in the Kansas City platform, is a second mistake of short-sighted politics—more and
worse "trimming."
3. The declaration of "opposition to trusts and combinations
that oppress the people and stifle healthy industrial competition" is feeble and pointless.
4. The selection of the four delegates-at-large was another
mistake.   The names are disappointing.   They will command
neither respect at home nor influence at St. Louis.   [They

were David B. Hill, Senator Edward Murphy, Jr., George
Ehret, a wealthy brewer, and James W. Ridgway.]

To add to the incongruities between the platform and the
men selected to represent it the name of James T. Woodward,
the astute President of the Hanover Bank and a prominent
member of the Morgan syndicate that bedeviled President
Cleveland's administration—a combination which The World
had the pleasure of smashing—appears as the first Presidential
elector-at-large!   Why and wherefore Woodward?

The World forced Woodward off the electoral ticket.
In effect it forced the party to stand by sound money.
But much mischief was already done.

When on July 6th the Democratic national convention
met in St. Louis the fact became manifest that, though
Mr. Bryan was not to be the candidate, his spirit ruled,
and that the party purposed to go down to a third defeat
without disavowing free silver.   *The World* had continued urging Judge Parker to speak out for "the accomplished fact" of the gold standard.   On the eve of the
adoption of the platform it reminded him that ten
words from him would insure a sound-money resolution.

The convention that nominated Mr. Roosevelt had
thus challenged Democracy:

> The maintenance of the gold standard, established by the Republican
> party, cannot safely be committed to the Democratic party, which
> resisted its adoption and has never given any proof since that time
> of belief in it or fidelity to it.

The answer of the St. Louis convention was silence.
There were delegates who wished a plank in the platform
recognizing the gold standard as an established fact, but
Mr. Bryan defeated them in an all-night struggle.   On
July 9th—the day he received the nomination upon the
final ballot—Judge Parker sent this telegram, which was
given out the following morning:

HON. WILLIAM F. SHEEHAN,
    Hotel Jefferson.

I regard the gold standard as firmly and irrevocably established, and shall act accordingly if the act of the convention to-day shall be ratified by the people.

As the platform is silent on the subject, my view should be known to the convention, and if it is proved to be unsatisfactory to the majority I request you to decline the nomination for me so that another may be nominated before adjournment.

ALTON B. PARKER.

It was too late to retreat. Democracy was committed in roundabout fashion to sound money. The Parker telegram was presented to the convention, and the following reply was drafted by John Sharp Williams, of Mississippi:

The platform adopted by this convention is silent on the question of the monetary standard because it is not regarded by us as a possible issue in this campaign, and only campaign issues are mentioned in the platform. Therefore there is nothing in the views expressed by you in the telegram just received which would preclude a man entertaining them from accepting a nomination on said platform.

Not an auspicious beginning for a campaign was this belated and grudging avowal!

There was still the Governorship of New York to be considered. The Republicans selected for that honor State Senator Frank Higgins, a man of good legislative record who could be trusted not to be too restive under the machine yoke. Not without much urging Mr. Higgins was later to do the state as fine a service as lies to the credit of its greatest executives.

Of the choice of a Democratic candidate *The World* spoke in reminiscent mood:

David B. Hill . . . nominated himself for Governor twice, and was twice elected. He allowed Croker to nominate him a third time, and was overwhelmingly defeated. . . .

Hill and Croker together nominated Roswell P. Flower for Governor, a man who could not write a grammatical sentence, but who had the money to secure Croker, and through him the nomination.

In 1898, when Robert B. Van Wyck, the most corrupt and incompetent Mayor New York has known since the Tweed Ring, was scandalizing the party in this city, Croker, with Hill's acquiescence, nominated Augustus Van Wyck for Governor. No grosser insult to public decency could have been conceived. . . . Yet such was the vitality of the Democratic party that this candidate came within 18,000 votes of being elected.

Two years later Hill nominated his law partner, Stanchfield, a cheap country politician, the defender of Brockway's enormities in the Elmira Reformatory, an advocate of imperialism, the type of everything that a Democratic leader should not be.

Why not let the Democracy this year make its own nomination?

In 1902 there was every prospect of Democratic victory. . . . But Hill had White-House hopes himself at that time. He did not want a candidate of Presidential size, and so he nominated Coler, . . . against whom even Odell managed to scrape out a victory by 8,000 plurality. . . .

The question was settled by the selection of Judge D-Cady Herrick, of Albany, a man of marked ability. Judge Herrick, *The World* said, had "wide knowledge of the State government. He has courage. He fought Hill. He fought Tammany in the past. He has no passion for money-making. He is above pecuniary influences. He wears no man's collar."

The tariff was the great historic issue upon which Democracy had twice carried the country. By its folly at St. Louis it was jockeyed into a defensive position upon finance. Vain was the effort to draw attention to the purpose of privilege to retain its hold. "Mr. Roosevelt," said *The World*, "adopts the cant of the spellbinder about the tariff as a prop to the standard of living of our wage-earners (the Carnegies, the Fricks and the Schwabs), but he does it with an air of sheepishness which shows that the Harvard free-trader is a little ashamed of his enforced disguise." Useless was the attempt to get people interested in the facts as to the recent hard times, that "the panic which occurred under the McKinley tariff was caused by the Republican Sherman silver law, and that under the Wilson tariff the times began to improve." The tariff was not the issue that counted most.

Toward the end of the campaign the growing scandal of the appointment of George B. Cortelyou as chairman of the Republican National Committee made a new issue that superseded even silver. Here *The World* succeeded better than with the tariff in shifting the fighting-ground; and, though the contest was lost, momentous results have continued to flow out of the controversy.

Mr. Cortelyou, beginning work in Washington as a stenographer in the Post-office Department, had risen to be the Secretary to the President, and later Secretary of the Department of Commerce and Labor, under which the work of collating facts concerning trusts was carried on by the Bureau of Corporations. The impropriety of taking the head of this department to be the "fat-fryer" of a campaign for protected corporations scarcely needed to be stated.

On October 1st Joseph Pulitzer personally signed in *The World* an editorial article addressing to President Roosevelt ten questions which have become famous:

1. How much has the Beef Trust contributed to Mr. Cortelyou?
2. How much has the Paper Trust contributed to Mr. Cortelyou?
3. How much has the Coal Trust contributed to Mr. Cortelyou?
4. How much has the Sugar Trust contributed to Mr. Cortelyou?

5. How much has the Oil Trust contributed to Mr. Cortelyou?

6. How much has the Tobacco Trust contributed to Mr. Cortelyou?

7. How much has the Steel Trust contributed to Mr. Cortelyou?

8. How much has the Insurance Trust contributed to Mr. Cortelyou?

9. How much have the national banks contributed to Mr. Cortelyou?

10. How much have the six great railroad trusts contributed to Mr. Cortelyou?

"I observe," the article continued, "by your letter of acceptance that in spite of the secrecy and silence of your Bureau of Corporations you are still in favor of publicity." Mr. Pulitzer suggested that President Roosevelt, if he really favored publicity, should write a letter to Mr. Cortelyou demanding that he make public all the information he possessed concerning contributions by corporations or others interested in Republican success, or concerning agreements, express or implied, entered into with such contributors. If the information were given, the article continues—

. . . would it not fully explain why, after 583 days, there has been no official publicity as to the affairs of the corporations whose business has been investigated by Mr. Cortelyou and his successor?

Would it not explain why the corporations that opposed you in March are supporting you now?

Would it not explain the rearrangement of your Cabinet? . . .

Would it not explain the princely contributions to your campaign fund which are pouring in from every corner of the country?

Would it not explain why all the kings of finance who were clamoring for your political life now believe that the best interests of the country will be served by your election? . . .

Would it not reveal to the American people how preposterous

is your pretext of danger to the Republic from foreign enemies
and how real is the danger to the Republic from its enemies
at home?

Of the workings of the Bureau of Corporations as a
preliminary to trust legislation or court prosecution the
article said:

The first thing to do, as you said in your speech at Wheeling,
was to "find out the facts." Your initial step was to appoint
as your Secretary of Commerce your private secretary, George
B. Cortelyou. The Bureau of Corporations was organized
February 26, 1903—more than 19 months, more than 80 weeks
—exactly 583 days ago—yes, exactly 583 days ago.

Will you kindly tell the country:

1. After these 583 days of supposed activity and official
duty how much more does the public know about the conduct
and management of these great corporations than it knew
before?

2. After these 583 days of supposed activity and official duty
what single witness has been subpœnaed? . . .

3. After these 583 days of supposed activity and official duty
what documentary evidence has been produced?

4. After these 583 days of supposed activity and official duty
what corporation magnate has been compelled to testify under
oath as to secret rebates on freight charges or other acts of
conspiracy in restraint of trade? . . .

Is there a corporation in the United States, Mr. President,
whose affairs are administered in greater secrecy than are the
affairs of your Bureau of Corporations?

Yet in your letter of acceptance you have—may I call it the
magnificent audacity?—to declare of the act creating this
bureau and of the related acts:

"These laws are now being administered with entire
efficiency."

The cry had been heard that moneyed interests were
building up a vast fund to elect Judge Parker; so much
harm the association of Belmont and Sheehan and Ryan

had done him.   "Cortelyou" was the retort.   *The World*
hammered at these queries day after day.   Finally upon
October 24th Judge Parker, in a speech at his home in
Esopus, asked, "Would the public interests be safe in
the hands of a party the greater part of whose campaign
funds have been contributed by corporations and trusts?"
Of this speech *The World* said:

Better late than never!   At last, within two weeks of the
election, the foremost representatives of the Democratic party
have struck the true keynote of an aggressive campaign:
"Cortelyou and Corruption!"

The vigorous speech of Judge Parker on Monday, following
the virile address of Mr. Cleveland in Carnegie Hall, showed
that at last the leaders understand and appreciate the real
burning issue of this election. . . .

How the country is governed by interests Judge Parker
indicated with perfect clearness in his speech on Monday:

"When such forces united to furnish the money which they
are promised will control the election, their purpose is as clear
as noonday.   It is to buy protection, to purchase four years
more of profit by tariff taxation, or four years more of extortion
from the public by means of monopoly."

Finally on October 29th Judge Parker said with a certain solemnity of phrase: "The trusts are furnishing the
money with which they hope to control the election.   I
am sorry to be obliged to say it: If it were not true I
would not say it to gain the Presidency or any earthly
reward."

Upon the "Great Moral Issue of the Campaign" *The
World* on November 5th summed up the campaign in an
editorial article of a full page.   This review said:

The President does not explain why the protected industries
are pouring money into his campaign fund.

He does not explain why the trust potentates that were
clamoring for his political life six months ago are now enthusi-

astically supporting his candidacy and generously assisting in financing it.

He does not explain the extraordinary changes in his Cabinet made in the interests of the corporations—the removal of Mr. Knox to the Senate; the appointment of Mr. Metcalf, the political agent of the Southern Pacific, to be Secretary of Commerce; the appointment of Mr. Morton, a vice-president of the Santa Fe, to be Secretary of the Navy.

He does not explain why there has been no publicity during the 619 days of supposed investigation by the Bureau of Corporations.

He does not answer the ten questions asked by The World.

He does not deny that Mr. Cortelyou, who has been Secretary of Commerce and is now Chairman of his Campaign Committee, is to be Postmaster-General, to make important contracts with railroads that have contributed or have refused to contribute to the Republican campaign fund.

Experienced politicians assumed that Judge Parker possessed proof of his assertion. He doubtless did have assurances that proofs would be furnished; but he was disappointed. Had he been able to cite one-half of the evidence now in existence he need not have been so badly beaten.

Shortly before midnight of November 4th President Roosevelt issued his famous reply to Judge Parker. With his characteristic skill in controversy he first restated Judge Parker's challenge to his own satisfaction, ignoring the exact wording of the main charge, and to the attack as thus shifted he replied: "The statements made by Mr. Parker are atrociously and unqualifiedly false."

This audacious denial produced its intended effect. Nothing in recent political history is comparable to the stir it made, with the exception of the "Rum, Romanism, and Rebellion" incident at the close of Mr. Blaine's campaign in 1884. The word of a President carries enormous weight. Mr. Roosevelt would in any case have been elected; but Judge Parker lost votes by failing to prove his case.

Mr. Roosevelt was elected by a plurality of 2,545,515, not so much because Democrats voted for him as because they did not vote. The Bryan wing of the party was disgusted with the control of the campaign by Judge Parker's Wall Street friends, and they ill concealed or openly avowed their dissatisfaction. The number of ballots cast was smaller than it had been eight years before. In New York Judge Herrick was badly beaten, and, like Judge Parker, obliged to return to private practice.

So the election was over. Reduction of taxation was again postponed. Reforms were sidetracked for the Juggernaut car of the trusts.

Upon Mr. Roosevelt's triumph *The World* commented:

It can truly be said of the people's choice of Mr. Roosevelt, as Disraeli said of the man who married a second time: "It is a triumph of hope over experience." If President Roosevelt will be satisfied with this splendid vote of confidence, the climax of his whole career, the greatest personal triumph ever won by any President—if he will strive for four years for the place in history to which his earlier ideals would have bid him aspire—the popular mandate resisted and deplored by Democrats and Independents may yet redound to the welfare and the true glory of the Republic.

It added that "his announcement that he will not be a candidate for re-election is a first, firm and most sagacious step in the right direction."

So *The World* was beaten in its fight—badly beaten. When next it met the President it was to win for itself and for the independent press of the country a notable victory.

XVI

"EQUITABLE CORRUPTION"

1905–1906

James Hazen Hyde and the Struggle for the Control of the Equitable—
"The World" Moves for a General House-Cleaning—Sale of the Company
to Thomas F. Ryan — Governor Higgins's Reluctance to Move for an
Investigation—The Armstrong Committee and Mr. Hughes—Mr. Perkins
and the Republican Campaign Fund—The Permanent Good Results of the
Probe—The Equitable Now in the Control of J. Pierpont Morgan—What
Remains to Be Done.

THE WORLD'S unique achievement in 1905–06 was its
success in forcing, single-handed, the reform of life insurance in New York State, against the opposition of the
Governor and the Legislature and great business interests.

The Equitable Life Assurance Society was and is one
of the strongest in the world. It was a proprietary company. It had vast assets whose control was an important
factor in finance, and over this control a dispute broke
out in the directorate in the latter part of 1904. It became
public in an attack upon James Hazen Hyde, son of
Henry B. Hyde, who had inherited his majority stock.
James Waddell Alexander was the president of the society
and the trustee to whom the senior Hyde had left the
control of his son's shares during a period he thought
sufficient to develop independent judgment. At the end
of the trusteeship, which was now approaching, Hyde
could oust the president and upset all his arrangements.
This was the real reason of the attack upon him. The
feud was at once embittered by counter-charges in Hyde's
interest against the Alexander management.

Hyde was an esthetic soul with literary and artistic tastes, no match in strength or cunning for the capitalists who used the Equitable millions for investment. The campaign against him gave *The World* its opportunity for a wider purpose. The vastness of the undertaking is indicated in the first of the series of editorial articles, headed "Equitable Corruption," which forced a remedy:

The most astounding, far-reaching financial scandal known to the history of the United States is approaching its climax in the battle for the control of the surplus and assets of the Equitable Life Assurance Society.

It is a scandal which directly involves the savings of 600,000 policy-holders and the 2,500,000 or 3,000,000 ultimate beneficiaries of these policies. . . .

The charges against James H. Hyde are:

First—That the cost of his dinner to M. Cambon, the French Ambassador; his expenses in Paris, and his French Ball at Sherry's were charged to and paid out of the Equitable's advertising account.

Second—That he placed on the Equitable's pay-roll his personal employees and servants, who rendered no service to the Equitable for the salaries they received.

Summed up in the language of the petition to Attorney-General Mayer, the charges against the notable financiers in the Equitable directorate are that the funds of the society were "wastefully and wrongfully taken" by them. The specifications of this general accusation are numerous:

First—That the stock in the Equitable Trust Company, owned by directors in the Equitable Society, and worth $150 per share, was sold by them to the Equitable Society for $500 per share, and that the said officials "were benefited to the amount of $2,000,000 or more."

Second—That Jacob H. Schiff, through his firm of Kuhn, Loeb & Co., sold to the Equitable Society bonds and securities of great value and received "large sums in the way of commissions, of which sums said Jacob H. Schiff has received a part."

Third—That the securities of E. H. Harriman's system of

railroads and the Gould railroads were sold to the Equitable Society, although Mr. Harriman and Mr. Gould were members of the Board of Directors.

Fourth—That by organizing banks and trust companies, the stock of which they own, and by depositing the money of the Equitable Society in these banks and trust companies, individual directors personally profited.

Fifth—That individual directors used the funds of the Equitable Society to secure control of great corporations, which they reorganized, and then sold to the Equitable Society bonds and other securities of the reorganization.

The World saw in the quarrel the opportunity to secure an investigation by a legislative committee of the whole subject of life insurance as conducted in New York. The insiders in the Equitable would have been more than satisfied with an investigation by the State Insurance Department. This important office had long been the prey of hack politicians. "Does any legislator think," *The World* demanded, "that the 600,000 policy-holders will be satisfied with a secret inquiry by a Lou Payn deputy in the Insurance Department or by a committee of the very directors, some of whom may have forever forfeited their rights to act in that capacity?" A committee of the directors, the Frick Committee, was, in fact, appointed. It dipped gingerly into the mud and made recommendations, excellent as far as they went, which the directors rejected.

Day after day *The World* hammered at the disclosures. Day after day it reminded the Governor of his duty. It was to be Mr. Higgins's unkindly fate to be subjected to an ordeal more stern than had faced any predecessor since the Civil War, to hesitate long, to put his name, finally, to some of the best laws ever passed in the state, and yet to be denied a renomination when his party was in the best repute it had enjoyed for years.

The World applied other pressure by printing the names

of the directors of the Equitable; though these names included some of the best known in New York—names such as Jacob H. Schiff, John Jacob Astor, Levi P. Morton, Alfred G. Vanderbilt, E. H. Harriman, and Marvin Hughitt—nearly all were dummy directors. They did not own the stock in the company that would legally qualify them to act. Some were doubly dummies, taking no share in the administration of the company; some were in schemes of promotion and investment, in which the company was staged as the rural dunce who buys the gold brick. Under this management the returns to policy-holders had fallen from the best standards, though their principal was not impaired. How the deal was operated *The World* explained:

When Mr. James Hazen Hyde had come of age he was elected Vice-President of the Equitable, the office which his father had honorably filled for so many years. . . . The owners of rail-roads, the officers of banks, the partners of banking firms, saw in young Hyde's weakness, his vanity, his social aspira-tions, his fads, the opportunity for them to use for their own venal purposes the funds which should have been held sacred to the widows and orphans of the future. . . .

These men made James Hazen Hyde director in their trust companies, banks and railroads. In return Mr. Hyde had them recorded in the stock book of the Equitable as the owners of five shares each of his stock, and thus ostensibly qualified them to be trustees of this great fiduciary fund.

All told, they made James Hazen Hyde director in forty-six corporations—this young man not yet out of the swaddling clothes twined round him by his father's will.

They made him director in these railroads:

The Southern Pacific and the Union Pacific and their depen-dent lines, the Oregon Railroad and Navigation Company, the Oregon Short Line Company, the Texas and Pacific, the Mis-souri Pacific, the Wabash, the Western Maryland, the Long Island, the Delaware and Hudson, the Manhattan Elevated, the New York City Railway Company, the Metropolitan

Securities Company, which controls the surface lines of New York; the constituent companies of the Brooklyn Rapid Transit system and the London Underground Railway.

They made him director in these banks:

National Bank of Commerce, American Surety Company, Fifth Avenue Trust Company, Greenwich Savings Bank, Commercial Trust Company of Philadelphia, Crocker-Woolworth National Bank of San Francisco, Fidelity Trust Company of Newark, First National Bank of Chicago, First National Bank of Denver, Franklin National Bank of Philadelphia, Mellon National Bank of Pittsburg, Missouri Safe-Deposit Company of St. Louis, Security Safe-Deposit Company of Boston, Union Exchange Bank of New York, Union National Bank of Newark, Union Savings Bank of Pittsburg.

They made him director in these trust companies:

Equitable Trust Company, Mercantile Trust Company, Mercantile Safe-Deposit Company, Lawyers' Title and Trust Company, Lawyers' Mortgage Company.

They made him director in these corporations:

The Colorado Fuel and Iron Company, Continental Insurance Company, International Mercantile Marine, or "Shipping Trust," Mercantile Electric Company, Westinghouse Electric Company, Western Union Telegraph Company.

In return Mr. Hyde made them directors in the Equitable and gave them in this one directorate immeasurably greater opportunity for personal benefit than he had in his forty-six.

Gradually the old directors of the Equitable had dropped out, and in their places were put the dummy directors qualified by Mr. Hyde's stock, until thirty-seven of the fifty were not directors, but directed; not elected, but selected; not the guardians, but the manipulators of the assets. . . .

This was the situation when the clash came between Alexander and Hyde. The term of the deed of trust was presently to expire, when Mr. Alexander's trusteeship would cease and Mr. Hyde would become sole controller of the society.

At this juncture President Alexander presented to Mr. Hyde a request, signed by many officers of the company, that Mr. Hyde should withdraw from the Equitable and surrender its control.

Governor Higgins was most reluctant to interfere; but by a series of startling disclosures by *The World*, culminating in the publication of a report by Superintendent Hendricks upon the Equitable troubles which had been withheld from circulation in the hope that the storm would blow over, he was forced in the end to capitulate and advise the appointment of a legislative committee to investigate "Equitable corruption" and the cognate corruption its discussion had revealed. A committee was selected with Senator William W. Armstrong, of Rochester, as chairman. On the Republican side it was of excellent quality. The Democratic members revealed the poverty of talent to which the boss system reduces a great city's representatives in a great state. Whatever character the committee possessed came from the country districts. Representing the metropolis, where the insurance business had its home, sat two Democrats of the familiar machine type; of one of whom, Dan Riordan, *The World* said his "strength in the politics of the lower East Side" had come largely from "the multiple voting of Monk Eastman's gang." That such men should be set to cleanse and cure insurance corruption seemed a grim joke.

But the investigation would depend for success upon the chief counsel chosen. Another of *The World's* long fights had recently ended in the appointment of a legislative committee to investigate the Gas Trust in New York as a preliminary to cutting down its charges. The Gas Committee had appointed as counsel an attorney little known to the people, though of high repute in his profession, who had shown in the inquiry a patience and persistence that brought admirable results. Charles Evans Hughes was forty-three years old. He had been a teacher, a law professor and lecturer, and was then in private practice.

The World was asked on behalf of the Armstrong Committee to suggest plans for procedure and to name a

15

chief counsel. Flattering as was this recognition of its work in forcing the inquiry, acceptance could not be considered. Those who represented the committee next stated that they had thought of employing Mr. Hughes. Would that be satisfactory? Certainly, was the reply. All *The World* wished was action.

Mr. Hughes was the most appropriate choice that could have been made. He was named; in that act the majority members made it clear that they were in earnest.

Mr. Hughes's conduct of the investigation was a legal masterpiece. Step by step he led it along, never hurried, never impatient, never neglecting to glance down a side-path that might flank a concealed position. He seemed to care more about eliciting facts than about impressing committee-room loungers with his brilliance. The sessions of the Armstrong Committee often made good reading next day; listened to, they were tedious, dull, long-winded. The chief counsel wound his way through mazes of technicalities until from weariness the witness relaxed his guard. Then some innocent-seeming question would elicit a piece of information that dovetailed into the elaborate pattern of facts the state was weaving.

It might seem that with the forcing of an inquiry the need of driving-power on the part of *The World* was past. To reason thus would be to take no account of the dry-rot in the Republican state machine, the fruit of long victory and the boss system. The men in charge hoped that the insurance exposures could be hushed up. They saw daily unfolded the proofs of fraud, theft, and perjury committed in the state to the hurt of its citizens and with the connivance of its Banking and Insurance departments; yet they thought to keep those departments unchanged as the refuge of unfit place-holders and as the protectors of dishonest practices.

The World in the latter part of 1905 was day by day urging Governor Higgins to reform these departments with an ax. "Your two Superintendents," it told him, "have been tried before the bar of public opinion and found guilty. For six years Francis Hendricks has certified to false statements and allowed the seal of the State of New York to be stamped upon a snare. For nine years Frederick D. Kilburn has supervised the banks and trust companies in which the cooked accounts were kept and through which policy-holders were robbed.

"You are yourself now on trial. . . . You say, 'I cannot discuss the matter now. I cannot try a case in advance.' There is nothing for you to discuss. There is nothing to try. A plea of guilty has been entered. It is for you to pronounce the sentence. It should be dismissal."

Because of the capacity for procrastination of the Republican machine men and the Governor, and because the county of New York lacked a district attorney capable of seeing his opportunity for jailing rich offenders, the revelations of the Hughes inquiry failed in part of their just effect. Governor Higgins kept Superintendent Hendricks in the Insurance Department, in spite of proof of his incompetency, until May 2, 1906. He then named for superintendent Otto Kelsey, another friend of the machine, whose incumbency meant that the cleaning up of the department would be postponed.

Toward prosecuting the rich culprits whom the Hughes inquiry revealed nothing was done by William Travers Jerome as district attorney. The most piquant of his exploits in this field was to cause the exculpation of George W. Perkins from the charge of larceny from the New York Life Insurance Company, by submitting his case to the courts practically as a moot question upon affidavits of three of Perkins's associates. The sum improperly taken was that indirectly contributed to the Roosevelt campaign fund of 1904 by the New York Life. The officers of the company, aware of the impropriety of the gift, had sought to conceal it. Mr. Perkins made the payment by personal check. After the campaign the money was refunded to him by company check. The sum taken was not an even $50,000, as in the case of two other insurance companies, but $48,702.50. Mr. Perkins gave his own money. The impropriety rested in his repayment from company funds.

The World urged Governor Higgins to appoint a special prosecutor to punish insurance crimes and to let Mr. Jerome "confine himself to the prosecution of such criminals as have neither wealth nor social standing." But Governor Higgins had no wish to send to jail contributors to Republican campaign funds, even if they did improperly reimburse themselves from policy-holders' money. So the proceedings dragged out to a natural death before the Court of Appeals, which decided for Perkins, absolving him on the ground of motive. Justice has been obliged to content itself with the moral victory contained in Chief Judge Cullen's dissenting opinion that Perkins's act in reimbursing himself was as much larceny as if he had taken insurance money to buy a necklace for a woman; with Perkins's refunding of the money; and with the aid the episode has rendered in hastening better laws limiting campaign contributions. Since the inquiry Mr. Perkins has partially retired from business and has devoted much time to Progressive politics and to the forwarding of reform measures.

But if the results of the investigation were disappointing, so far as the Governor and the district attorney were concerned, nothing could be more admirable than the manner in which the 1906 Legislature rose to its occasion. Not without friction, not without opposition, the Armstrong insurance code, based upon the report of the committee, was forced through the Legislature and past the Governor. No large element in the state would now dispute that the net result of the agitation had been healthful for insurance and beneficial to policy-holders. What had been done may be summarized in *The World's* words, printed upon April 28th, the day after Governor Higgins signed the last of the Armstrong bills, in No. 202 of the "Equitable Corruption" series:

The law now calls it crime for any corporation, excepting such as are organized for political purposes, to contribute to any political fund. No railroad, bank, trust company or manufacturing or mining corporation may hereafter lawfully give one cent to politics. Neither may any corporation maintain in Albany a secret lobby.

The crime of perjury has been made more easy of punishment. The making of conflicting sworn statements in writing is henceforth presumptive evidence of guilt. . . . The new insurance code provides for real representation of the policy-holders, for the abolition of deferred dividends, for restriction of the cost of getting business, for annual apportionment of surplus, for truthful and intelligible statements, for the punishment of rebating.

But the greatest of all in its service to the community is the blow the Armstrong laws strike at the system of high finance which uses the savings of the people to convert public franchises into instruments of oppression. The prohibition of any participation by any life-insurance company in syndicates, flotations or stock speculations cuts off the great source which Wall Street promoters draw upon for speculative funds.

This summary of the practical achievement of the Armstrong Committee and its counsel, Mr. Hughes, was followed by a review of the history of the case:

For beginning the exposure credit is due to James Hazen Hyde. Unintentionally young Mr. Hyde has done his best to atone for what his father did. The system which Henry B. Hyde founded, James Hazen Hyde toppled over. . . .

Older men, whom he had been taught to look up to, young Mr. Hyde had seen take the policy-holders' money to buy railroads for themselves and banks and trust companies. He had no desire to accumulate railroads and banks and trust companies. What he did want was a special car and flowers out of season and French plays. They had taken millions for what they wanted. He saw no reason why he should not take a few thousands to gratify his taste. . . .

This shocked the "staid and conservative" financiers, who never took the policy-holders' money except to get railroads, banks and trusts. . . .

The Board of Directors of the Equitable stirred in its sluggish sleep. The majority were only dummies, invited to seats for the respectability of their names and accepting the office as an honor instead of a responsibility. The honest dummies tried to reorganize the company and to make it mutual in fact, as it was in law. Against this uprising Hyde and Alexander combined their forces, and, dropping recrimination in the face of a common danger, rallied enough votes to defeat the respectable dummies. . . .

As a concession to public opinion, a committee was appointed, with Henry C. Frick as chairman, to hear both Alexander and Hyde. . . . It found that both charges were sustained, both complainants guilty.

Francis Hendricks, State Superintendent of Insurance, began by trying to force a reconciliation between the Hyde and Alexander factions. Struggling under the traditions of his department and his political training, he yielded, inch by inch, until he also investigated and brought to light additional facts. . . .

The World printed the full testimony taken before him, only parts of which he had made public. This testimony disclosed Senator Depew, former Senator Hill and Elihu Root as recipients of Equitable money. It made public the Harriman and Schiff syndicates, the thefts by trustees. It lifted the lid.

Gov. Higgins sought to leave the matter of investigation in the hands of Superintendent Hendricks. Day after day he announced that he would not authorize a legislative investigation. The Legislature was in special session, called to try Justice Hooker. The last day of its session came, when Governor Higgins realized that no one man can dam back the public conscience. So he too yielded and authorized the Legislature

to appoint the committee of which Senator Armstrong was
Chairman, and of which Mr. Charles E. Hughes was later made
chief counsel. . . .

At the first meeting of the Armstrong committee President
McCall appeared and said that he had employed no lawyer,
because the New York Life needed none. . . . He had stood
against Bryanism, socialism, anarchy, free silver and all
attacks upon the institutions of the United States, including
the attempt to elect Judge Parker President in 1904. To aid
in these noble causes he had regularly contributed the policy-
holders' money. . . . No sooner was Mr. McCall's confession
published than public opinion rose in greater wrath. Such
was the effect that within a fortnight he sent out an official
statement that never again would he do what he had boasted
of doing.

When President McCurdy of the Mutual testified, his attitude
was the same as Mr. McCall's—that he had done a great public
service, worthy of commendation. He told how, during his
twenty years as President, the dividends to the policy-holders
had diminished and their money was taken for the "missionary
and philanthropic purpose" of spreading the blessings of life
insurance. He told of the furniture of his office, the real gold
on the walls, the $12,000 rug on the floor, the furnishings, which
cost more than $50,000, and justified the expenditure; it added
to the dignity of life insurance. . . .

Deposition, disgrace and disaster followed speedily upon
confession and conviction. President Alexander of the Equitable broke down in mind and body. Young Hyde went into
voluntary exile. John A. McCall died. Missionary McCurdy,
shattered and crushed, seeks peace in alien lands. . . .

The high financiers fought among themselves for the Hyde
stock. Thomas F. Ryan, the strongest, grimmest wolf in the
Wall Street pack, won. He reorganized the Equitable by making Paul Morton president and supplanting the Hyde dummies
with Ryan dummies. . . .

But even Thomas F. Ryan quailed before the power of public
opinion. He had regarded his purchase of the Hyde stock as
a private affair. The public did not so regard it. . . . Mr.
Ryan's next yielding was to induce former President Grover

Cleveland, Morgan J. O'Brien, Presiding Justice of the Appellate Division, and George Westinghouse to act as his proxies to name his dummy trustees. . . .

The public conscience is sound. However private consciences may differ in their apologies for the weaknesses of their possessors, the collective conscience has no personal evasions, no excuses for wrong-doing. The force of moral ideas in the community is omnipotent. What it has done to insurance corruption it can do wherever and whenever the public safety is menaced.

The mention of Thomas F. Ryan takes us back again to the summer of 1905, whence may be traced the amazing story of the successive transfers of ownership, as a private property, of this vast undertaking of public interest and wide participation.

Mr. Hyde, as has been said, had literary and artistic tastes. He had figured in arrangements for an exchange of American and French college professors to promote international understanding. His dinner to Ambassador Cambon, however unfortunate the manner of payment of the cost, was a sincere expression of his personality and his tastes. He had no mind to war in Wall Street. His ambition was to seek his ease and congenial company in Paris.

Early in June, 1905, he sold his five hundred and one shares to Thomas F. Ryan. Their par value was $50,100. They were limited to a seven-per-cent. dividend, and as investment securities were worth at most $75,000. Ryan paid about $2,500,000. The excess represented the value of the control of the company. Edward H. Harriman, who had been a power with Hyde, expected to share the ownership with Ryan, but was, as he later explained under oath, cheated out of his share. His purpose to get even with Ryan—an ambition "not yet" accomplished, as he once testified—left him only with his life. Of the Ryan acquisition *The World* said:

Thomas F. Ryan has bought James H. Hyde's stock in the Equitable Life Assurance Society. Mr. Ryan is one of the choice spirits in the Consolidated Gas Company and the Metropolitan Securities Company, two corporations notorious for their corrupt alliances with corrupt politicians.

Mr. Ryan has elected Paul Morton chairman of the Equitable board. Mr. Morton is a self-confessed violator of the Interstate Commerce law, and is the distinguished gentleman who used to manipulate the rebate business for the Atchison, Topeka and Sante Fe Railroad Company. . . .

Mr. Ryan has invited Grover Cleveland, Judge M. J. O'Brien and George Westinghouse to act as trustees of the stock which he has purchased. Without discussing Mr. Ryan's motives in acquiring this Equitable stock, which can yield him only $3,500 a year in legal dividends, The World can only say that the necessity for a legislative investigation into Equitable corruption is more acute now than ever.—*June 10th.*

Except the people of the State of New York, and the 600,000 scattered policy-holders, everybody concerned in Equitable affairs is satisfied with the present situation.

The Dignified Dummy Directors, who did not know what was going on, have nearly all resigned. Several of the Predaceous Dummies have also quit. The other Predaceous Dummies and the Hereditary and Parasitic Dummies and the Satellite Directors remain. Instead of the Dignified Dummies who formerly furnished the respectability, Mr. Cleveland, Justice O'Brien and Mr. Westinghouse will provide a new set of directors fully equal in respectability to those who have resigned.—*June 14th.*

Mr. Ryan did not long hold the stock. He in turn gave it up to a stronger hand. The stock he bought from Hyde, with a few other shares, was taken at cost, plus 4 per cent. interest, the total then amounting to more than three million dollars, by J. Pierpont Morgan under an arrangement with George F. Baker and James Stillman, presidents of the First National and National City banks, to take half the stock off his hands if he wished to be relieved. The voting trustees as rearranged after Mr.

Cleveland's death were Judge O'Brien, Lewis Cass Ledyard and George W. Perkins. The directors are elected partly by the stockholders, partly by the trustees. They certify that no control over their action was exercised by Mr. Morgan.

Before the Pujo committee in Washington in December, 1912, Mr. Morgan explained that he bought the controlling stock, which could only yield him one-eighth or one-ninth per cent. upon the price paid, because he "thought it a desirable thing for the situation." Further testimony gave the meaning of the phrase, and at least hinted at the reasons why Ryan sold:

Q. That is very general, Mr. Morgan. Will you speak of the situation? Was not that stock safe enough in Mr. Ryan's hands? A. I suppose it was. I thought it was greatly improved by being in the hands of myself and these two gentlemen, provided I asked them to do so.

Q. How would that improve the situation over the situation that existed when Mr. Ryan and Mr. Harriman held the stock? A. Mr. Ryan did not have it alone.

Q. Yes, but do you not know that Mr. Ryan originally bought it alone, and Mr. Harriman insisted on having him give him half? A. I thought if he could pay for it that price, I could. I thought that was a fair price. . . .

Q. The normal rate of interest that you can earn on money is about 5 per cent., is it not? A. Not always, no. I am not talking about it as a question of money. . . .

Q. Was anything the matter with it in the hands of Mr. Ryan? A. Nothing.

Q. In what respect would it be better where it is than with him? A. That is the way it struck me.

Q. Is that all you have to say about it? A. That is all I have to say about it.

Q. You care to make no other explanation about it? A. No.

Q. The assets of the Equitable Life were $504,465,802.01 on Dec. 31, 1911. Did Mr. Ryan offer this stock to you? A. I asked him to sell it to me.

Q. Did you tell him why you wanted it? A. No, I told him I thought it was a good thing for me to have.

Q. Did he tell you that he wanted to sell it? A. No, but he sold it.

Q. He did not want to sell it, but when you said you wanted it he sold it? A. He did not say that he did not want to sell it.

Q. What did he say when you told him you would like to have it and thought you ought to have it? A. He hesitated about it and finally sold it.

By the death of Mr. Morgan the shares carrying control of the Equitable passed to his son, the present J. P. Morgan. Their final disposition is curiously awaited, in the expectation that means will ultimately be found to mutualize the society.

So closed the insurance war. The Equitable is not yet turned over to its rightful owners, the policy-holders. The anomaly of $50,100 worth of stock controlling asset trust funds now mounting above five hundred million dollars continues. But great has been the value of the house-cleaning.

Not the least of the beneficent results was the movement in the state that, by putting Charles E. Hughes in the Governor's chair, established a higher ideal of executive responsibility and taught a greater confidence in the power of the people over their representatives.

XVII

CHARLES EVANS HUGHES

1905–1909

Rise of Mr. Hughes to Power in New York—Mr. Hearst's Candidacies for Mayor and Governor—George B. McClellan as Mayor—Governor Hughes's Bitter Conflicts with the Republican Bosses—His War upon Race-Track Gambling—Roosevelt Compels his Renomination—His Fruitless Fight for Direct Primaries—Why Hughes was Side-Tracked from Politics to the Supreme Court—Mayor Gaynor's Administration.

INSURANCE reform made Charles Evans Hughes a logical candidate for high office. His friends could see his road lying straight before him through the Governorship of New York to the White House. He traveled that road some distance. How he was forced to step aside, taking up, indeed, a position of usefulness and honor, but abandoning his ambition for the Presidency, is the political story of 1906 and the troubled years that followed it.

Mr. Hughes was a constructive, progressive statesman. He made a record of unbroken success at the polls and of a gratifying measure of success in his executive policies. His brief political career was one of constant struggle with the bosses of both parties, with whom he did not always come off second best. Appeal direct to the people was the method of warfare which he might almost be said to have rediscovered.

The first campaign Mr. Hughes made for elective office brought him into conflict with William Randolph Hearst.

Mr. Hearst had become conspicuously a factor in

politics by his fruitless effort to secure the Democratic nomination for the Presidency in 1904. In the following year he was a candidate in one of the hottest political contests ever waged in the United States. His campaign for Mayor of New York City upon the Municipal Ownership ticket presented much to remind one of the Henry George campaign of 1886, with William M. Ivins, the Republican candidate, playing the rôle of Theodore Roosevelt as third in an unequal contest, and with Mayor McClellan repeating the part of Mayor Hewitt. Mr. Hearst's doctrines and his emphasis again alarmed citizens who had taken anxious thought of Henry George's single-tax beliefs in the earlier campaign. Again, many Republicans went to the Mayor's support, and the Republican machine was not unfavorable to McClellan's election. Again the devotion of a part of the attacking force had about it something almost of exaltation. To complete the parallel a dispute arose whether McClellan was fairly elected.

The World in this three-cornered contest had no candidate, although in the end it practically supported Ivins, who had no hope of success. McClellan it could not praise, his administration having until then exhibited its most unlovely phases. Hearst it opposed, though mindful of the aid he was giving to the habit of independent voting. It put forth its best effort in electing Mr. Jerome district attorney as an independent, against both the Republican and Democratic parties. Jerome had promised to pursue financial criminals concerned in the transit plunder of New York City, the Shipbuilding Trust, and other money scandals. His continuance in office was a disappointment; he did not pursue these criminals, nor those exposed in the insurance investigation; but the remarkable example of independent voting given in his election remains a healthy reminder of what New York, when it wills, can do to political machines.

Mr. McClellan's plurality over Hearst, on the face of the returns, was 3,468 in a total of nearly 650,000. Charges of fraud were made, and a bill was introduced in Albany, which *The World* supported, to permit a recount. This was later secured, but did not materially alter the result. Mr. McClellan's second term, of four years, was an improvement upon his first of two years. Much of the time he was in conflict with Boss Murphy. His appointments grew better toward the close of his service, but his administration will remain notable chiefly for its financial sins. Never before had the ruinous system of keeping tax rates down by charging current expenses to debt been carried to such extremes. Six years of this policy, with a financial panic toward its close, left the city in an embarrassing plight, facing its new problems of rapid-transit and dock development.

Upon this Mayor of New York, so attractive yet so disappointing, *The World's* judgment at his leaving of office ran as follows:

It cannot be said that Mr. McClellan has proved himself a great Mayor, but it can be said that he has made it easier for his successor to be a great Mayor. Let us give him credit for that.

Whatever his reasons, Mr. McClellan broke with Murphy and emancipated his administration from boss servitude. That in itself was a long step in the direction of better government.

The great reproach of Mr. McClellan's administration has been its unparalleled extravagance and its indifference to the transportation necessities of the people of New York. . . . No justification in sound administration can be found for the tremendous increase in the debt limit during the last six years, which has put the gross bonded debt of New York City above the national debt and left it seven times as great as that of any other American city.

In 1904 Mr. Hearst had accepted a renomination for Congress from Boss Murphy. In 1905 he had assailed

Murphy as the power behind McClellan. In 1906 he made terms with Murphy, and in one of the most turbulent conventions ever held in New York gained the Democratic nomination for Governor. The issue was made plain by the Republican convention in nominating Mr. Hughes—weighted down, however, by a weak ticket for minor offices.

There was now no need of *The World's* concentrating its effort on a side issue, as it had done the previous year. Mr. Hughes would furnish an excellent administration. Not much could be expected of the Independence League-Tammany alliance, which alienated thousands of rural Democrats, as well as many in the metropolis who had supported Hearst for Mayor. *The World* made telling use of previous Hearst cartoons picturing Boss Murphy in prison stripes, and of the Hearst newspapers' editorials of denunciation. Thus in its article of October 1st:

When Mr. Hearst makes his speech at the Tammany ratification meeting which Murphy is arranging for him, will he repeat his statement of August 22, "I repeat now that I am absolutely and unalterably opposed to the Murphys and the McCarrens, and also to the Sullivans and the McClellans and to the kind of politics that they all represent"?

Will Mr. Hearst repeat his speech at Durland's, October 29, 1905, in which he said, "Murphy is as evil a specimen of a criminal boss as we have had since the days of Tweed. Murphy grows rich and insolent on corrupt contracts"?

Will Mr. Hearst repeat the editorial printed in his New York American, October 16, 1905, which said, "Murphy, the most hungry, selfish, and extortionate boss Tammany has ever known, is fighting for his life and for his plunder"?

Will Mr. Hearst repeat the editorial statement of his evening Journal, December 30, 1905, "Murphy should be in Sing Sing wearing stripes instead of at Delmonico's"?

The contest was by no means a walk-over for Hughes. Toward the end of the campaign a vigorous blow was struck by President Roosevelt, who sent Secretary Elihu Root of his Cabinet to attack Mr. Hearst in a bitter speech at Utica. Thus aided by the power of the President, who was then at the summit of his popularity, Mr. Hughes won by 57,879, but the remainder of the Hearst-Murphy ticket was elected. The Democratic state officials, however, worked in harmony with Governor Hughes. Lewis Stuyvesant Chanler as lieutenant governor and Martin Glynn as comptroller were specially efficient.

The changes of the Independence League were not yet at an end. In 1907 there was no state election of importance, but Mr. Hearst, deserting Murphy, arranged with Herbert Parsons, chairman of the New York Republican Committee, representing Odell and his state machine, to run fusion candidates for aldermen, for the assembly, and for county offices. The attempt at fusion failed in the main, and *The World's* comment states the lesson:

This year, when an honest fusion might have greatly reduced the Tammany majorities, Mr. Hearst packed the ticket with hacks and hired men and gave Tammany a walk-over. Thanks to Mr. Hearst, Murphy's leadership is more securely established to-day than at any other time in his whole political career. Honor to whom honor is due.

To win in New York, fusion must represent character, conscience and conviction. If it be merely an appetite for office it is foredoomed to disaster.

Governor Hughes was fulfilling expectation that he would give the state a live administration. He had against him the machine of the party that elected him as well as the party that opposed him. He early asked for the Senate's concurrence in the removal of Otto Kelsey as superintendent of insurance. It was refused. *The World*, outraged that the reform of insurance methods which it had compelled should be hampered by the neglect of the department, filed charges against Kelsey; the Governor appointed Matthew C. Fleming to take testimony; and the inquiry revealed such ignorance of his duties upon Kelsey's part that it made the Senate a laughing-stock. Fleming's report was filed February 2, 1908, and presently Kelsey resigned and was "taken care of" by an appointment in the comptroller's office. The Insurance Department was provided with an abler head in William H. Hotchkiss.

The World had supported the Governor in the Kelsey matter. It supported him in forcing the recount bill, to silence the complaint that Mr. Hearst had been counted out for McClellan in 1905. It upheld the Governor in his demand for the public-utilities bill. This act provided Public Service Commissions for city and country, put a check on stock-watering by public-service companies, and gave the people a representation and a control. It is the model for the New Jersey public-service law and others that have since been passed. Though mutilated by the most regrettable court decision in the Third Avenue case, that its provisions do not apply to reorganizations, as was intended when it was enacted, it has proved of great value.

A hotter contest in which Governor Hughes had the support of *The World* as well as that of Mr. Hearst's newspapers was his war upon gambling at race-tracks. The constitution of New York prohibits gambling. Under the Percy-Gray law pool-selling at race-tracks was permitted by legislative connivance in failing to provide penalties. To reconcile the rural conscience to this hypocrisy, part of the huge revenue from the betting-rings of metropolitan tracks was paid to agricultural-society fairs. But the people did not approve of the arrangement, nor could it have been retained so long but for the influence of race-track lobbyists at Albany.

The Legislature refused to provide penalties for acts

16

within race-track fences which were punished outside them. Governor Hughes went beyond the Legislature to the people and threatened a special session. Of this threat *The World* said on April 10, 1908:

His message is a constitutional threat that if the Legislature does not fully and honestly consider Wall Street and race-track gambling, the regulation of telephone and telegraph companies, the rapid-transit law, the improvement of the highways, certain economies in administration, a direct-nominations law, banking legislation, immigration, the condition of the unemployed and reform in the procedure of the courts of criminal jurisdiction, he will call a special session and use his constitutional executive power to see that the Legislature exercises its constitutional legislative power. . . .

With all its duties undone, the Legislature was calmly arranging to adjourn, that its members might be more free to play national and state politics. The fault lies specifically in the Senate. That is the reason the Governor's message cuts like a lash those Senators who are now writhing under it.

The special session was called. To fill a Senate vacancy a by-election was held before the Legislature could re-assemble; upon the race-track issue Governor Hughes's supporter won against odds. The people were aroused, and legislators heard from their constituents. Two months later the bills were passed. In the following autumn many men who had opposed the Governor failed of renomination or re-election; and as they were generally of the hide-bound and sometimes corrupt "Old Guard," the state gained by the upheaval.

These stirring scenes brought the state campaign of 1908 to alert public attention. A Governor was to be elected, the Senate and the Assembly. The men who had been fighting Governor Hughes in the Legislature and getting worsted were forced to renominate him. They would have been willing to renominate Higgins two years before, but did not dare. They now longed to "turn

Hughes down," but were forbidden to do so by President Roosevelt, who knew how great a reputation Governor Hughes had acquired throughout the country, and how bad an effect would be produced upon the Republican campaign by denying him a renomination; and the political graveyard was already full enough of men who had tried to stop the Governor in his course. Mr. Hearst named an Independent ticket, headed by his counsel, Clarence Shearn. The strength of Mr. Hughes *The World* discussed with its usual candor September 16th:

There is bitter opposition to him within his own party. There is dissatisfaction in this city with the work of the Public Service Commission. There is intense hostility against the Governor among the elements that patronized the race-tracks. There is the indirect issue of personal liberty, many of whose defenders scent danger in certain of the Governor's puritanical tendencies. And, finally, William Travers Jerome is still District Attorney of New York County.

At the same time Mr. Hughes is fortunate beyond any other Republican nominated for Governor in a generation. He owes nothing to his party's organization. He owes nothing to the Republican partnership with Wall Street and high finance. He is a free man, under obligations to nobody but the people of the State of New York.

The nominee of the Democrats was Lewis Stuyvesant Chanler, the Lieutenant-Governor who had beaten the Republican candidate two years before when Hearst was defeated; a popular young man, with an excellent record. As the campaign developed and Mr. Chanler proved weak in debate and chary of decided policies *The World* more strongly urged Hughes's cause. He was re-elected by a majority of 69,462 against the bitterest opposition any candidate in New York had faced in years. The Hearst party neither aided him nor could have defeated him, since Shearn received but 34,000 votes. But Hughes was greatly aided by the Presidential election, in which Taft, against Bryan, received 202,000 plurality in New York.

Governor Hughes in his second term was even more hampered by the Republican machine. His Wall Street investigation brought out valuable facts, but failed to produce results in legislation. As, prior to 1898, the state punished gambling outside race-track inclosures while permitting it inside them, so it continued to penalize usury outside of Wall Street, but permitted it within that charmed area, and made no attempt to curb gambling transactions on 'Change.

In both his terms Governor Hughes served New York City by removing unfit officials. Three borough presidents fell at his hands after careful hearings. In the case of President Ahearn of Manhattan, the Tammany aldermen showed their sense of justice by re-electing him to the office in which he had been found unfit, raising curious questions as to the *de facto* status of a member of the Board of Estimate who *de jure* was not a member, until the courts ousted him. After long consideration, however, Governor Hughes failed to remove District-Attorney Jerome upon charges preferred by minority stockholders of the Metropolitan street Railway Company that he had failed to move zealously against rich criminals.

Governor Hughes, again with the support of *The World*, compelled the Legislature to include telegraph and telephone companies under the jurisdiction of the Public Service Commission. The new law has been followed by reductions in tolls and by better control over an important business affecting the public. The Governor was less successful in his last great fight with the political machines—his attempt to secure a direct-primary law.

While Governor Hughes was still in the thick of the fray President Taft selected him as an associate justice of the United States Supreme Court. The appointment was made in May, 1910, though Justice Hughes did not

take oath until October 10th.   Mr. Taft's selection was
widely approved, perhaps by no one more heartily than
by the bosses of his own party in New York, whose folly
and feebleness Mr. Hughes had exposed.   This appointment removed from political life an official to whom *The
World* had tendered more active support than to any
other since Grover Cleveland.   In after-time men may
be puzzled to know why one so strong in leadership as
Governor Hughes, so secure in the confidence of the people, so progressive in his policies, should have been lost
to political life.   The reason is indicated in the following
article, which appeared in *The World* two years after his
retirement to the bench, when the panic-stricken New
York leaders of Republicanism were facing defeat by the
Bull Moose schism:

Surveying the wreck of a once splendid political organization,
what would the Republican bosses at Saratoga give for another
Charles E. Hughes? . . .
The Republican chickens have all come home to roost.
After Mr. Hughes was elected Governor in 1906 Mr. Roosevelt
discovered that he was not going to be subservient to the White
House, and cunningly set to work to destroy the Governor
politically.   Mr. Roosevelt's visitors were told that "Hughes
is an ingrate," and Mr. Roosevelt used to boast that he would
never permit the Republican National Convention to nominate
Hughes for President.
Mr. Barnes, who was a Roosevelt office-holder, and all his
associate Republican bosses in New York ardently played the
Roosevelt game. . . . Thanks to their efforts, Mr. Roosevelt
had no difficulty in controlling the Republican National Convention in 1908 and in nominating Mr. Taft.   Then he compelled these same bosses to renominate Mr. Hughes for Governor, because he knew that the Hughes candidacy was essential
to Republican success.   But even then the bosses went their
way blindly and stupidly.   Throughout his second term they
continued their fight against the Governor.   The Republican
machine worked with Tammany; Grady (Tammany spokes-

man) was the leader of both parties on the floor of the Senate, and the Hughes administration fought, inch by inch, for every popular measure that it won.

But in the summer of 1910 Mr. Roosevelt came back from Africa, ambitious to be the only third-term President. He needed a moral issue, and Governor Hughes had provided one. So Mr. Roosevelt seized it, turned upon the up-State bosses who had been his henchmen while he was in the White House, and launched himself as the champion of progressive policies.

In the mean time Governor Hughes went to the Supreme bench; the Republican bosses were left without a shred of moral leadership, and to-day their party organization is annihilated, and they are facing political extermination. They helped Roosevelt destroy Hughes, and now Roosevelt is destroying them.

Had they stood by Governor Hughes after his election in 1906 . . . it is very likely that Charles E. Hughes would be President of the United States. They could have made him President in spite of the Roosevelt machine. If Mr. Hughes had been nominated for President instead of Mr. Taft, there would be no Roosevelt third-term candidacy, no Progressive party, no wreck of the Republican organization, no certainty of Republican defeat.

The campaign of 1909 was to New York City as important as that of Presidential year. A Mayor and Board of Estimate were to be elected for four years. *The World* had long urged as a candidate for Governor or Mayor William J. Gaynor, whose prowess against McKane, of Gravesend, has been described. Justice Gaynor was one of the strongest men of the city. Upon the Supreme Court bench he had refused to be lost to sight. His energy, his interest in public affairs, and the piquancy of phrasing that made his public utterances readable kept him prominent.

The Republican machine after futile negotiations for fusion nominated Otto Bannard as a "straight" candidate. The Civic Alliance that had succeeded to the

Independence League repented of its former friendship
for Gaynor, and nominated Mr. Hearst himself.   Fusion
was fortunately accomplished in nominations for some
other offices.

Boss Murphy, once more showing the boldness that had
impelled him to draft Grout and Fornes from the Fusion
ticket of 1903, caused the indorsement of Justice Gaynor
by the Democratic City Convention.   He had already been
nominated by petition.   *The World* in supporting Judge
Gaynor had no fear of his proving putty in Murphy's
hands.   Gaynor was, in fact, selected for Mayor by public opinion.

Mr. Hearst's vote was weaker than in 1905.   He was
third in the race; Gaynor led Bannard by 73,074 votes.
In minor offices fusion fared well.   Said *The World* the
day after election:

Tammany was beaten by Democrats and lost the city government to Democrats.

John P. Mitchel, elected President of the Board of Aldermen,
is a Democrat.   George McAneny, elected President of the
Borough of Manhattan, is a Democrat.   Alfred E. Steers,
elected President of the Borough of Brooklyn, is a Democrat:
Lawrence J. Gresser, elected President of the Borough of
Queens, is a Democrat.   Cyrus C. Miller, elected President of
the Borough of the Bronx, is a Democrat.

These were some of the men upon whom the Hearst
party had fused with Republicans.   Although Gresser
was later forced out of office, the fusion city and borough
government thus provided for was much better than
its Tammany predecessors.   It was no small thing for
New York to have as Borough President of Manhattan
Mr. McAneny instead of the incompetent Ahearn; and
Mr. Miller in the Bronx to replace the impossible Haffen.
With a Republican Comptroller, with so excellent a
Republican District Attorney of New York County as

Charles S. Whitman and a fusion Board of Aldermen, New York for the four years beginning with January 1, 1910, was anything but a Tammany preserve.

In its first few months Mayor Gaynor's administration so far surpassed all predecessors as to seem almost magic. The tax rate was bravely put up to stop borrowing money for current expenses, and an appropriation of ten million dollars was made to clear off bad assets upon which the city had been borrowing. Sluggish Commissioners were forced out of office. Excellent appointments were the rule. Economy intruded where it had long been a stranger. Waste was cut off in the Board of City Record, in aqueduct appraisals, in many departments. Borough appointments were generally excellent. When after less than seven months of new life for the city the Mayor was stricken down by the bullet of a would-be assassin the country was appalled at the threatened loss of one of its great figures.

If in succeeding years Mayor Gaynor's administration lost strength and popularity the causes are easy to estimate. First among them all, the conduct of the Police Department, always a Mayor's toughest problem, was cast into discredit by the murder of Herman Rosenthal, a gambler who had promised to reveal secrets of the complicity of the police "system" with protected vice and law-breaking.

Rosenthal had complained to the Mayor that Lieutenant Charles Becker, who commanded a squad of "strong-arm" police, had been his partner in the illicit venture of conducting a gambling-house, but was now persecuting him. For that reason he was willing to become an informer. Rosenthal got little sympathy from the Mayor, and took his story to *The World*, which prepared it for publication. Rosenthal was also about to go before the Grand Jury, and this became known by his old associates. Early in the morning of July 16, 1912, he was called out of the Hotel Metropole, Forty-third Street near Broadway, and shot dead within sight of a number of people by men who fled in a gray automobile.

Circumstances pointed to a prearranged escape. Policemen in the vicinity got the number of the gray automobile wrong. A civilian who took down the correct number and reported it at the station-house was locked up, to his amazement. By good fortune the news promptly reached District-Attorney Charles S. Whitman, who went to the station-house in the early morning hours, released and questioned the imprisoned witness, and set the detectives of his own office upon the trail.

The World at once published Rosenthal's long story of his underworld experience of police protection and persecution. His death set the seal of truth upon every sordid detail of the recital. The murder explained the story; the story explained the murder. This publication, coupled with Mr. Whitman's prompt action, prevented the crime from dropping into the class of "mysterious" killings in New York due to gang and gambler warfare, for which often no culprit is found guilty. The city was aroused. The crime would not blow over. Soon, through the tracing of the gray automobile and its chauffeur, four "gunmen" who did the shooting became known, and with them evidence to connect Lieutenant Becker with the crime. Out of the slime of the underworld witnesses were haled who knew and who, to save their own lives or liberty as accomplices, were compelled to tell how Becker had ordered the gunmen to kill Rosenthal, had assured them of immunity from punishment, had arranged that "getaway money" be paid them by a wealthy gambler.

Instead of offering the district attorney assistance, the Mayor made, and afterward adhered to, the grave error of treating him as the enemy of the police force and the city administration. He bade Police Commissioner

Waldo retain Lieutenant Becker on the force until his arrest. He criticized Becker only for having sat at table with "a scoundrel like Rosenthal." Even after Becker's conviction Mr. Gaynor spoke of this man, who had held the power of life and death and had boasted of his ability to give immunity to murderers, as "only a little lieutenant." It almost seemed as if the police authorities were willing to see the accused men and the witnesses balk justice. But the district attorney gradually rounded them up, some in the city, one witness from as far away as Hot Springs, Arkansas, and brought the whole crew into a court of justice.

Becker was tried first, and on October 24th, less than three months after his arrest, he was convicted. The four gunmen—young degenerates of an ordinary type, members of a criminal gang—were convicted on November 19th. *The World* sought to read "New York's Great Lesson" in these famous trials and to enforce the need of vigilance:

> The murder of Rosenthal brought the hideous meaning of the System home to every man and woman in New York, but the sequel has demonstrated the capacity of this crime-ridden community to re-establish a government of law. New York is no longer at the mercy of its criminals, whether in or out of the Police Department.
>
> This city found in Charles S. Whitman a District Attorney who measured up to every responsibility of his office. It found in John W. Goff a just and upright Judge who never hesitated to do his duty as he saw it. It found in the jury that convicted Becker and in the jury that convicted the four young crooks who did the actual killing twenty-four citizens who have helped restore public respect for the administration of justice.
>
> Even though the Mayor missed the great opportunity of leadership that he owed to the community, even though the Police Commissioner deluded himself into believing that the System was a myth, organized government has again vindicated itself.

For the time being the alliance between the police and the criminals is broken, and by vigorous administration it will stay broken. . . . A body of intelligent public opinion has been created that will make it easier to reorganize the Police Department, purge it of its debauched elements and re-establish the ascendancy of its majority of honest men.

Besides vigilance there was needed, for permanent reform, the abandonment of hypocrisy:

A death-sentence of Becker, a death-sentence of the four gunmen, a death-sentence of gang rule, a death-sentence of the System. And then what?

For a little while a purified city; and then a new Becker, new gunmen, a new gang rule, a new System, a resurrection of all the evils which we think we are burying, unless there is also passed a death-sentence on the conditions which directly created these evils. . . .

So long as an Anglo-Saxon hypocrisy persists in making felonious everything that it considers shocking, so long as it brands as crimes those practices which other broader-minded and equally civilized nations handle as public nuisances, so long as an Albany Legislature takes it upon itself to decree a rigid, standardized, criminally enforceable code of manners and of morals for a city nearly half of whose inhabitants come from a score of foreign lands each with its own customs and standards, so long as such a Legislature strives to create fiat chastity, fiat sobriety and fiat frugality in conformity with its own professed ideals, and binds our local authorities by oath to treat any divergence from these ideals as crimes, just so long will human nature, following the dictates of its foibles, evade such laws by subterfuge and by corruption. And as soon as corruption is employed to evade laws which the enforcers of those laws themselves consider unreasonable, just so soon shall we again have a debauched police force, a System, a Becker, gangs, gunmen, a city shamed before the world.

With the mass of evidence bearing upon bribery of the police brought out in these trials District-Attorney Whitman went swiftly ahead to prosecute extortioners high upon the force who had grown wealthy by selling privileges to break the law, but against whom evidence had been lacking. Policemen of lower rank were convicted of bribery, and following their trials Inspectors Sweeney, Hussey, Murtha, and Thompson were brought into court upon the minor charge of conspiring to silence a witness against them, one Sipp, the proprietor of questionable resorts and a state's witness, by causing a vile charge to be made against him upon which he was arrested. Sipp was rescued by the district attorney. The evidence was untangled and the inspectors convicted in a group, with the graver charges of bribery and extortion still hanging over them.

These bombshells bursting in the police force had not caused general agreement with Mayor Gaynor, who continued constant in praise of the Police Department; who said that there were not more than fifty dishonest men wearing the blue, even after several of them were wearing prison stripes; and who voiced the police grievances against the district attorney. Naturally also *The World*, which had begun the clean-up process with the Rosenthal revelation, continued it in caustic editorials criticizing the Mayor and urging and commending the activity of Mr. Whitman.

Another matter in which *The World* opposed Mayor Gaynor was the settlement of the subway problem. The Mayor and other members of the Board of Estimate had been elected upon an understanding that they favored the municipal construction of further rapid-transit lines, without leasing them to the existing Brooklyn and Manhattan monopolies.

The McClellan administration had used the city's credit even beyond the legal debt limit, so that the new administration had to begin by canceling some $20,-000,000 of commitments against which bonds were not yet issued.   The debt limit had been increased by exempting bonds issued for self-supporting purposes, like docks and subways, and by higher assessments which automatically raised the borrowing power.   Thus provided with funds, it seemed to *The World* that the city did not need to go again into partnership with the monopolies which had shown such scant consideration for passengers and, in their stock-jobbing manipulations of transit rights in the public streets, such slight regard for honesty.   The Mayor joined what became the dominant element in the Board of Estimate, and after long negotiation the complicated "dual system" agreement with the Interborough Company and the Brooklyn Rapid Transit Company was struck.   This strange bargain was a disappointment to a great many of the people, as it was to *The World*.   Under it the city's credit was the vivifying force in hundreds of millions of fresh investments, the Interborough's profits, unduly swollen by overcrowding upon its inadequate lines, were guaranteed by spreading them over old and new capital alike, the watering of stocks in the elevated railroads was condoned by the acceptance of their capital as entitled to profits; and the city's return upon its own portion of the investment was, in the opinion of many, made uncertain except in conditions of renewed overcrowding, such as the people wished to end.   Yet, however owned, the new subways will be a potent force in building a vaster New York than was dreamed of thirty years ago.

As Mayor Gaynor's administration is not complete the time has not come for any journal to pass judgment upon it.   In 1911, before the final disposition of the rapid-transit bargain, and before the Rosenthal murder, *The World* said of it and of the Mayor:

We think that Mr. Gaynor has been a very good Mayor. Up to the time he was shot last summer, we think he was probably the best Mayor New York had had within the memory of any man then living   We still think he is a better Mayor than Mr. McClellan or Mr. Low or Mr. Van Wyck, and that the municipal service is in better condition than at any other time since consolidation. . . .

If anybody chooses to say that Mr. Gaynor is irascible and irritable in his discussions of public affairs, we shall agree with him; but we are aware of no provision in the Constitution of the State or the charter of the city which asserts that the Mayor of New York must be sweet-tempered and gentle and lovable.   Mr. Gaynor is rather difficult to get along with at times and we are glad that we have no personal relations with him; but these infirmities of disposition do not greatly concern the public welfare.   Most of the people that the Mayor scolds are office-holders and they are competent to take care of their own troubles.

Many citizens are undoubtedly disappointed because the Mayor has not done better, because he has not accomplished more.   This is an honest disappointment.   The World would be very reluctant to accept the Gaynor administration as the highest possible achievement in the way of city government; but it spells progress, and we fervently hope that New York may never have a worse Mayor than William J. Gaynor.

XVIII

"THE MAP OF BRYANISM"

1906-1908

Mr. Bryan's Return from a Trip Around the World—He Conquers "The Enemy's Country" — Practically Nominated Two Years in Advance— "The World's" Strong Protest—Mr. Taft's Selection Becomes Certain— A Big-Stick Convention—The Nation's Need of An Opposition—Untimely Death of Gov. John A. Johnson of Minnesota—Taft Elected by His Opponent's Weakness—The Hard-Times Issue Goes for Naught.

RETURNING from a trip around the world, during which he had been received with honors in many lands and had made notable addresses, William Jennings Bryan reached New York Wednesday, August 29, 1906. He was greeted by Democrats from every section and hailed as their next candidate for the Presidency.

The World did not wait to hear Mr. Bryan's speech to an immense audience in Madison Square Garden the following night before warning Democrats of the folly of "tying their own hands and closing the door of opportunity against themselves two years in advance of the campaign." It told Mr. Bryan that the well-heralded appeal he was about to make for government ownership of the railroads was "a scheme of state socialism absolutely revolutionary." It described the premature Presidential demonstration as the "most impolitic, foolish abdication of power on the part of a great political organization ever recorded" in the United States.

Mr. Bryan's speech was rapturously applauded in what was once "the enemy's country," and government ownership was temporarily added to the patchwork which Democratic policy had become under his leadership. Less than a year later the pattern was again changed when, on July 20, 1907, Mr. Bryan in a formal statement said:

> Government ownership is not an immediate issue. A large majority of the people still hope for effective regulation. While they so hope they will not consider government ownership. While many Democrats believe, and Mr. Bryan is one of them, that public ownership of railroads is the ultimate solution of the problem, still those who believe that the public will finally in self-defense be driven to ownership recognize that regulation must be tried under the most favorable circumstances before the masses will be ready to try a more radical remedy. Regulation cannot be sufficiently tried within the next year. There is no desire anywhere to make government ownership an issue in 1908.

It was no new thing for Mr. Bryan to modify or defer his policies in response to party sentiment. In 1896 he had subordinated his tariff opinions to press the silver cause. In 1900, while not consenting to disavow free silver, he had recognized that it was not an "immediate issue" by making anti-imperialism paramount. Between his home-coming address and the statement of July, 1907, he had espoused in his Jefferson Day speech in Brooklyn a new issue, the initiative and referendum. Thus was illustrated the peril, against which *The World* had warned the party, of selecting a candidate two years in advance. "What new Populistic or Socialistic issue he will have by 1908 for the Democratic party to subscribe to," was its comment upon the July statement, "is beyond the ken of human foresight." And it repeated a query of the preceding year: "If the American people considered Mr. Bryan unsafe in 1896 and in 1900, wherein is he safer now? In what respect is he a cooler counselor or a wiser leader than he was then?"

After the disastrous elections of 1907 Mr. Bryan's

previous boast that "the prospects of the Democratic
party are very bright and are constantly growing brighter"
was recalled by *The World* in the rejoinder that became
famous as "The Map of Bryanism." This pictorial representation of the harm "16 to 1" had done the party
and the country was devised by Mr. Pulitzer himself, a
blind man, to convince those who, having eyes, saw not.
The map, which first appeared November 11, 1907, showed
the entire country north of Oklahoma, Arkansas, Tennessee, Virginia, and Maryland solidly Republican. For
months the map was repeated in every form the ingenuity
of the cartoonist could devise; as the Denver convention
drew near it was usually drawn upon the side of a Con-
estoga wagon, or "prairie-schooner," headed for "Pike's
Peak or Bust." Eventually the "Map of Bryanism,"
by which *The World* protested against the courting of
defeat in advance, was made the text of a vigorous
pamphlet which was widely circulated. The power of
this appeal to Democracy to seek the way of success and
usefulness may be indicated by a citation. The date is
February, 1908. The appeal is to Mr. Bryan himself:

Your leadership of the Democratic party, Mr. Bryan, began
with the National Convention held in Chicago in 1896. It was
an unfortunate year for a national campaign.

The American people were paying the penalty of thirty years
of trifling with their currency and their monetary standard
of value. Industry was half paralyzed, commerce semi-
prostrate. Crops had been poor, the price of farm products
was low; the farms themselves were generally mortgaged.
The National Government itself, with a demoralized treasury,
was borrowing money to pay its current expenses under the
form of maintaining the gold reserve. Bond sales to favored
syndicates had aroused the indignation of the people, without
regard to party. Probably a million men in the cities were
out of work. Soup-houses had been opened during the two
preceding winters, and in every large center of population police-
stations had been filled nightly by homeless wanderers.

17

Armies of tramps moved sullenly along the highways. A Democratic Administration was in power, which seemingly had no friends except its own appointees and beneficiaries. Discontent was almost universal. It was the hour of the agitator, and the Democratic National Convention was his opportunity.

There were orators, there were demagogues, there were self-seekers; there were in plenty Jack Cades, with seven half-penny loaves on sale for a penny; but something more was needed, and that was a man who gave evidence of zeal, who had not been conspicuously identified with ancient party feuds, and who, by his demeanor, might inspire the despairing, satisfy the frantic, excite the luke-warm and appeal to the imagination of the doubtful voter.

That man appeared in the person of you, William Jennings Bryan, then thirty-six years old, at that moment editor of an Omaha newspaper by grace of the silver-miners, and affectionately known in the West as "the Boy Orator of the Platte."

The "Map of Bryanism" from this point traced Mr. Bryan's career through the reverse of 1896, the four following years of experiment, the more decided disaster of 1900, the fresh coquettings with strange doctrine—in short, the twelve years of division and defeat. *The World* argued that there were men who could make appeal to the new spirit in the Democracy—the spirit that four years later was to bear it past all obstacles to a notable victory. Foremost among them at this time was John A. Johnson, Governor of Minnesota, who had been elected in 1904 by a plurality of 6,352 on the same day that his state gave Roosevelt 161,464 plurality. Governor Johnson had been re-elected by 76,633 plurality in 1906. One of the strongest, simplest figures in American political life, he was the candidate of his state for the Democratic nomination for the Presidency; his death in September, 1909, was a loss to Minnesota and the Union. Judge Gray, of Delaware, known throughout the country for his able and patriotic action as chairman of the commission that settled the coal strike, was another man, strong with the people and in his Democracy unquestioned, with whom the party might have retrieved disaster.

That *The World* in later supporting Mr. Bryan, after exhausting all arguments against his candidacy, was under no illusions as to his chance of election was shown in its article of April 24, 1908:

William H. Taft will be nominated for President by the Republican National Convention.

If William J. Bryan is to be the Democratic candidate, Judge Taft's election is certain. There need be no anxiety as to the outcome of another Bryan campaign; no increased industrial suspense, no further shutting down of factories, no new recruits to the army of unemployed.

Not that *The World* shut its eyes to the graver dangers which lay behind immediate confidence in "Taft and Prosperity." It found no cause for congratulating the public in the convention which in June nominated Mr. Taft. That ratification meeting swayed at will by an imperious Executive it described as "A Big Stick Convention."

It was the Big Stick that prodded the Federal employees, in defiance of civil-service-reform law or principle, into frantic activity for Taft; that marshaled the delegates; that clubbed contestants out of court. The Big Stick wrote the keynote speech, selected the committees of the Convention, called it to order, directed its nominal deliberations. Familiar Big-Stick phrases and ideas fill the platform that was given out in Chicago before the Convention had even assembled—and the Big Stick brands this same platform, full of praise of the Big Stick's past performances and promises for the future, as a "mere tentative draft." The Big Stick scrawls on the Convention door the names of approved Vice-Presidential candidates, to the impotent anger of Republican managers, and nails down the anti-injunction plank while conservative leaders shriek themselves hoarse in vain protest. The Big Stick, waved over apprehensive monopolies, will provide the campaign funds; it will admonish the spellbinders, lead the bands, conduct the campaign for both parties and wear the credit of the result.

The Republican platform, while declaring for tariff revision, contained for the first time the doctrine that protection should maintain "such duties as will equal the difference between the cost of production at home and abroad, *together with a reasonable profit to American industries.*" It made no reference to a federal income and inheritance tax, which President Roosevelt had recommended to Congress. Mr. Taft's speech of acceptance was quite as disappointing. While *The World* admitted that it would "strengthen him with the very large business interests of the country," it found objection to his "fulsome eulogy of Roosevelt, his obvious evasion on the income tax, his hedging on the Philippines, his disheartening apology for unprecedented Republican extravagance," and added:

His speech leaves the one great problem of the campaign still unsolved. In the minds of intelligent, thoughtful voters everywhere lies this grave question of the Republican candidate's personal and political dependence upon Roosevelt.

Will Taft be a President or a Proxy?

The Democratic National Convention in July was also a mere indorsing body. Mr. Bryan's nomination was inevitable. The platform was much better than those of 1896 and 1900. It made no mention of free silver. It contained no attack on the courts. Its tariff plank was "far more moderate and restrained than was the 1892 platform upon which Mr. Cleveland was elected, in which a protective tariff was denounced as unconstitutional." It upheld the civil-service law. It favored the income tax. Its declaration in favor of campaign-fund publicity and a corrupt-practices act gratified the enemies of political fraud. In comment *The World* said on August 1st:

Mr. Bryan will be wise indeed if he carries out his announced purpose of "standing squarely on the platform," and on the platform alone, subordinating everything else to the issues of the campaign as officially defined by the Chicago and Denver Conventions.

Mr. Bryan will be wiser still if he sticks to half a dozen vitally Democratic planks in preference to the Denver platform as a whole:

1. Jingoism, with its bigger armies, bigger navies, crazy war-scares and reckless expenditures—an issue on which the Democratic party is sane and sound, as proved by the over-whelming refusal of the Denver Convention to tolerate the insensate war-shrieks of Hobson.

2. Philippinism.

3. Publicity of campaign funds.

4. Roosevelt extravagance.

5. Tariff reform.

6. Centralization.

These issues represent fundamental Democratic principles.

Upon the following day *The World* gave at greater length its reasons for a hearty support of a candidate whose nomination it had fought and still regretted. This reason was the need of Opposition. However objectionable the action of the Democratic Convention might have been, greater dangers lay in unrestricted power in Washington, with a Proxy President and a Big Stick still brandished over the country:

We opposed Mr. Bryan's nomination on the ground of principle and expediency. In advocating the nomination of Gov. Johnson or Judge Gray The World's aim was the rehabilitation and revitalization of the Democratic party.

Even as a minority party the Democracy has an important duty to perform. There are grave wrongs to redress. There are shocking abuses of power to correct. There is waste and extravagance in the National Government, so scandalous that it finds no parallel in modern government. No adequate punishment has yet been dealt out to the eminent pirates of American finance who have reduced law-breaking to a fine art. There is jingoism, militarism, imperialism, rough-riderism, government by denunciation, Executive contempt for Congress and the courts—Rooseveltism in all its worst manifestations, unchecked and unrestrained.

Mr. Bryan, the article continued, was "fortunate in the strength of the issues which the Republicans have presented to him." First among these was the refusal of the Republican convention to "adopt a plank demanding an efficient corrupt-practices act and publicity of campaign expenditures." Mr. Taft had advocated the latter of these measures, yet the Convention that nominated him voted down a plank upon the subject by 880 to 94! Besides this great cause there was the issue of " administrative economy ":

Never before was there such a debauch of extravagance in modern government as that which the Roosevelt Administration is responsible for. In place of the sensational Billion-Dollar Congress, which Speaker Reed was compelled to defend, we have the Two-Billion-Dollar Congress, spending a thousand millions of public money at each annual session. . . .

But the first practical issue that must be faced and squarely met, is that of dislocated business and industry. The people of the United States need peace, they need prosperity, they need employment, they need bread. No campaign can be successful which does not take this great factor into consideration. In place of an indiscriminate crusade against all business and a continuation of the Roosevelt reign of terror must come a realization that guilt is always personal, and that the only effective way to deal with corporation crimes is to send the one responsible man to jail.

Throughout the campaign *The World* had often to repeat its question whether in the election of Mr. Taft the country was getting "a President or a Proxy":

There is need of real statesmanship at Washington. We are spending a thousand millions a year. We are playing a strong hand in the war game. We are involved ten thousand miles away in colonial adventure. We have privilege and prostration. We have plutocracy and depression. We are giving the world a fairly successful imitation of imperialism.

But empires that endure have statesmen, economists and financiers who look after resources, and who note with care the state of the country and the welfare of the people. Imperialism must not rest wholly upon extravagance or upon epaulets and ribbons. Money must be had. It must be drawn from the people by taxation. If the people are to pay the taxes they must be prosperous, and if discontent is not to appear, the imports must be just and reasonable, and not too severe a burden upon enterprise and industry. Expenditure must be wise.

Much of our thousand millions of outgo is waste and worse. A spendthrift government makes a spendthrift people. A large percentage of our taxation is laid discriminatingly, for the benefit of favored interests. A government that shows partiality is in no position to establish comprehensive justice. A nation that wastes is sure to come to want. A government that can do no more than denounce injustice is certain to be a failure.

Since Mr. Taft has refused to discuss the important questions bearing upon business and industrial revival, the re-employment of the idle, the fairer distribution of public burdens and the reduction of the cost of living, it is gratifying to note the fact that Mr. Bryan promises to devote his first speech of the campaign to these problems. The subject has been too long neglected by our public men. . . .

If Mr. Taft aims to be President he should have some ideas on these highly important questions, even if they do involve criticism of Mr. Roosevelt, and he should express them fearlessly. If he is content to be a Proxy he will continue as he has begun, with eyes turned toward Oyster Bay, and in a posture of adoration.

"The first speech of the campaign" by Mr. Bryan when it came was something of a disappointment:

Legitimate and proper as this arraignment of Republicanism must be considered, it loses much force by reason of its studied avoidance of the equally glaring errors of Rooseveltism. In some respects it resembles a Roosevelt message to Congress. It leaves the impression that Mr. Roosevelt has been in the right at all times; that his policies have been wise and just; that his methods have been correct, and that his failures have resulted through no fault of his own. That is not the case. There can be no true estimate of the wrongs, follies and disasters that are to be forever associated with this administration which does not take into the fullest account the personal responsibility of the President.

Probably the favor thus shown to Mr. Roosevelt accounts for the astonishing fact that in all of Mr. Bryan's 5,000 and more words, the word "extravagance," the word "retrenchment," and the phrase "waste of public money" do not appear. Such an oversight would be considered extraordinary and unprecedented in a leader of any Opposition, and it is emphatically so in the leader of a Democratic Opposition to crazy Republican profligacy at Washington. What would Tilden have said under such provocation? What oratorical thunderbolts would Gladstone, in opposition, have hurled at a ministry having such a record?

Mr. Bryan's speech of acceptance was a notable state paper. He advanced three reasons for the failure of reform measures under the Republican administration even when advocated by the Republican President: (1) The Republican party as an organization has drawn its campaign funds from the beneficiaries of privilege; it has sold legislation and immunity to favored interests, and it has naturally refused to provide for publicity in the matter of campaign contributions and expenditures. (2) The Republican Senate of the United States, the very citadel of privilege and plunder, has stubbornly refused to pass the resolution for an amendment to the Constitution permitting the election of Senators by the people. (3) The Republican party, through the despotism of the Speaker and the rules governing the House of Representatives, has made that body a creature of the interests rather than a servant of the people.

As to such of his personal ideas as were not contained in the party declaration of principles Mr. Bryan said "a platform is binding as to what it omits as well as to what it contains. . . . A platform announces the party's position on the questions which are at issue, and an official is not at liberty to use the authority vested in him to urge personal views which have not been submitted to the voters for their approval." These sentences were tombstones over the graves of free silver, of government ownership of railroads, of the initiative and the referendum, and of hostility to the courts. This guarded utterance encouraged *The World* to hope that Opposition might be aggressive, unsensational, and not without a generous support at the polls:

Although Mr. Roosevelt in his stump speeches for two years vehemently insisted upon the restriction of "swollen fortunes" by means of income and inheritance taxes, not one word appears in Mr. Roosevelt's Chicago platform in favor of these just and equitable measures.

In spite of all his frenzied denunciation of malefactors of great wealth, all "the malefactors of great wealth" are praising the platform and pledging their support on the ticket.

To make assurance doubly sure that the work of his convention would command the approval of Wall Street and the predatory elements in general, Mr. Roosevelt made James S. Sherman the party candidate for Vice-President. Mr. Sherman represents the very tendencies in politics that Mr. Roosevelt pretends to oppose so violently. Yet Mr. Roosevelt elevates this astute representative of Wall Street politics to the dignity of a Man of My Type. . . .

The World will treat Mr. Bryan with scrupulous fairness and justice. It will endeavor to treat him more than generously because it so vigorously argued against his nomination. Our conviction is stronger than ever that Governor Johnson or

Judge Gray could have polled tens of thousands of votes which Mr. Bryan cannot get. But if Mr. Bryan should adhere to his admirable speech of acceptance and the gratifying pledges to bury the past, and should prove during the campaign that he has profited by defeat and unlearned his past follies in the school of experience; if he should resolutely keep his back turned upon the delusive issues which he has hitherto advocated; if he should refrain from attacks upon the courts; if he should avoid all appeals to class prejudice; if he should prove that he is not the old Bryan, courageously leading the popular protest against the excesses of Rooseveltism, he can then appeal with fair prospects of success to the great independent vote—in some States the deciding vote—that will be governed not by clamor but by reason; not by claptrap but by conscience; not by noise but by facts and truth; not by appeals to class hatred and ignorance but by appeals to public intelligence— public intelligence.

The World's anxiety lest Mr. Taft should prove a Proxy and not a President continued to be complicated by evidence that Mr. Bryan also had been affected by the glamour of the retiring President's power and the appeal of his policies, and was in danger of conducting his campaign as a Proxy candidate. In September, at the outset of the active campaign, *The World* thus treated "An Amazing Situation":

The Democrats have stout rods in pickle for the Republicans this year, as is proved by their campaign book of 300 pages, but they apply none of them to the Republican President.

They are opposed to jingoism, militarism and imperialism, and yet the most warlike of Presidents escapes criticism. They denounce extravagance at Washington, and yet the man who is largely responsible for this reckless expenditure finds no accuser. They make war upon the privileged plutocrats of the tariff, the combines and the trusts, and yet the only President who ever sent for a Harriman and arranged for the collection of a campaign corruption fund is nowhere condemned. . . . They reproach the Republican party for its failure to enforce the laws against the pirates of interstate commerce, and yet the President who holds that the laws are too drastic and that they must be modified, goes free of censure. . . .

Mr. Roosevelt appears to have talked everybody but the socialists to a standstill. Democrats as well as Republicans are shy of him. His party is harshly condemned for the things that he has done and for the things that he has not done; but the man of profligacy, the man of Privilege, Protection and Plutocracy, the man of imperialism, the man of jingoism and war and the man of campaign-fund secrecy is set so high above the mischief he has wrought that nobody undertakes to call him to account.

In his letter to Conrad Kohrs President Roosevelt himself, while emphatically repudiating Bryan as a disciple, proclaimed Taft his lawful heir, and declared that "The policies for which I stand are his policies no less than mine." This public acceptance of Taft as a Proxy made the Republican candidate shoulder the burdens of the Roosevelt administration, which *The World* had thus summarized:

1. It has been extravagant and wasteful.
2. It has attempted to popularize war.
3. It has glorified in Philippine imperialism.
4. It has menaced the States with Federal usurpation by means of constructive jurisprudence.
5. It has recklessly undermined confidence in our business methods, causing panic, depression and suffering.
6. It has profited by the political contributions of corporations seeking legislative favors.
7. It has spoken vociferously against the malefactors of great wealth, but it has not brought one of them to justice.
8. It has bullied Congress, threatening to do as it pleased, law or no law.
9. It has assailed the courts when their judgments were contrary to its wishes.
10. It has maintained the highest tariff ever known in a free

country and has made no move in favor of income and inheritance taxes.

11. It has constantly demanded law and more law for the protection of trusts, although existing laws are held by it to be too drastic for enforcement.

12. It is now attempting to round out a career of wilfulness, greed, ambition and tyranny by forcing the election of a personally excellent and amiable Proxy.

These, said *The World*, "are legitimate issues; they are timely issues; they are Democratic issues." Mr. Bryan's "opportunity lies not in an appeal to the Roosevelt Republicans, most of whom will naturally go to Mr. Taft, but in an appeal to Democrats and to that great independent element in the electorate that is tired of extravagance, of militarism, of imperialism, of rough-riderism, of centralization, of personal government, of big-stick administration and political partnership with predatory plutocracy. Let Mr. Taft be the Proxy. Let Mr. Taft be the heir to My Policies. But let Mr. Bryan be the Democratic candidate for President of the United States."

In this view of the campaign of 1908 the function of Opposition was opposition.

Those who with *The World* supported Mr. Bryan in that spirit did not expect his victory. They looked beyond to the heartening of the opposition party, the healing of its wounds, the promotion of its chances of success in later contests. And in this, at least, they were successful.

Mr. Bryan stood far higher in public estimation in the East than in 1896. His honesty of purpose, his gifts, and capacity for leadership were more fairly appraised. But many distrusted him not more for heresies he had espoused than for the fact that he had so lightly turned from one "paramount" idea to another. "What assurance have we," men said, "that Mr. Bryan might not in the Presidency invent yearly new ideas for government innovation which, in that high seat, would shock the country and upset industry?" Between the twice-beaten candidate, with his handicap of innovation, and the Proxy of a President still powerful and popular, a Proxy whose own character and ability were known, the choice was easy to predict.

Moreover, there was an impression that the tariff would really be "revised by its friends." The Republican platform was discouraging, but Mr. Taft was committed to "honest downward revision." As to Congress, the people trusted to the political effect of the strong protest within the Republican party to compel reasonable lowering of duties upon the necessaries of life.

The defeat was crushing. Mr. Bryan had a million more votes than Judge Parker in 1904. But Mr. Taft's plurality was the second largest ever received by a President; Mr. Bryan's vote was smaller by 343,000 than in 1900; smaller by 487,000 than in 1896. In the House of Representatives the Republicans retained a majority of only fifty; the complexion of this body reflected public dissatisfaction. Three Congresses successively since 1904 had shown a Republican majority decreasing. In the next election it was to vanish.

The World's comment upon Mr. Bryan's defeat follows. It was singularly good-natured for a commentator whose hopes of reform in the national field had been blasted for twelve years by the silver folly:

Mr. Taft owes his election less to his own strength than to Mr. Bryan's weakness. . . . Day after day we warned the Democracy against it. The morning after Mr. Taft's nomination this newspaper declared without reservation that "Bryan's nomination means Taft's election," and the vote yesterday abundantly vindicated this prediction.

Mr. Bryan's friends insisted, however, that he was entitled to another nomination backed by a united party. They had their way. Mr. Bryan received his nomination and a party more united than it has been since 1892 loyally supported him; but even a united party could not overcome the handicap of Mr. Bryan's political record. He was weaker than his party, as shown by the vote for Governor in New York, Minnesota, Illinois and elsewhere; weaker than his issues which he made still weaker by the stupendous folly of posing as Roosevelt's heir. . . .

The Republican candidate had to bear the burden of general hard times; of a million men out of employment; of business interests complaining and dissatisfied; of a steadily increased cost of living; of an unparalleled disaffection of labor leaders; of an unparalleled disaffection of the negro vote; of Republican factional fights in the great pivotal states of New York, Ohio, Indiana and Illinois; of a reactionary platform which he was obliged to modify in his speech of acceptance.

The hard-times issue alone was a burden under which a far stronger candidate than Mr. Taft might have succumbed. It is the first time in the history of the country that a great panic, so far as the popular vote is concerned, has not defeated the party in power.

The echoes of the expected defeat of Mr. Bryan in a hopeless campaign were soon forgotten in an amazing legal battle between the President of the United States and the leading newspaper of the Opposition.

XIX

THE PANAMA LIBEL SUIT

1908–1911

The Narrow Bar between Seas at Panama—De Lesseps and the Crash of the French Canal Company — Failure of Colombia to Ratify the Hay-Herran Treaty—The Prepared "Revolution"—President Roosevelt Takes the Isthmus—William Nelson Cromwell and the Panama Companies—Mr. Roosevelt's Answer to "The Indianapolis News"—"The World" Denounces his Statements as False—Federal Libel Suit Ordered Under a Charles I. Law of 1662—Failure of the Government's Case—Crushing Defeat Before the Supreme Court—Later Developments.

AT Panama the American continent is thirty-five miles across; the height of land is some three hundred feet.

To avoid transshipping for this land passage freight may sail from Colon to Panama through the Strait of Magellan, some seven thousand miles. By no northern sea route can the isthmus be turned; to open a northwest passage was the vain dream of early Arctic navigators.

A canal at Panama has been talked of almost four hundred years. Familiar is the story how Ferdinand de Lesseps, conqueror of the Suez sands, formed a company in Paris in 1876 to cut through the isthmus; how by 1894 $449,000,000 of securities had been sold, $240,000,000 of money expended, one-third of it in France, and the work scarcely more than begun; how corruption reigned at the isthmus and in the Panama lobby in Paris; how workmen perished in the swamps, and costly machinery rotted in the jungle, and the work halted, and the company failed, and a new one was patched up and went on spending money, but more slowly and with little result; how fraud blighted the undertaking, doomed by physical conditions, and the great work came to a standstill.

In 1876 an American Canal Commission reported that the best route lay through Nicaragua. Warner Miller and others formed a company to dig a canal there, spent some $4,500,000, and gave up the task.

In 1896 a strong lobby came into existence whose press-agents extolled the Panama route for an American canal, urged and predicted its acquisition by the United States, and painted dark pictures of danger to the Nicaragua Canal by earthquake if it were ever taken over by the United States and completed. In 1902 the American Canal Commission, changed in personnel, reported that if the French company would sell its rights for $40,000,000 Panama would be a better route than Nicaragua—in shopping phrase, a "bargain."

Steps had been simultaneously taken to secure this modification of the report of 1876 and to prepare the way diplomatically for the transfer of the canal. In 1901 the Hay-Pauncefote treaty, succeeding to the Clayton-Bulwer treaty between Great Britain and the United States, left the road clear for an all-American canal at Panama, if the French company could be bought out. The Hay-Herran treaty, negotiated with Colombia in January, 1903, would have permitted the transfer. But when the Colombian Congress was called in special session for the purpose it failed to ratify this treaty.

This action on the part of Colombia was possibly unwise, but it was not unpatriotic, nor was refusal due, as has sometimes been said, to the desire to "blackmail" the United States. Colombia's financial interest in the canal and railway was great. By the contract of 1867 she had ceded the trans-isthmian railway to the Panama Railroad Company for $1,000,000, an annuity of $250,000 and the reversion of the property after ninety-nine years. By the contract of 1878 she had granted De Lesseps and

his associates a ninety-nine-year concession for the construction of the Panama Canal, for $250,000 a year from
the opening of the canal to the expiration of the term,
when the property was to revert to Colombia.   Both contracts forbade transfer to any foreign government.   In
case of infraction of this fundamental stipulation such
concession was to become null and void, and Colombia
was to enjoy her right of re-entry without compensation.
Colombia was also the largest individual stockholder in
the new French company.   If the canal, as reported by
the American Commission, was worth $40,000,000,
Colombia had in the right of re-entry, in the reversion of
the whole property at the end of the term, and in her stock-
holdings something of value to sell.   And she was not unreasonable in desiring a price.

Nor would it have been courteous to the greater republic to suppose that a violent seizure was about to take
place.   In the treaty of 1848 the United States had guar-
anteed the sovereignty of Colombia over the Isthmus in
compensation for freedom of transit over it and the
abolition of the differential duties then levied; thus enabling the United States to develop the Northwestern
territories and California before railroads were stretched
across the continent.

This treaty, from which the United States had so im-
mensely benefited, was still in force in 1903.   Nevertheless, the Panama "revolution" was already prepared
months before the Colombian Congress finally adjourned
on October 31, 1903, without ratifying the Hay-Herran
treaty.

The revolution was planned, not in Panama, but in New
York and Washington.   Its master mind was William
Nelson Cromwell, general counsel for both the Panama
Railroad and the new Panama Canal Company.   His
agent in Panama, Captain James R. Beers, seems to have
suggested secession to the Panamanians.   Dr. Amador and

18

Señor Arango, respectively the physician and land-agent of the Panama Railroad, were leaders in forming a secret junta of seven members. At the house of one of these, Señor Arias, the movement was launched in the presence of Colonel Shaler and Herbert G. Prescott, superintendent and assistant superintendent of the Panama Railroad, and of some United States army officers who were inspecting the canal.

On June 13, 1903, four and a half months before the revolution occurred, Mr. Cromwell had a conference with President Roosevelt in the White House. There was no secrecy as to the subject discussed or the policy decided upon; the next morning, June 14th, *The World* published an accurate forecast of the revolution, the recognition of the fake republic, and the making of the canal treaty with Panama exactly as these events afterward occurred. Colombia learned of the plan, not unnaturally, and her minister protested, threatening to recommend to the Colombian government the cancellation of both concessions. Cromwell disavowed Amador and left for Paris. Arrived in his stead M. Philippe Bunau-Varilla, a director of the French company. Arrangements were made with the Bowling Green Trust Company to give the revolutionists a hundred thousand dollars; and Amador returned to Panama carrying the flag of the Panama republic, designed by Mme. Bunau-Varilla, and a long cable code, partly in his own writing, in which "abbot" stood for "Ask Bunau-Varilla for the $4,000" and "sorry" denoted "Send 500 Remington rifles and 500,000 cartridges." Amador also wrote to his son on October 18th, detailing just how the revolution was to be accomplished.

The plan went like clock-work. One day before hostilities commenced President Roosevelt issued an order forbidding Colombian troops to go within fifty miles of the canal to fight rebels; a United States vessel was conveniently at hand; cable wires were cut to delay the transmission of news to Bogotá; forty-two marines were landed; Colombian officers in Panama were bought up. Independence was declared in Panama on November 3d, three days after the Colombian Congress adjourned; in seven days the "Republic of Panama" was recognized; in eighteen days the new nation ceded the canal zone to the United States for $10,000,000; in two days more than a month the treaty was ratified. As Mr. Roosevelt said in his speech at the University of California, March 23, 1911, "I took the isthmus, started the canal, and then left Congress, not to debate the canal, but to debate me."

The Colombian government could easily have put down the revolution had it not been prevented from landing troops in Panama by President Roosevelt's warning, and by the formal notification of the American Admiral in command of a squadron of eight war-ships, that the forces would not be permitted to disembark in any part of the Isthmus. Ten thousand men who had been ordered to arms were thus rendered of no avail. A thousand upon the spot could have crushed the rebellion. Forty times a thousand could have been furnished if necessary.

The taking of the canal, imperfectly understood by the general public at the time, was probably accepted by most of them as a state necessity owing to Colombia's obstinacy in refusing to permit a transfer of the French company's rights. The evidence, plain upon the face of events, that men outside the original French bond-holders' group were interested in the sale of the company and the made-to-order revolution attracted what now is seen to have been surprisingly little attention. Even as late as August 29, 1908, the Democratic National Committee, giving out a statement about wealthy men as "Guardians of Reform" in the Republican machine, barely mentioned William Nelson Cromwell as "the great Wall Street lawyer, attorney for the Panama Canal combine, etc."

It was Mr. Cromwell through whom the scandal broke. On October 1, 1908, William J. Curtis, one of his partners, complained to District-Attorney Jerome of New York that certain persons were trying to blackmail Cromwell in connection with the Panama affair. Learning of this the next day, *The World* sent a reporter to the district attorney, who refused any information.

Late that evening Jonas Whitley, employed by Mr. Cromwell as a press-agent, came to *The World* office and warned the managing editor not to print a Panama article that was false. The managing editor had heard of no such article, and consulted the city editor, who told him of Curtis's complaint. Mr. Whitley had related its substance and had insisted that if anything were printed Mr. Cromwell should be allowed to make a statement. A synopsis of his account was dictated to a stenographer, and the typewritten copy given Mr. Whitley to revise. The news article with his corrections was printed the following morning, October 3, 1908. This summary of the Curtis complaint ran as follows:

In brief, Mr. Curtis told Mr. Jerome it had been represented to Mr. Cromwell that the Democratic National Convention was considering the advisability of making public a statement that William Nelson Cromwell, in connection with M. Bunau-Varilla, a French speculator, had formed a syndicate at the time when it was quite evident that the United States would take over the rights of the French bond-holders in the de Lesseps Canal, and that this syndicate included among others Charles P. Taft, brother of William H. Taft, and Douglas Robinson, brother-in-law of President Roosevelt. Other men more prominent in the New York world of finance were also mentioned.

According to the story unfolded by Mr. Curtis, it was said that the men making this charge against Mr. Cromwell had averred that the syndicate thus organized in connection with Bunau-Varilla had gone into the French market and purchased for about $3,500,000 the stock and bonds of the defunct de

Lesseps company, and of the newer concern which had taken over the old company and had for a time prosecuted work on the canal.

These financiers invested their money because of a full knowledge of the intention of the Government to acquire the French property at a price of about $40,000,000, and thus—because of their alleged information from high Government sources—were enabled to reap a rich harvest.

The World naturally desired a statement from Mr. Cromwell. Mr. Whitley telephoned him, and late that night Cromwell made a statement by telephone to a stenographer, whose notes were read to him and pronounced correct. This statement, denying improper dealings by the persons named was printed with the Curtis complaint.

Only this Curtis complaint, which was never submitted to a grand jury by District-Attorney Jerome, brought the names of Charles P. Taft and Douglas Robinson into discussion. Mr. Taft denied any connection with the Panama syndicate, and his denial was at once accepted by *The World* as conclusive. Mr. Robinson refused to make any statement. Like Mr. Taft, he owed his appearance in the news article solely to Mr. Cromwell and Mr. Cromwell's press-agent.

The Panama mystery was discussed in a desultory way during the campaign, but it was not regarded as an issue. Mr. Roosevelt, who was managing Mr. Taft's campaign from the White House, paid no attention to the articles.

On November 2d, the day before election, however, *The Indianapolis News*, the leading paper in Indiana, which had refused to support the Republican national and state tickets, printed an editorial asking who got the $40,000,000 the United States had paid. Morally, the election in Indiana was a Republican defeat, for, although Mr. Taft carried the state by 10,731, a Democratic Governor and Legislature were elected, a Democrat was sent to the Senate in place of Mr. Hemenway, and only three Republican Representatives were elected out of thirteen. Mr. Roosevelt and his friends attributed the result largely to *The Indianapolis News.*

William Dudley Foulke sent to the President on November 9th the Panama editorial from *The Indianapolis News* and suggested that "if the statements of *The News* are true our people ought to know it; if not true, they ought to have some just means of estimating what credit should be given in other matters to a journal which disseminates falsehoods." Mr. Foulke's curiosity was shared by many citizens; its expression brought forth on December 1st a reply from Mr. Roosevelt, made public December 7th.

In this the President denied many statements referred to in Mr. Foulke's letter and said of the editor of *The Indianapolis News*, "Mr. Delavan Smith is a conspicuous offender against the laws of honesty and truthfulness." Dealing with the purchase of the Canal, he asserted that the United States "paid $40,000,000 direct to the French Government, getting the receipt of the liquidator appointed by the French Government to receive the same"; that "the United States Government has not the slightest knowledge as to the particular individuals among whom the French Government distributed the sum"; that "this was the business of the French Government"; that "so far as I know there was no syndicate"; that "there certainly was no syndicate in the United States that to my knowledge had any dealings with the Government, directly or indirectly"; that "the people have had the most minute official knowledge" of the Panama affair; that "every important step and every important document have been made public," and that the "abominable falsehood" that any American citizen had profited from the sale of the Panama Canal "is a slander not against the American government, but against the French government."

We now come to the real beginning of the Panama libel suit unsuccessfully waged against two newspapers in the name of the Government of the United States.

The World had not previously discussed the Panama matter editorially. But when Mr. Roosevelt said that the United States Government "paid the $40,000,000 direct to the French Government," it decided that the time had come when the country was entitled to the truth, and it challenged Mr. Roosevelt upon the official records and demanded a Congressional investigation. In this history-making editorial *The World* accused the President of "deliberate misstatements of fact in his scandalous personal attack upon Mr. Delavan Smith." The article continued:

The Indiananapolis News said, in an editorial for which Mr. Roosevelt assails Mr. Smith:

"It has been charged that the United States bought from American citizens for $40,000,000 property that cost those citizens only $12,000,000. There is no doubt that the government paid $40,000,000 for the property. But who got the money?"

President Roosevelt's reply to this most proper question is for the most part a string of abusive and defamatory epithets. But he also makes the following statements as truthful information to the American people:

"The United States did not pay a cent of the $40,000,000 to any American citizen.

"The Government paid this $40,000,000 direct to the French Government, getting the receipt of the liquidator appointed by the French Government to receive the same.

"The United States Government has not the slightest knowledge as to the particular individuals among whom the French Government distributed the same.

"So far as I know, there was no syndicate; there certainly was no syndicate in the United States that to my knowledge had any dealings with the Government directly or indirectly."

To the best of The World's knowledge and belief, each and

all of these statements made by Mr. Roosevelt, and quoted above, are untrue, and Mr. Roosevelt must have known they were untrue when he made them.

Only one man, William Nelson Cromwell, knew the whole story of the transaction. President Roosevelt and Secretary Root aided Mr. Cromwell in consummating the Panama revolution and arranging the payments for the old canal—"$40,000,000 for the canal properties and an additional $10,000,000 for a manufactured Panama republic, every penny of both of which sums was paid by check on the United States Treasury to J. P. Morgan & Co.—not to the French Government, as Mr. Roosevelt says, but to J. P. Morgan & Co." The history of the case is then resumed:

The old French company organized by Ferdinand de Lesseps in 1879 failed in 1889, years before Mr. Cromwell's relations with President Roosevelt began. As Mr. Cromwell testified before the Senate committee on February 26, 1906, "we never had any connection with the so-called de Lesseps company. Neither did the United States Government conduct negotiations with the old French Panama Canal Company."

What Mr. Cromwell did represent was the new Panama Canal Company, the American Panama Canal Company and the $5,000,000 syndicate which he formed to finance the new companies. After Mr. Cromwell had testified "I do not recall any contract," Senator Morgan produced a contract reading (Panama Canal Hearing, Vol. II, page 146):

"Mr. William Nelson Cromwell is exclusively empowered, under the formal agreement with the Board of Directors of the Compagnie Nouvelle du Canal de Panama of France, to effect with an American syndicate the Americanization of the Panama Canal Company on the following basis."

Senator Morgan unearthed a copy of the $5,000,000 syndicate agreement, which provided that the subscribers should contract with William Nelson Cromwell to pay in $5,000,000 in cash and to take their several allotments in the enterprise.

Five million dollars was more than ample to buy the majority of the old Panama stock. . . .

Following that, to quote from Mr. Cromwell's testimony, "in May, 1904, I, representing the new Panama Canal, and Judges Day and Russell, representing Attorney-General Knox, consummated" the transfer and sale to the United States.

Mr. Roosevelt says "the Government paid this $40,000,000 direct to the French Government."

Mr. Cromwell testified that the United States paid the money to J. P. Morgan & Co.

Mr. Roosevelt says "the French Government distributed the sum."

Mr. Cromwell testified as to how he distributed it.

Mr. Roosevelt talks of "getting the receipt of the liquidator appointed by the French Government to receive the same."

Mr. Cromwell testified: "Of the $40,000,000 thus paid by the United States Government $25,000,000 was paid to the liquidator of the old Panama Canal Company under and in pursuance of an agreement entered into between the liquidator and the new company. . . . Of the balance of $15,000,000 paid to the new Panama Canal Company, $12,000,000 have already been distributed among its stockholders, and the remainder is now being held awaiting final distribution and payment."

As to Mr. Roosevelt's statement that "there was no syndicate," he could have read the "syndicate subscription agreement" on page 1150, Vol. II, of the testimony before the Committee on Interoceanic Canals—if he had cared for the truth.

That the United States was not dealing with "the French Government" or the "liquidator appointed by the French Government" or any one save Cromwell and his associates was made clear by the account of Gabriel Duque. Señor Duque said that Cromwell offered him the Presidency of the Panama republic, and told him that he might rely upon the help of the United States. "We bought this general and that one," said Duque, "paying three to four thousand dollars per general." Accord-

ing to Duque, "Mr. Cromwell made the revolution."
Then . . .

Mr. Cromwell, having been elected by the Panama Republic
as general counsel, and he and J. Pierpont Morgan having
been appointed a "fiscal commission," negotiated with President
Roosevelt, by which the United States paid $10,000,000 more
to "the fiscal commission" for Mr. Cromwell's Panama Republic. Of this money three-quarters is still under the control
of "the fiscal commission.".

Why did the United States pay $40,000,000 for a bankrupt
property whose control could undoubtedly have been bought in
the open market for less than $4,000,000?

Who were the new Panama Canal Company?

Who bought up the obligations of the old Panama Canal
Company for a few cents on the dollar? . . .

Whether all the profits went into William Nelson Cromwell's hands or whatever became of them, the fact that Theodore
Roosevelt as President of the United States issues a public
statement about such an important matter full of flagrant
untruths, reeking with misstatements, challenging line by
line the testimony of his associate Cromwell and the official
record, makes it imperative that full publicity come at once
through the authority and by the action of Congress.

The election was over. More than two months had
elapsed since the publication of Mr. Cromwell's complaint to the New York district attorney. No man mentioned in any article had appealed to the courts, which
were open to punish libel.

*The moving cause of the extraordinary action that fol-
lowed was not the "libel upon the United States government"
of October 3d, as alleged by President Roosevelt. The
government had not been libeled. The cause was that the
President himself had been pilloried on December 8th as a
publisher of falsehood.*

December 15th President Roosevelt sent to Congress a
long special message upon Panama containing the state-

ment that the $40,000,000 in payment for canal rights was distributed in Paris to the owners of the new and old Panama companies. That Mr. Roosevelt's powers of invective were in working order is indicated in these passages:

These stories were first brought to my attention as published in a paper in Indianapolis, called the *News*, edited by Mr. Delavan Smith. The stories were scurrilous and libelous in character and false in every essential particular. Mr. Smith shelters himself behind the excuse that he merely accepted the statements which had appeared in a paper published in New York, *The World*, owned by Mr. Joseph Pulitzer. It is idle to say that the known character of Mr. Pulitzer and his newspaper are such that the statements in that paper will be believed by nobody; unfortunately, thousands of persons are ill informed in this respect and believe the statements they see in print, even though they appear in a newspaper published by Mr. Pulitzer. . . .

Now, these stories, as a matter of fact, need no investigation whatever. . . . In form, they are in part libels upon individuals, upon Mr. Taft and Mr. Robinson, for instance. But they are in fact wholly, and in form partly, a libel upon the United States Government. . . .

The real offender is Mr. Joseph Pulitzer, editor and proprietor of *The World*. While the criminal offense of which Mr. Pulitzer has been guilty is in form a libel upon individuals, the great injury done is in blackening the good name of the American people. It should not be left to a private citizen to sue Mr. Pulitzer for libel. He should be prosecuted for libel by the Government authorities. . . . The Attorney-General has under consideration the form in which the proceedings against Mr. Pulitzer shall be brought. . . .

Attorney-General Bonaparte's proceedings took the form of indictments procured from a District of Columbia Federal Grand Jury charging *The World*, Mr. Pulitzer, and certain of *The World's* editors, and *The Indianapolis News* and its editors, with criminal libel in articles circulated in the District of Columbia, libeling the United States Government and also Elihu Root, William Nelson Cromwell, Charles P. Taft, Douglas Robinson, ex-President Roosevelt, and President Taft. These indictments were found upon a section of the District of Columbia code based upon the English law of 1662 enacted in the tyrannous time of Charles I. for the muzzling of the press.

President Taft, who succeeded on March 4, 1909, to Mr. Roosevelt, properly made no effort to halt proceedings with whose inception he had nothing to do. Early in the Taft administration Joseph B. Kealing, United States District Attorney in Indianapolis, resigned his post, which he had held almost eight years, rather than be a party to the suit. In his letter to Attorney-General Bonaparte Mr. Kealing said:

> As to the guilt or innocence of the defendants on the question of libel I do not attempt to say. If guilty, they should be prosecuted; but properly indicted and prosecuted, in the right place—*viz.*, in their homes. It is only with the question of removal that I have to do. I am not in accord with the Government in its attempt to put a strained construction on the law, to drag the defendants from their homes to the seat of the Government, to be tried and punished, while there is a good and sufficient law in this jurisdiction in the State court.
>
> I believe the principle involved is dangerous, striking at the very foundation of our form of Government. I cannot, therefore, honestly and conscientiously insist to the court that such is the law, or that such construction should be put on it. Not being able to do this, I do not feel that I can, in justice to my office, continue to hold it and decline to assist.

Preparations for the issue were unceasing up to October 11th, when the Indianapolis case was taken before Federal Judge Anderson, who dismissed it the following day. In his opinion Judge Anderson did more than decide a technical point, as these extracts will show:

> It is the duty of a public newspaper, such as is owned and conducted by these defendants to tell the people, its subscribers, the facts that it may find out about public questions or matters of public interest. It is its duty and its right to draw inferences from the facts known, to draw them for the people. . . .
>
> So far as the record has been read—and that is all the part that I have an acquaintance with—Mr. Cromwell stood upon his privilege whenever questions were asked [by the Morgan Senate Committee investigating the Panama matter], the answer to which would or

might reflect upon him and his associates, but whenever a question was asked which gave him an opportunity to say something in their behalf he ostentatiously thanked the examiner for the question and proceeded to answer it. To my mind that gave just ground for suspicion. I am suspicious about it now.

There are many very peculiar circumstances about the history of this Panama Canal, or this Panama Canal business. . . . Now, there were a number of people who thought there was something not just exactly right about that transaction, and I will say for myself that now I feel a natural curiosity to know what the real truth was. . . .

Here was a matter of great public interest, of public concern. I was interested in it; you were interested in it; we were all interested in it. Here was a newspaper printing the news, or trying to. Here was a matter up for discussion, and I cannot say now, I am not willing to say, that the inferences are too strongly drawn. . . .

To my mind, that man has read the history of our institutions to very little purpose who does not look with very grave apprehension upon the success of a proceeding such as this—if the history of liberty means anything, if the constitutional guarantees mean anything—if the prosecuting authorities should have the power to select a tribunal, if there be more than one tribunal to select from, at the capital of the United States; that the Government should have that power and drag citizens of distant States there to be tried.

The defendants will be discharged.

No action was taken by the Government to remove Mr. Pulitzer and *The World's* news editors to the District of Columbia; but another attempt was made to stretch the law to permit the prosecution of *The World* in the Federal Courts without raising the question of removal.

Under instructions from President Roosevelt United States Attorney Henry L. Stimson had also obtained indictments for criminal libel from the Federal Grand Jury in New York against *The World* and an editor, charging the circulation of twenty-nine copies of the issues complained of within "the fort and military post and reservation of West Point" and within "the tract of land" whereon stands "a needful building used by the United States as a post-office."

This indictment, couched almost in the language of the

Sedition Act, charged that it was the purpose of *The World* "to stir up disorder among the people." The Sedition Act reads, "to stir up sedition among the people."

The law on which the government relied for this prosecution was that of July 7, 1898, entitled "An Act to Protect the Harbor Defenses and Fortifications Constructed or Used by the United States from Malicious Injury, and for Other Purposes." It was founded on an act of March 3, 1825. It had never before been invoked by the federal authorities as giving them the right to punish libel.

It was asserted by United States Attorney Stimson in a letter to District-Attorney Jerome of New York that:

These publications . . . appear to have been circulated by the newspaper in question in a number of distinct and independent jurisdictions. . . . In each of these jurisdictions, under well-known principles of law, each of these publications would constitute a separate offense.

As there were 2,809 government reservations corresponding to West Point and the Post-office building, a newspaper might under this theory of law be prosecuted from one end of the country to the other for an article that was neither written nor printed on any of these reservations.

At the suggestion of counsel for *The World* court orders for the examination of witnesses were addressed through diplomatic channels to the judicial authorities of the French and Panama governments. It was necessary for *The World* to pay the expenses of United States Attorney Wise and Deputy Attorney-General Stuart MacNamara to Paris, and of Mr. Knapp, of the United States Attorney's office, to Panama, as the government refused to assume any part of the cost.

The State Department notified De Lancey Nicoll, of

The World's counsel, that the American Ambassador to France would assist Coudert Brothers, *The World's* counsel in Paris, in obtaining the authorization of the Minister of Justice for the examination of witnesses. But there was difficulty in getting at the records, and the attempt failed. *The World*, however, collected much evidence in Paris and in Panama. A staff correspondent was sent to Bogotá, and by the courtesy of the Colombian government secured certified copies of records and other documentary evidence.

When the case came up for trial in the United States Circuit Court in New York City on January 25, 1910, before Judge Charles M. Hough, *The World* was prepared to sustain the defense of justification. But the form in which the prosecution was brought forced responsibilities which could not be disregarded. *The World* could not go to trial upon the merits of the case without conceding the existence of a federal libel law and placing the press of the country at the mercy of the President. Not merely in its own interest, but to safeguard the free discussion of national questions, it felt obliged to resist every pretense of the federal authorities that they had a co-ordinate jurisdiction with state authorities in prosecuting libel.

Argument was therefore directed upon jurisdiction. Distinguished counsel were engaged: Henry A. Wise, Stuart McNamara, and James R. Knapp for the government; De Lancey Nicoll, John D. Lindsay, and Thomas Steven Fuller. After hearing testimony and the summing up of counsel Judge Hough announced a decision which invited an appeal to higher authority. The disposition of the case is indicated by the record:

JUDGE HOUGH: I am of the opinion that the construction of this Act claimed by the prosecution is opposed to the spirit and tenor of legislation for many years on the subject of national territorial-jurisdiction. It is a novelty, and the burden of upholding a novelty is on him who alleges it. . . . This very interesting question can be lawfully presented to the Supreme Court of the United States, and I am sure that the judgment of that Court should be obtained before either the time of this Court or the time of jurors be occupied in going into a matter which could not, in my judgment, if exploited with a question of law of this kind hanging over it, be determined with any profit to the public, or any benefit to the administration of justice.

It is, therefore, ordered that a judgment of this Court be entered quashing the indictment herein, because upon the construction of the statute, hereinbefore stated, the indictment is not authorized by the statute upon which it rests.

MR. WISE: Before that is done, I ask that a juror be withdrawn, in order that no question of jeopardy may enter into the case.

THE COURT: Motion granted.

President Taft was a skilled lawyer and had been a judge. Doubtless he had little liking for the prosecution begun by Mr. Roosevelt and would gladly have seen it drop with defeat before Judge Anderson and Judge Hough. *The World* was not satisfied with any decision short of the highest tribunal; and in a series of articles it demanded an appeal by the government to the Supreme Court. The initiative was with the government, in form; in fact it rested with the paper which prodded the government. Yielding finally to the demand for a conclusive settlement the Department of Justice took an appeal, and on January 3, 1911, the Supreme Court handed down an opinion sustaining Judge Hough in quashing the indictment, on the ground that the federal government had no jurisdiction.

The Supreme Court did not discuss the point at issue— "Who got the money?"—which had so interested Judge Anderson. Like Judge Hough, it followed the question of jurisdiction, of reasonable inference as to the intent of Congress in passing the laws appealed to. There was no rebuke of a co-ordinate department of the government which had grasped at tyrannous power. But the decision was unanimous.

At the Columbia Club in Indianapolis shortly before

the 1910 election President Roosevelt had enlivened a social occasion by calling Judge Anderson a "jackass and a crook" for his decision in *The Indianapolis News* case. He did not now denounce all the members of the Supreme Court, but their decision may have added emphasis to his later statement that our courts are "fossilized."

The World on January 4, 1911, thus summed up its victory:

The unanimous decision handed down by the United States Supreme Court yesterday in the Roosevelt-Panama libel case against The World is the most sweeping victory won for freedom of speech and of the press in this country since the American people destroyed the Federalist party more than a century ago for enacting the infamous Sedition law.

In unanimously sustaining Judge Hough's decision quashing the Roosevelt indictments against The World on the ground that the Federal Government had no jurisdiction, the Supreme Court upholds every contention advanced by The World since the outset of this prosecution. . . .

Federal jurisdiction was claimed by Mr. Roosevelt and Attorney-General Bonaparte under the pretext that the regular circulation at West Point of twenty-nine copies out of 382,410 of The World containing certain Panama news articles, and the sending of one copy free to a Post-Office inspector in the Government Building in New York City in compliance with the postal regulations, constituted the publication of a libel in these reservations, and that under this statute the Federal Government could criminally prosecute The World.

There were few newspapers, the argument continues, that could not be ruined by the government by the mere legal expense of having to defend itself in a "number of distinct and independent jurisdictions" under District Attorney Stimson's interpretation of the law. In carrying the case to the court of last resort President Taft and Mr. Wickersham had rendered a notable service to American liberty. The article concludes:

19

The decision of the Supreme Court is so sweeping that no other President will be tempted to follow in the footsteps of Theodore Roosevelt, no matter how greedy he may be for power, no matter how resentful of opposition. . . .

As De Lancey Nicoll, The World's counsel, said in his argument before the Supreme Court:

"As a matter of fact this prosecution is premature. It is born before its time. It belongs to that new dispensation when the Federal Government shall have taken to itself all power and all authority, when the States shall have been reduced to mere geographical divisions of the national domain, and when Federal tribunals shall no longer decide cases in accordance with precedent and authority and the law of the land, but in accordance with the need and spirit of the time as they may be interpreted by some great steward of the public welfare."

It was indeed premature. With the smashing of the New Nationalism at the November elections comes the smashing of the Roosevelt doctrine of lese-majesty and the smashing of the Roosevelt doctrine of Nullification by the highest tribunal of the Nation. We are still living under a government of laws and not of men. We are still living under the old Constitution as interpreted by the Supreme Court of the United States, not under the New Nationalism as interpreted by some "steward of the public welfare" in Washington.

While the Panama case was still pending in the courts a curious side-light was thrown upon it by the publication in *The World*, October 17, 1910, of a photographed facsimile of the account of Kuhn, Loeb & Co. with the late E. H. Harriman, covering a series of transactions in Panama shares. This account was opened in January, 1902, the month and the year when President Roosevelt instructed the Isthmian Canal Commission, in effect, to reverse its report recommending the Nicaraguan route, and to favor Panama instead. At the very time, therefore, when Mr. Harriman was called to the White House by President Roosevelt in October, 1904, and went back to Wall Street to raise $260,000 for the Republican campaign fund he was carrying a speculative account in Panama shares. The account showed a profit of $86,447.38 upon total investments of $253,060.47.

The "taking" of the Panama zone by Mr. Roosevelt, though it hastened the digging of the canal, intensified distrust of the United States throughout Latin America. It immeasurably harmed American relations with these countries, whose development is so interesting a political and commercial study. Colombia had a just claim upon the United States. *The World* had opposed the payment of $10,000,000 to the made-to-order republic of Panama, but favored some friendly arrangement with Colombia which should admit and mend her grievance by such reparation as agreement or arbitration might decide.

The slate is clean for such accommodation. Colombia's early protests against the taking of the canal were ignored. In 1906 Secretary Root stated to Señor Don Diego Mendoza, then Colombian Minister in Washington, that the United States had followed its sense of right and justice in espousing the cause of a weak people, the Panamanians, against the stronger government of Colombia. Senor Mendoza in reply specified grounds for asking arbitration, but his request was ignored. His successor, Minister Cortez, signed the Root-Cortez-Arosemena treaties, which were rejected by the Colombian Senate. So unpopular were they that on his return home Señor Cortez was driven back on board ship by infuriated Colombians. After Colonel Roosevelt's statement on March 23, 1911, that he took the Canal Zone, a new minister, Dr. Borda, filed a new protest; so did his successor, General Ospina, equally without avail.

Following General Ospina's letter, pointing out that Secretary Knox's proposed visit to Colombia in February, 1912, might be inopportune if his country's claims remained unconsidered, Colombia sent Señor Don Julio Betancourt to Washington, and by prolonged negotiations through him and through the American Minister to Colombia, James T. Du Bois, the latter was authorized to offer Colombia $10,000,000 in cash, special privileges in the canal, and the arbitration of reversionary rights in the Panama Railroad. Mr. Du Bois intimated unofficially that the money payment might be raised to $25,000,000. These offers were rejected, Colombia requiring instead that all differences relating to the acquisition of the Canal Zone be submitted to arbitration, or that the United States should make a direct proposal of both moral and material reparation to Colombia.

At the time of writing, therefore, there remains no proposal pending between the two countries which should hamper a new attempt at settlement. Diplomacy has apparently exhausted its resources for directly dealing between the two nations. The case has seemed to *The World* eminently one for arbitration.

And, since the operation of the canal will chiefly benefit the great Republic, *The World* not only opposed the action of Congress in exempting American coastwise traffic from canal tolls in defiance of treaty obligations with Great Britain, but it has urged that the new way be made toll-free to all the nations of the world.

XX

PUBLIC SERVICE

1883–1913

"The World's" Long Fight for the Income Tax—"Reversing the Court" as to the Gas Trust—Working-men's Acts—The Japanese War—The Founding of the School of Journalism—Opposing the Catskill Water Folly— "The World" and the Courts—Opposition to the Recall of Judges and of Judicial Decisions—The Initiative and Referendum.

"THE WORLD'S" Platform of Public Service has been printed in an earlier chapter. Much water has flowed under bridges since May 17, 1883. How has the Platform fared?

Reform of the civil service has been furthered by the examination system in the federal departments and in those of most states and çities.

Vote-buying and the coercion of employees are less prevalent since the passage of secret-ballot laws.

A tariff for revenue has been vetoed by government extravagance. All that reformers now expect is a tariff lowered to moderate height.

The income tax has been the bone of hot contention. In the months following Mr. Pulitzer's purchase of *The World* he called it "the fairest and most democratic tax a government can impose"; cited the vast fortunes of the Vanderbilts, Goulds, Sages, and Fields, and denounced the outrage that "while the middle classes pay taxes on all that they consume these millionaires should escape their proper share of the public burdens"; explained how the British income tax had been "re-established after a suspension of twenty years by a Parliament composed of the representatives of property" because it was "necessary for the public safety" and how it had been "continued ever since in obedience to the popular will."

In 1894 an income-tax law passed Congress. It has been seen how, although such a tax had already been levied in the United States, the Supreme Court declared the re-enactment illegal, in a five-to-four vote. Difference of opinion between those who thought a Constitutional amendment should be passed, those who denounced the Supreme Court and wished to pack it to reverse its decision, and those who thought, with *The World*, that a valid law if properly framed could be passed without an amendment, delayed action. In 1906 *The World* was still unweariedly advising that the United States should "borrow the best ideas" of England, France, and Germany, and adopt "progressive inheritance taxes, with a liberal exemption of small estates" and "graduated income tax, with liberal exemption both for persons and families."

On February 9, 1907, *The World*, approving President Roosevelt's demand for a graduated income tax and a federal inheritance tax, thus summarized the principles of income taxation on which the "common sense of Europe" agreed:

1. There should be a generous exemption. This is $800 in England and is to be $1,000 in France. A much larger exemption would be required in this country.

2. There should be a distinction made between earned income and income from investment.

3. The tax should be graduated, falling most heavily upon those colossal incomes whose fortunate recipients would otherwise most nearly escape taxation.

4. Income tax should be supplemented by graduated succession taxes upon inherited estates. Already in England this tax rises to 8 per cent. upon the largest fortunes.

In a special message on June 16, 1909, President Taft followed President Roosevelt in urging the income-tax amendment upon the attention of Congress, and it was soon passed in the following form:

The Congress shall have the power to levy and collect taxes on incomes, from whatever source derived, without apportionment among the States and without regard to any census enumeration.

Two weeks before the assembling of the New York Legislature *The World* was already urging Governor Hughes to recommend ratification of the amendment. Much time would have been saved if he had seen the matter in the same light as President Taft. Instead, he advised against ratification because of the inclusion of the words "from whatever source derived." This phrase was construed to permit the taxation of state and municipal bonds by the federal government. Said *The World* on January 6, 1910:

Gov. Hughes has furnished to the opponents of the income-tax amendment the one thing that they have been seeking— a plausible argument from a highly respectable source. . . .

Regardless of the distinction he makes, Gov. Hughes's message will be hailed with delight by all the interests that oppose an income tax. . . . Wall Street is always for State rights when there is any money in it. . . . It will turn Gov. Hughes's message, his arguments, his influence and his great reputation to its own account in every State capital in which there is a chance to prevent ratification of the amendment.

What *The World* predicted happened. Enemies of the measure divided the counsels of its friends, now hesitating anew whether to amend the amendment by omitting the four offending words or to pass it unchanged. The latter course prevailed, and state after state ratified the measure. The accession of New York came only with the election of a Democratic Legislature, and it was with difficulty that the measure was pushed by public opinion past the barrier erected by the "Old Guard" in Albany. No organ of public opinion aided so steadily and powerfully as *The World* to bring this great measure to triumph.

The taxation of monopolies and corporations covered two planks in the platform of *The World;* and in securing the Franchise tax of New York it led the way in squeezing out of these combinations some assistance in bearing the public burdens.

Akin to the Franchise-tax campaign was the long struggle of *The World* to compel lower indirect taxation by the Gas Trust, through a reduction of its rate first to one dollar a thousand cubic feet, and then to eighty cents. Every step was fiercely fought. The Legislature under persistent prodding authorized an investigation committee which, with Charles E. Hughes as counsel, brought out in 1905 a mass of facts upon which an eighty-cent law was passed. The Gas Trust went into the federal courts upon a plea of confiscation, and won victories before Referee Masten and in the United States Circuit Court in New York City. When these decisions were rendered *The World* caused some sarcastic comment by "reversing" them; as when on May 22, 1907, it said: "It is doubtful whether the Supreme Court of the United States will concur with Referee Masten's findings"; as when it said of Judge Hough's decision, based upon Referee Masten's finding that the eighty-cent bill was unconstitutional:

This view of the fourteenth amendment makes the Railroad Rate law unconstitutional. The free street-car transfer law could be set aside on the same ground. No franchise could be repealed, for that would destroy "property." No franchise once capitalized could be amended if profits were thereby reduced.

Whether New York City has eighty-cent or ninety-cent or one-dollar gas is of little consequence compared with the great question of whether a franchise is superior to legislative restriction or legislation.

Referee Masten's decision as accepted by Judge Hough menaced more than the eighty-cent gas law:

Baldly expressed, he decides that a public franchise becomes private property when in the possession of a corporation, and that the value of the capitalized profits cannot be diminished by the Legislature. In other words, that the people once having granted a franchise are thereafter helpless to protect themselves from extortion, once that extortion is capitalized.

Obviously, a grant of sovereign power cannot be irrevocably made to a corporation unless the sovereignty of a State is divisible. If a franchise grant is not revocable the people can divest themselves of their sovereignty, and the moment that any people has divested itself of sovereignty, either in whole or in part, that people ceases to be free and independent to the extent that its sovereignty has been parted with.

The decision of Referee Masten is revolutionary. Should it by any misfortune be sustained by the Supreme Court of the United States the governmental powers of this country would henceforth be divided. The most profitable part of these powers would be exercised by public-service corporations. The remainder, constantly dwindling, would be all the people would have left.

On January 4, 1909, the Supreme Court found, as *The World* had done, that a public-service company cannot capitalize good will; that no reasonable rate can be called confiscatory until it has been tried; that if the eighty-cent rate did not provide a fair return the Gas Trust could appeal for relief; that a corporation cannot capitalize at its own valuation and require a rate profitable thereon.

In questions affecting working-men *The World* has kept the spirit of its 1883 program. It long sustained the efforts made in New York for a workmen's compensation act. It held that the system under which employers intrust to insurance companies the task of fighting damage suits by injured workmen, and every effort of delay is used to defeat just claims, is costly and repulsive. When the Court of Appeals decided that a Compensation act passed by the New York Legislature was invalid, *The World* urged that a constitutional amendment should be adopted enabling the Legislature to pass an act that would stand review. *The World* has also pressed advanced child-labor laws and factory acts upon attention.

The World has naturally been interested in the efforts of democracy abroad. It kept a friendly attitude toward the Portuguese Republic, the short-lived reforms of the Young Turks, the attempts at self-government and national union in Persia, China, the Balkans. It led the fight against the machinations of American capitalists and jingoes who would use the State Department to bully weaker nations in the interest of schemes of exploitation; and, as often before, it gave the contest a name that was a weapon. As "Dollar Diplomacy" it made the attempt to force a loan upon China that China neither needed nor asked for, and various menaces of Central American states, odious to the people. It has tried to avoid the error of taking its views of British politics from Tory London, and parroting the cry that more democracy is ruining England. Its sympathies have been Home Rule and Liberal; it has not been democratic at home and Tory abroad.

The Russo-Japanese War appealed to *The World* because of its hatred of Russian autocracy and its hope that defeat might further domestic reforms in the Cossack Empire. From the beginning of the conflict in 1904 it was never deceived by the giant proportions of Russia. It called the fear of Russia's power "a pricked bubble." It hailed the Czar's acknowledgment of the "right of the people to participate in the government" through the Duma, and his resolve, as the Imperial rescript ran, "henceforth, with the help of God, to convene the worth-iest men possessing the confidence of the people, and elected by them, to participate in the elaboration and consideration of legislative measures."

When Rojestvensky's fleet was on its ill-starred way half round the world to attack Japan, and when naval experts were fighting shy of predicting defeat or victory, Mr. Pulitzer sent peremptory instructions to say "with-out ifs or buts" that the Russian fleet would be destroyed. There was accordingly printed on April 11, 1905, a prediction that attracted much attention from its boldness:

Rojestvensky's fleet plunging northward into the China Sea to its doom is to-day the most thrilling spectacle in the world.

All the elements of dramatic effect are combined in its dogged advance. The element of heightened tension, since for six months the world has read with slowly mounting interest of its progress, its haltings, checks, feints, coalings, target practice; the element of tragedy, for the whole air about it is heavy with the menace of death; the element of valor and of sacrifice, for never were brave men pushed forward to slaughter with more cynic cruelty. . . .

And so the battle-ships with their weed-grown bottoms, which will matter little enough when they rest under the waves from their last voyage, and the old cruisers, such as Great Britain has just been throwing upon the scrap-heap, and the converted merchantmen that curb their fleetness to the lumber-ing train, and all the other elements of a mighty Russian fleet—on paper—are going up, to be smashed or beached or blown up or sunk. . . .

Was ever wickedness in a ruler more foolish? Was ever folly more wicked than to insist upon the sacrifice?

So interested was Mr. Pulitzer in seeing the Russian giant beaten and still beaten, until the Czar in good faith rendered up to the people the power, that *The World* predicted that peace was impossible, even as peace was being made. Calling the "great Russia" of the Czar a "shown-up sham," it said: "To give back one inch of Chinese territory to Russian hands would be to expose millions to exploitation. To forego one penny of the ransom the bankers of the world are willing to provide Russia in her dilemma would leave her so much the more able to launch new war-ships, to raise new regiments, to forge new arms, to buy new knouts for Cossacks to lay on women students' backs." These were excellent reasons for crushing Russia; but there were also reasons why Japan was satisfied to let Russian democracy do its own crushing.

The attitude of *The World* upon the Portsmouth peace was Mr. Pulitzer's personal attitude. He dictated many of the editorials printed at that time. It was one of the few occasions when his ardent sympathies led astray his keen perception of the trend of events.

It was the contention of *The World* and of its founder that the expression and information of Public Opinion was one of the highest tasks in a republic. Mr. Pulitzer held that one great need of the country was a body of trained journalists, bound together by professional standards of honor. He wished to see journalists subscribe to ethical rules as well defined as those of the legal and medical professions. He early evolved a plan for such training, and on the completion of twenty years of ownership of *The World* he offered Columbia University $1,000,-000 to establish a School of Journalism, with another $1,000,000 conditional upon its successful operation. What he thought of the reasons which demanded such a school he told in *The World* of August 16, 1903. There were one hundred schools for lawyers in the country; for journalists not one. It was the fashion in the newspaper world to say that "journalism alone of all arts, sciences, trades, and professions in the world cannot be systematically taught, but must be picked up as a boy picks up a knowledge of swimming when he is thrown into the water. Some boys drown." And yet . . .

— every newspaper is a daily sufferer from the lack of training in its staff. The first question an editor asks of an applicant for a position is, "What has been your experience?" In other words: "Have you picked up some knowledge of your duties at the expense of some other newspaper, or must I waste my time teaching you the rudiments of the trade?"

In former years a boy began the study of law by sweeping out a lawyer's office, or of medicine by mixing pills for a country doctor. Instruction for newspaper work is still in the same stage. That law and medicine are now studied in professional schools, while a knowledge of newspaper work must be "picked up" in an office, does not mean that journalism is any less capable than law or medicine of being systematically taught, but merely that the methods of preparation for one profession have stood still, while those for the others have advanced.

From these practical considerations *The World* proceeded to the underlying ethical ones:

The object of this School of Journalism, as described by its founder, is to make the newspaper profession a still nobler one— to raise its character and standing, to increase its power and prestige, through the better equipment of those who adopt it, and by attracting to it more and more men of the highest capacity and the loftiest ideals.

Mr. Pulitzer in the last months of his life had begun work upon the organization of the School of Journalism. By his will an endowment upon substantially the terms quoted was released, and Columbia University opened the school in October, 1912. The new building which is to house it is now completed, and an able corps of instructors, headed by Dr. Talcott Williams, well known both as a scholar and a journalist, as director, is actively at work.

In the years when *The World* was supporting the

administration of Governor Hughes in Albany it energetically fought the wasteful Catskill Aqueduct.

The provision of water for New York had long been a
problem. Federal law forbade going into New Jersey or
Connecticut for a supply. Suffolk County, Long Island,
had secured a state act forbidding the extension of the
Brooklyn waterworks. Similar exclusion acts hemmed
in the Croton waterworks on the North. These acts were
passed partly because of a feeling in rural counties that
the people needed the supply of their own streams, but
more because of the machinations of private water
companies, of which the "Great Chartered Ramapo" conspiracy was the chief, to compel the city to buy their
rights. Honest local objection to extension could have
been met by making a plan under state authority for a
metropolitan water district within which all the towns
could have obtained supply from a common source, as
Massachusetts has done. The engineers called into consultation said that a small plant for temporary supply
could at a not exorbitant price be placed across the
Hudson. From this suggestion, reasonable in the circumstances, grew a great bi-partisan waterworks undertaking with "millions in it" for speculators in land options, for contractors and appraisers.

The World was not slow to denounce this scheme.
On October 14, 1905, it said:

The city must pay $161,000,000 for the extension of its
waterworks. The entire present system in all the boroughs is
valued at only $125,000,000. Its present cost to the city—the
bonds upon which the people pay interest—is only $77,000,000,
the original debt having been reduced by instalments from the
water rates. For the northward extension of its mains the city
must more than triple the water debt upon all its plants.

The fight continued for years. On January 25, 1908,
The World printed as part of an editorial upon the squan-

dering of millions a photograph of the water rushing to waste over Croton dam. This article said:

More water has been going over this spillway in the last two months than has flowed through the aqueducts. For several weeks a daily average of 969,000,000 gallons has gone to waste, or three times as much as daily flows through the aqueducts to New York City.

This waste occurs not one year, but every year.

Computing the value of water on the estimated cost of the Esopus scheme and the amount of water which it would supply, which gives an equivalent of $85 per million gallons, there is every day $82,365 flowing over the Croton dam. . . .

Why should the city of New York be called upon to go eighty miles further away, to the foot of the Catskills, at a minimum cost of more than $161,000,000, when more water which the city already owns is now going to waste than flows through Esopus Creek? . . .

Owing to the greater evaporation during the summer there will always be an annual danger of an August or September water famine unless the city provides more storage capacity. This can be done either by going to the Catskills, buying millions of dollars' worth of land there and building an aqueduct one hundred and ten miles to New York; or it can be done by cleaning out the present reservoirs, by building new storage reservoirs in the Croton watershed, where the city already owns the land, and then laying more pipes from the Croton, thirty miles, instead of from the Catskills, one hundred and ten miles.

The money saved would be enough to build four long interborough subways or eight short ones, to build all the new schoolhouses New York would require for ten years, and to equip the Fire Department with ten thousand lengths of hose that would not burst.

If an engineer had been asked to say how New York should be provided with water he would have said, as *The World* did: first, stop waste and bring consumption nearer to a generous but reasonable allowance; then stretch the Croton Aqueduct gradually northward as needed, always under state authority, always supplying the towns along the line. If a practical politician were asked how to get more water he would have replied: "Let the people use all the water they want. Get up a big scheme." This is what the Catskill Aqueduct plan did. Beginning at the wrong end of water extension—the end farthest from the city—a state commission irresponsible to the city planned the huge Ashokan reservoir before it was even shown how the water would be brought across the Hudson River. This problem was only solved after long experiment by an extremely deep and costly inverted siphon.

The fight on the water folly was continued until the election of Mayor Gaynor. The city was then so far committed that it might have been almost as wasteful to drop the project as to carry it on. But *The World* had the satisfaction of seeing some of the waste of public money cut off by the appointment of a special Assistant Corporation Counsel to fight extravagant condemnation awards and excessive bills of appraisal commissioners.

When serious charges were brought against Mr. Justice Hooker, of the New York Supreme Court, in 1905 *The World* waxed sarcastic over the plea of his friends that the acts complained of were performed before he became a judge, while he was in Congress; that these were "political practices" and did not touch his "judicial integrity." "This view," it said, "seems to appeal to the Gas Senators, to the Sugar Senators, to the Corporation Senators. It is whispered by the loftily virtuous McCarren. It thunders in the eloquence of the ascetic and impeccable Grady."

Yet while quick to denounce impropriety in individual judges *The World* has been a defender of the courts; has insisted upon better payment of judges; has opposed limitations to the writ of injunction, sought by people who do not always clearly see the meaning of their endeavors; has fought the modern panacea of the judicial recall. In 1911 this doctrine became prominent in discussion because of the struggle in Congress over the admission of Arizona as a state, with a constitution including provision for the recall of judges. Said *The World:*

The initiative and referendum is dubious enough itself, but when it is coupled with the recall of judges it means a revolution in our system of government. The checks and balances are overturned. The barriers against sudden outbursts of popular passion are thrown down. The majority can do what it will. The minority has no rights which the majority is bound to respect.

One of the last editorials which Mr. Pulitzer personally suggested was that of August 11, 1911, upon this subject. The whimsical references to Tammany judges and to Judge Archbald were contained in his memorandum. The article runs in part:

The World is gratified by the report that President Taft is preparing a ringing veto message upon the Statehood bill just passed by Congress for the admission of Arizona and New Mexico. . . .

The dangers of the recall are insidious. If we had it now in full force in State and Nation, The World would certainly wish to recall some of our boss-appointed Tammany judges. We should recall United States District Judge Archbald, who lets off with fines the worst Wire Trust offenders and releases the $1,400,000 smuggler who jumps his bail bond, while sending the $2,500 smuggler to jail. But individual èxceptions do not disprove the general value of our well-tried system of government by checked and balanced powers. . . .

These checks do not hamstring progress. They may sometimes compel a salutary pause for reflection, discussion, the wiser second thought. Against a dictator we may never need them. They are as stanch to resist the firebrand and the demagogue.

20

Judge Archbald was later placed under impeachment charges by the House of Representatives for causes other than those mentioned, and on January 13, 1913, was found guilty by the Senate. *The World* said of this verdict:

The Institution of Impeachment is revived and invigorated by the proceeding against Robert W. Archbald, a Circuit Judge of the United States sitting in the Commerce Court, which has resulted in his conviction and removal from office.

Impeachment is an institution because it is the method prescribed by the Constitution for the punishment of public officers who betray their trust or otherwise prove their unfitness. . . . That this institution has fallen into disfavor of late has been due wholly to negligence. . . .

We now see that Robert W. Archbald never should have been made a Judge. He was a self-seeker on the bench. His relations with litigants in his court were scandalous. He accepted favors and gratuities. He was interested financially in matters that came before him. He exhibited a bias in favor of the rich and the powerful. He had no true appreciation of the position that he held or of his responsibilities to the people. He was a man misplaced.

The vote of the Senate by which he loses his office and is forever debarred from holding another is the most impressive judgment rendered by that body for many a year. . . . It is a death-blow to the demagogy of the judicial recall by popular uproar.

Naturally *The World* looked with no more favor upon the gloss on the judicial recall which Colonel Roosevelt described as the "recall of judicial decisions." This device would keep the electorate of every state—and as to federal decisions, the voters of all the states—in a perpetual stew of constitutional revision through the reversal of court decisions. The doctrine was annexed by Mr. Roosevelt in his speech before the Ohio Constitutional Convention on February 21, 1912. As he

expressed it, "The decision of a state court on a constitutional question should be subject to revision by the
people of the state":

> If any considerable number of the people feel that the decision is
> in defiance of justice, they should be given the right by petition to
> bring before the voters at some subsequent election, the question
> whether or not the Judge's interpretation of the Constitution is to
> be sustained. If it is sustained, well and good. If not, then the
> popular verdict is to be accepted as final, the decision is to be treated
> as reversed and the construction of the Constitution definitely decided
> —subject only to action by the Supreme Court of the United States.

Said *The World* in comment:

> In other words, the majority is to enact the laws through
> the initiative and referendum, and the majority is to interpret
> the laws through another initiative and referendum. If a
> State court undertakes to protect the rights of a minority, if
> a State court ventures to say that an act of the majority tran-
> scends the Constitution or transgresses against human rights
> and human liberties, the Judge may be recalled and the decision
> reversed by the majority which enacted the law.
> In these circumstances there would be no State Constitution
> except from day to day. No man would have any stable
> guarantee that the majority would respect his rights and no
> man would know to-day what his constitutional rights might
> be to-morrow. Every instrument that makes for stability of
> government would have been crippled or destroyed. State
> government would become a matter of mob-rule—a quiet,
> orderly mob, perhaps, but a mob that was lawless and unre-
> strained and responsible only to itself for its actions.

The World has been no more zealous in praise of the
extension of the principle of initiative and referendum,
especially for the more populous states, where vast masses
of people are herded in the large cities. It has been content to see these cure-alls tried in the far West, where
cities are smaller, the illiteracy percentage lower, and wrong
decisions likely to be made upon a scale less disastrous.

It was in the spirit of *The World's* platform of 1883 that on the first day of January, 1913, with its thirtieth anniversary rapidly approaching, it put forth a programme of immediately practicable reforms. "An increase of more than 100 per cent. in the Socialist vote," it said, "the support that more than 4,000,000 citizens gave to the semi-Socialist Roosevelt candidacy is sufficient proof of a rapidly growing unrest that will no longer be satisfied with perfunctory reforms or with government that does not adjust itself to the changing needs of the general welfare." The programme follows:

1. Tariff revision to reduce the cost of living, with unremitting opposition to all forms of governmental waste and extravagance.

2. Enforcement of the criminal provisions of the Sherman Anti-Trust law against all deliberate offenders.

3. Incorporation of the New York Stock Exchange, and such other legislation as may be necessary to safeguard legitimate business from the public evils of stock-gambling and stock-jobbing.

4. An elastic currency system that is not subject to Wall Street control and manipulation.

5. Strict regulation of child labor.

6. An employers' liability law, by Constitutional amendment if necessary.

7. Effective protection of women wage-earners.

8. Direct nomination of candidates for State office, with a constitutional provision for the short ballot.

9. Home rule for New York City, with complete municipal power over gambling, vice and liquor-selling, and a reorganization of the Police Department.

10. The overthrow of Murphy, and the election of a capable anti-Tammany Mayor next fall.

"This programme," said *The World*, "is in harmony with True Democracy. The principles which it represents are principles which *The World* has championed for nearly thirty years."

XXI

*Payne-Aldrich Act Repeats the Story of the Wilson Bill—Mr. Taft's Dilemma
—He Reluctantly Sides with the Tariff Stand-patters—Revolt in the House of
Representatives, and Party Lines Broken—Failure of the Special Session—
Arbitration Treaties Negotiated by Mr. Taft Beaten in the Senate—Canada
Rejects Reciprocity Proffer—Two Fine Peace Measures thus Defeated—
Mr. Taft, the Corporations and the Courts—Undeserved Humiliation of an
Able President.*

THE success or failure of Mr. Taft's administration
rested on the tariff.

The Republican tariff plank of 1908 was reactionary.
For the first time a political party promised not only well-
paid employment to protected working-men but undertook to guarantee profits to protected capital. But the
people had some reason to hope that the party's bite
would prove less vicious than its bark. Many Republican leaders, like Senator Dolliver and Senator Cummins,
were known to favor tariff reduction. Mr. Taft was committed in word and in belief to honest "revision downward." The sentiment of the country was so over-
whelming that it was supposed no party could defy it.

The passage of the Payne-Aldrich tariff repeated to
some extent the story of the Wilson bill under the second
administration of President Cleveland. The House prepared a measure which did not answer the expectations of
the people but was an improvement upon existing law.
The Senate oligarchy headed by Nelson W. Aldrich, then
doing his last services for high protection, tore the bill
in pieces, made its enormities more absurd, piled higher

its burdens. Again, as with the Wilson bill, many members of Congress consented against their judgment to the passage of the Payne-Aldrich bill because they despaired of other action. Again a President reluctantly assented as a choice of evils. But in the manner of assent there was a difference. Mr. Cleveland refused to sign the mutilated Wilson bill. Mr. Taft was expected to refuse to sign the mutilated Payne bill. He disappointed expectations.

In the end he signed. He admitted that it was "not a perfect Tariff bill or a complete compliance with the promises made, strictly interpreted." He said that "in a number of cases" excessive tariff duties had not been reduced. He denounced the wool schedule as "indefensible." He declared that "it should have been lowered," and that "it was not, because a combination of representatives from the manufacturing and wool-growing sections of the East and West had a majority in Congress that was overwhelming." But whatever good effect might have come from these reservations was thrown away later by excess of good nature. In a speech in the East the President praised Senator Aldrich, the chief architect of the abomination; in his Winona speech in the West he forgot how faulty he had found the act, and referred to it before a hostile audience as on the whole "the best tariff bill that the Republican party has ever passed and, therefore, the best tariff bill that has been passed at all."

The World, protesting against the Payne-Aldrich bill at every step, did not abandon the contest. Taking the President at his word that he desired revision, it began on January 18, 1911, a series of editorials headed, "Give Us a Special Session, Mr. Taft." The new House, elected in November, 1910, was Democratic by sixty-five votes—the reply of the people to the Payne-Aldrich act. Even Republicans in Congress might be ready under the chastening of such a smashing overturn from their majority of fifty in the previous House to look upon tariff reform as inevitable.   Said *The World:*

By impressive majorities the people in November condemned privilege in laws and in taxation.   In particular they passed judgment upon the taxes which under the manipulation of trusts have so oppressively increased the prices of food and clothing.

This is not the first time that they have done this thing. A generation has come and gone since 1876, when tariff reform and retrenchment swept the country.   The demand was repeated insistently in 1884, in 1892 and in 1908.   Both of the great parties have promised to undertake the work.   Both have been tried.   Both have failed. . . .

If the fruits of recent political activity are to be gathered; if popular rule is to be spared another staggering blow; if fresh energy is not to be given to all the socialistic and revolutionary influences which even now are undermining representative government, the President cannot fail to perceive that it is his highest duty to call the new Congress in extra session in March. . . .

It happens occasionally in the affairs of nations that one man finds himself so placed as to be able by a word or the stroke of a pen to leave his impress for good forever upon his time.   We believe that President Taft is thus situated to-day. Honor and fame hang on his initiative.

The World was able to marshal such aid in its demand that Mr. Taft was constrained on March 5th to call a special session for April 4, 1911.   *The World* hailed his message as "A Victory for the People":

Making claim to nothing more than public service in revealing from day to day the drift of opinion, The World nevertheless feels that, through its efforts and those of other newspapers that ably seconded it, the President has been made acquainted with the people's views and strengthened in his disposition to give them proper effect.   Champ Clark, who will be Speaker

of the House when Congress convenes, calls The World's battle
for an extra session "one of the most effective campaigns I
have ever known a newspaper to make." For once plutocracy
and privilege did not monopolize all attention at Washington.

If this courageous act shall be followed at the proper time
by a Presidential recommendation that the new Congress
remove the extortionate taxes upon food and clothing, Mr.
Taft will have the distinction of promoting a reform that
cannot fail to give him lasting fame.

Congress, by an alliance between Democrats and Progressive Republicans, passed in the 1911 special session
bills reducing duties upon cotton and woolen goods and the
so-called Farmers' Free List bill. Mr. Taft vetoed them
all in turn on the ground that they made excessive cuts,
and that they were not based upon exact knowledge derived from the Tariff Board's inquiries. Since in his
Chicago pledge of December 3, 1910, the President had
said "We are bound to promote the *prompt* elimination of
instances of injustice in the Tariff law,"there seemed little
point in advising Congress to wait for the reports of a
board which had no status as its informant but was
merely empowered to advise the President upon maximum
and minimum schedules.

The World commented upon the vetoes in repeated
articles headed, "Has Mr. Taft Committed Suicide?"
Thus on August 23, 1911:

With his veto of the Cotton bill Mr. Taft completed the
slaughter of all the tariff-reform measures passed by Congress.

No President could have been committed more unqualifiedly
to the reduction of the wool and woolen duties than Mr. Taft
was by his verbal and written pledges. His veto of the Wool
bill is inexcusable. He had denounced the woolen schedule
of the Payne-Aldrich tariff as "indefensible."

The Farmers' Free List bill was the logical complement of
Canadian Reciprocity. It was designed to affect directly the
cost of living and of supplies at a time when prices to consumers

are again rising. Mr. Taft wrote his veto of the bill before
Congress had passed it.

It was on the cotton schedule in the Payne-Aldrich tariff
that the Republican Senator Dolliver made his great fight and
showed how the country was being imposed upon in the name
of protection. The cotton duties were raised in the Tariff
act of 1909, and by his veto of the Cotton bill Mr. Taft justifies
the increase and prevents reduction. . . .

With how much faith does Mr. Taft imagine the people,
whose just hopes he has mocked, will listen to him when next
he offers himself as their leader in a campaign for real tariff
revision?

The question was answered the following year. But
before the verdict was rendered that put the Republican
party third in popular strength at the polls indisputable
proof was given that the country was against Mr. Taft.
On April 4, 1912, the new House in regular session once
more passed the Wool bill, 182 to 92; and the Metal
Schedules bill, passed by both Houses and vetoed, was
actually passed over the President's veto in the House
by 173 to 83, with many absentees. The Senate, more
closely divided, refused. "So ends," said *The World*, "the
chief tariff-reform work of the session. Only a Republican
President and an occasional Senator stand between the
people and their relief from excessive taxation on the cost
of living. The issue is clear. If the people want relief
they know just how to vote to get it."

If *The World* was compelled to criticize President Taft
for his position upon the tariff issue it was his foremost
supporter for world peace and arbitration, and for
common-sense trade with Canada.

Arbitration with Great Britain was no new word. Our
first treaty in 1783 contained an arbitration clause. So
did that of 1814, under whose provisions the Maine
boundary question was arranged in 1828. The Oregon
dispute and many differences upon the eternal fisheries

question were peaceably settled before the Venezuela explosion brought war near. Instead of shedding their best blood upon that occasion the countries established a friendly understanding. Lord Salisbury's bluntness at the outbreak of the Spanish-American war in calling Spain a decadent nation shocked diplomatists, but it showed that we had one firm friend in Europe. On the other side, when the German Emperor sent his sympathetic despatch to President Kruger during the Boer war, when there was scant liking for Great Britain upon the Continent and when in America Boer sympathizers were many, President Roosevelt kept the diplomatic attitude of our State Department scrupulously correct; and the war bonds issued by Sir Michael Hicks Beach were largely subscribed in Wall street.

No public act of recent years gave *The World* more satisfaction than the signing in the East Room of the White House on August 3, 1911, of a treaty to insure perpetual peace between the two nations through an agreement to submit all differences to arbitral process. Said *The World:*

At the same time a similar treaty between France and the United States will be signed in the Foreign Ministry in Paris. Both treaties have yet to be ratified, but it is scarcely conceivable that the hope of humanity will be dashed by any failure to take this final step.

This, therefore, is a memorable day in the history of three great nations. To The World it brings the welcome fruit of ceaseless agitation for more than a quarter of a century to the end that wanton slaughter and destruction shall no longer be invoked in the settlement of international disputes.

Ex-President Roosevelt did not make easier the path of peace by repeating that the ratification of the treaties by the Senate would amount to "unctuous and odious hypocrisy." He leveled this charge of bad faith not only at the President, but at the Prime Ministers and Cabinets of Great Britain and France, who advocated the treaties.

This splendid movement was finally blocked by the insistence of the Senate upon its right to be consulted afresh upon every question arising between the two countries—an insistence that seemed to clash with any proposal to settle questions automatically by general procedure.

Said *The World* of this Bourbonism:

No treaties are required to bring nations into an arbitration of questions which they are always mutually willing to arbitrate at the time of a dispute. What these treaties sought to do was to create an obligation to arbitrate a broad or justiciable class of questions which they might not be willing to arbitrate in the heat of controversy. So provision was made for joint high commissions of both parties to interpret disputed points and determine the arbitral character of issues arising.

The Senate strikes out this vital provision. It adds others for the further emasculation of the proposed conventions. And then in solemn mockery it adopts the Lodge resolution which was intended to overcome the objections thus enforced....

It is not the Taft Administration which the Senate has injured. It is the Senate itself.

It is not the President who has been betrayed, it is a great cause of civilization.

Reciprocity fared as badly as the arbitration treaties, but in this matter it was not the United States but Canada that took an unprogressive attitude.

Blaine and Dingley reciprocity had been accepted by the Republicans as attempts to quiet public displeasure at tariff exactions. They were not meant to be put into effect. With Mr. Taft in the Presidential chair working for a trade arrangement with Canada real reciprocity once more seemed possible. *The World* seconded him. The five-column editorial of April 3, 1911, and its briefer successors, entitled "Hundreds of Facts in Favor of Reciprocity," had much to do with strengthening the sentiment among Democrats which made possible the passage of legislation providing for a reciprocity arrangement. Of that triumph of common sense *The World* said on July 23, 1911:

The measure passed the Republican House of Representatives February 14th by a vote of 221 to 92, but failed to secure Senate concurrence in the dying Congress. Foreseeing this The World in its articles headed "Give Us an Extra Session, Mr. Taft," named Reciprocity and lower taxation of necessaries as the two great reasons for calling the new Congress together. . . .

Early in the fray the wolves of Privilege donned their sheepskin robes and went hot-foot to Washington to stop Reciprocity. . . . On the Canadian side there was the same alignment of abhorrent and hypocritical forces. But there it was chiefly the railroad man and not the manufacturer who donned the farmer's clothes to oppose friendly relations; he argued that there is more money in hauling goods a thousand miles from east to west than in letting them take the shorter path. . . .

The "defenders of Empire" mixed mischievously in the struggle, and from London and Montreal came prophecies of annexation and British dismemberment. . . . The press of both countries refused to be buncoed. And talk of Empire failed, as everything had failed, to stem the tide.

A tide, in truth, it is; a great, unyielding force and fact of nature that no Mrs. Partington with her broom can hold at bay. The glacial drift that ground and grooved its broad paths down the continent decreed ages ago that trade shall forever pass north and south over short ways in level valleys or on the friendly lakes rather than toil over heavy mountain grades for twice the distance east and west. . . . Some day we shall be wise enough to see that New York has no more need of a tariff against Canada than against Pennsylvania.

Between the United States and Canada there lies the longest "unscientific boundary" in the world; the longest line between nations not made or marked by natural obstacles. Yet soon we are to celebrate the one-hundredth anniversary of unbroken peace along that boundary. We trust that the newer and closer relations which it now rests with her to conclude will forward and prosper Canada greatly in the swift industrial development for which she looks in the twentieth century.

The battle was not won. The arrangement—in form it was not a treaty but an agreement for legislation, since our House of Representatives wished to preserve its right to initiate revenue laws—was repudiated by Canada after the Liberal party had been overthrown in a hot political campaign.

The World also gratefully reviewed Mr. Taft's moderate position upon the proper relation to the federal government of the great corporations, and in the early summer of 1909 thus summed up the case for Government regulation so far as it had gone:

No corporation-tax law should be enacted which leaves the matter of publicity to the discretion of any Federal official, whether President or department clerk. This country has had enough personal government.

The act of February 26, 1903, creating the Bureau of Corporations, provided that the information obtained through its investigations, "or as much as the President may direct, shall be made public." What has been the result? Corporations have been investigated when it suited the whim of the President to have them investigated. Information has been made public when it suited his purposes to make it public. . . . There is lodged with the President of the United States the most powerful instrument of favoritism and oppression known to free government.

Not only in his views upon corporation law did President Taft use to public advantage his judicial training. His knowledge of the workings of the United States courts and of many of the men engaged in them enabled him to make judicial selections of the highest quality. This counted heavily in the fair words *The World* paid his administration as its rightful due on November 7, 1912, two days after he was so crushingly defeated at the polls:

History will deal much more sympathetically with Mr. Taft than did the popular majority at the polls, and its verdict will not be long delayed. . . .

As President Mr. Taft will leave a record of many triumphs and a single conspicuous and fatal blunder. He has been a constitutional magistrate, governing by law and not by caprice. He has given us the greatest Supreme Court since the days of Marshall and Story. He was the first President to enforce the criminal clauses of the Sherman law. He has urged the reform of judicial procedure. He has powerfully supported the cause of arbitration. He has worked for reciprocity. He has suppressed jingoism. He has promoted civil-service reform. He brought about the corporation tax. He has had regard for economy.

Mr. Taft's stumbling-block has been the tariff. He signed the Payne-Aldrich bill which he should have vetoed, and he vetoed the non-partisan bills reducing the cost of living which he should have signed. No doubt he deserved punishment for these errors, but not at the hands of men calling themselves high-tariff Republicans, not at the hands of States like Pennsylvania, not at the hands of industrial oligarchies like Rhode Island.

Not to Mr. Taft alone but to the better deeds of the great party he worthily represented *The World* again paid tribute of praise on March 3, 1913, the day before he was to yield office to President Wilson. In these words it described the "Rocks that Wrecked a Party":

Sixteen years ago, with William McKinley at its head, the Republican party was restored to power. It has been supreme in all departments of government during that time except for the last two years in the House of Representatives. It carried four national elections by tremendous pluralities. It polled in 1908 for William H. Taft the greatest vote ever thrown for a Presidential candidate. It goes out of office to-morrow a third party, its candidate the choice of but two small States, its ranks broken, its leaders implacably hostile to each other.

Yet this once invincible organization has a wonderful record of achievement which its successor must not belittle. During these sixteen years, with Democratic assistance it is true, the Republicans have established the gold standard, carried on the war with Spain, kept faith with Cuba, liberalized the government of the Philippines and Porto Rico, constructed the Panama Canal, given us postal savings banks, rural free delivery, the parcel post, new railroad-rate laws and enlightened labor laws, extended to some extent the principle of international arbitration, and, during the Administration now closing, enforced vigorously for the first time the civil and criminal law against trusts.

To Mr. Taft personally belongs the credit of upholding in the face of many obstacles ideas of economy and of carrying to success in Congress his proposition in favor of Canadian reciprocity. By the one he has given the people of all parties lessons of lasting value, we hope, on the subject of governmental extravagance. By the other he conducted a campaign of education against the folly and waste of tariff wars between neighboring nations which cannot fail to add much to public enlightenment. His most notable error, to which may be traced most of his own and his party's troubles, was his failure to veto the Payne-Aldrich bill and his later refusal to co-operate with Democrats and Republicans in Congress to revise the tariff downward, as he had promised. It was these blunders that split his party, gave free rein to Theodore Roosevelt's overmastering ambition and brought about his crushing defeat.

Reduced to the fewest terms, therefore, the fate of the Republican party may be attributed to privilege, plutocracy, and personal government. These are the rocks on which it went to pieces. . . .

Democrats may study this record with profit. They will find much to emulate and not a little to avoid. They also have their stand-patters and plutocrats. They also have their turbulent leaders, eager for power and crazy for violence. The forces that have humiliated the Republicans in spite of much good service will unfailingly undo the Democrats, if given the upper hand.

XXII

THE LONG BATTLE FOR REFORM

1880–1912

Indiana in 1880—Vice-President Arthur and "Soap"—"Frying the Fat" in 1888—"Floaters" in "Blocks of Five"—Corruption Stirs the States to Action—The Silver Campaign Fund in 1896—Mark Hanna and Hannaism —Trust Contributions in 1904—Harriman's $260,000 and "Where do I Stand?"—The Standard Oil Contribution not Sent Back, as President Roosevelt Ordered—Ryan and Belmont's Vast Gifts—Cleaner Fighting in 1908— Passage of Federal Corrupt Practices Acts.

WHEN the plot to buy the vote of Indiana in the Presidential campaign of 1880 was already hatched Joseph Pulitzer said on October 9th in a speech in Indianapolis:

We want prosperity, but not at the expense of liberty. Poverty is not as great a danger to liberty as wealth, with its corrupting, demoralizing influences. Suppose all the influences I have just reviewed [banks, railroads and protected industries] were to take their hands off instead of supporting the Republican party, would it have a ghost of a chance of success?

Let us have prosperity, but never at the expense of liberty, never at the expense of real self-government, and let us never have a government at Washington owing its retention to the power of the millionaires rather than to the will of the millions.

The "power of the millionaires" prevailed. When, three years later, Mr. Pulitzer assumed the editorship of *The World*, money control hung like a cloud over the country. The President of the United States, Garfield having been murdered, was the Chester A. Arthur who, when Vice-President-elect, had said at a banquet to S. W. Dorsey in New York City on February 11, 1881:

Indiana was really, I suppose, a Democratic State. It had always been put down in the book as a State that might be carried by close and careful and perfect organization, and a great deal of— [here the speaker paused a moment while somebody interjected "soap." Laughter.] I see the reporters are here and, therefore, I will simply say that everybody showed a great deal of interest in the occasion and distributed tracts and political documents all through the country. [Laughter.] . . .

The gentlemen in New York who stood at the back of the national Committee responded so liberally to the demands of the committee that Mr. Dorsey, with his matchless skill, cool head and wonderful courage was able to save not merely Indiana, and through it the State of New York, but the nation.

Two years later Dorsey was telling how the Indiana campaign of 1880 was managed. He had nearly five thousand aids in buying the state. "Each of these men reported what they could do . . . and how much it would take to influence people to a change of thought. We paid twenty dollars to some and as high as seventy-five dollars to others, but we took care that the three men from every township should know just what each got. There was no chance for 'nigging.'"

It was under such conditions that *The World* began its long fight thirty years ago against practices of corruption. It scouted the notion that "the great burning question of the day is that our clerks shall be able to pass examinations in fractions or geography." Electoral reform was the need. We must protect the ballot-box "against the open violence of the ruffian and against the subtler violence of the corruptionist."

The arts of the briber failed to stay the election of Grover Cleveland in 1884, the young efforts of *The World* proving to be the decisive power. The corruptionists did not look for the defeat and were taken unawares.

They made no such mistake in 1888.

21

On May 25, 1888, President James P. Foster of the Republican League sent out a letter saying that manufacturers enriched by protection were laggard in contributing. He added a phrase that became famous: "If I had my way about it I would put the manufacturers of Pennsylvania under the fire and fry all the fat out of them." Foster's letter closed with the remark: "If you give us the means to win the victory we will do it. Are you willing?"

On October 24th Col. W. W. Dudley, Treasurer of the Republican National Committee, showed how the "means" were to be applied. He sent out this confidential advice on the handling of purchased votes: "Divide the floaters into blocks of five and put a trusted man with necessary funds in charge of these five and make him responsible that none get away and that all vote our ticket."

The election was very close. Corruption decided it. Money elected Harrison, though Cleveland had a plurality of the popular vote. Classic among American editorial articles was that which *The World* printed under the title of "Triumphant Plutocracy" on March 4, 1889, the day when Benjamin Harrison took seat in the White House to which the stained title of purchase admitted him:

To-day at the capital of this Republic founded by a free people, Money seals and celebrates its triumph in the election. . . . What is the remedy?

There can be no cure for these evils that does not proceed from an enroused and imperative public opinion. It is the dreadful inertia of indifference that must first be overcome.

There is a work for the pulpit. Where sleep the thunders of righteous condemnation that rolled from the pulpit against human slavery? If the will of the people be the will of God, is not a crime against the suffrage a concern of religion?

It is a work for the press. Public opinion will never be aroused against corruption by the politicians. They will not quarrel with their trade. . . .

*The State can apply a remedy by providing ballots and protecting
the voters in secrecy in casting them, and by limiting the expenses
of campaigns, and by requiring publicity to expenditures, as has
been done with such good results in England.*

An official statement prepared for the Senate in 1908
enumerated nineteen states and territories that then
had laws for the publicity of election contributions or
expenditures.   These were, with the dates of enactment,
New York, 1890; Colorado, 1891; Massachusetts, 1892;
Alabama, California, and Virginia, 1893; Arizona, Connecticut, and Minnesota, 1895; Nebraska and Wisconsin,
1897; South Carolina, 1905; Pennsylvania, 1906; Iowa
and Washington, 1907.   In 1897, also, Florida, Kentucky,
and Tennessee passed laws forbidding corporations to
contribute; but without publicity acts these prohibitions
were ineffective.

With the passage of these earlier acts came Australian-
ballot laws in many states, which made corruption hazar-
dous by rendering it harder to be sure that the purchased
voter "stayed bought."   But the nation still took no step
to end corruption in federal elections.   Meanwhile the
scandal was recurrent at every general election.   Not all
the arts of bribery could prevent Cleveland's election in
1892.   But then came 1896 and the silver issue.

Always since the war the heaviest purse had been on
the side of the protected manufacturer in national elections, though in local contests neither party excelled in
unscrupulousness.   The silver issue brought to Mr.
Bryan's aid a competitive Democratic campaign fund
given mainly by Marcus Daly, Senator Clarke, and other
silver-mining magnates of the mountain states.   Mark
Hanna and his supporters, many of whom were more
moved by fear of financial panic than by interest in
tariffs, put into use the largest corruption fund yet gathered, none of which was wasted by the shrewd business

man who conducted the McKinley campaign as if it had been a factory or a mine.

What was the total thus gathered? No one knows. No record was ever made public. The outrage was this: that corruption was paid for in the dark; that the people whose rights and power were bought and sold could not even know who paid the price; that they could only infer how this price was repaid in turn.

The situation was not greatly different in 1900; and so we come to 1904. A means of "frying the fat" which out-Fostered Foster's wildest dreams had now been provided in the Bureau of Corporations, whose researches were conducted in secret and whose conclusions were disclosed only to the President. As late as 1911 its reports were refused even to an investigating committee of the House of Representatives.

When George B. Cortelyou, who as Secretary of Commerce and Labor had oversight of the Bureau of Corporations, was made Chairman of the Republican National Committee charged with the re-election of Theodore Roosevelt, "financial leaders" knew what was expected. Early in the campaign and at frequent intervals in the course of that struggle *The World* asked the famous Ten Questions already quoted. No answer was ever vouchsafed by Mr. Roosevelt or by Mr. Cortelyou. Yet the questions were by degrees answered in the current news; in the revelations of disappointed conspirators for profit; in the inquisitions of courts; in state and national investigations.

Most of the records are destroyed, and no scrutiny of the funds in the original entries is possible. But we know that the Beef Trust contributed to the Roosevelt campaign fund, though we do not know the sum.

That the Insurance Trust contributed was proved in the Hughes investigation. Without knowledge or consent of their policyholders the Mutual Life gave $50,000, the

Equitable $50,000, and the New York Life $48,702.50 through George W. Perkins.

The Coal Trust and the Railroad and Banking trusts were represented in funds gathered in New York and Philadelphia.

The Steel Trust contributed not only in 1904 but in 1906.   The Harvester Trust, a child of the Steel Trust, was favored by the Roosevelt Administration.   Permission to the Steel Trust to absorb the Tennessee Coal and Iron Company in 1907, in violation of the anti-trust act, was avowed and defended by Mr. Roosevelt.

There lingers unanswered from these revelations the question how much Mr. Roosevelt knew of corporation contributions when he denied Judge Parker's charges. That he knew of certain donations is admitted.   Controversy is keenest about the fund raised by E.H. Harriman and about the Standard Oil contributions.

By the publication in *The World* on April 2, 1907, of a letter from Edward H. Harriman to Sydney Webster it became known that Mr. Harriman had raised $260,000 in 1904 for Roosevelt, to be expended in New York State. Harriman understood that for this money Senator Depew was to be made an Ambassador, Frank Black was to become Senator in his stead and Harriman was to be consulted upon railroad recommendations in President Roosevelt's message.   None of these arrangements was carried out, and Harriman asked Webster, "Where do I stand?"

There is no proof beyond Harriman's word that President Roosevelt asked Harriman to raise a fund.   There is proof that Mr. Roosevelt asked Harriman to the White House, for upon his denying that fact Harriman produced the invitation.   There is no proof that Treasurer Bliss received assurances from Mr. Roosevelt as to the treatment he would accord Harriman.   Probably he did not. That was made unnecessary by the code of politics.   Long afterward Senator Platt explained upon the witness-stand that campaign contributions established "a moral obligation."

Harriman raised the money. He wrote to Webster that his fund had "turned fifty thousand votes" in New York. That he supposed he had an understanding with the President he gave proof by offering to return to the contributors of his special offering the money they had given, since the conditions had not been fulfilled. None of them cared to be reimbursed at Harriman's expense.

The facts about the Standard Oil contributions came out more slowly. During the campaign of 1904 it was said that the company had contributed $100,000 to the Roosevelt fund. On October 25th S. C. T. Dodd, counsel of the company, stated that it had taken no part in politics or in securing the nomination of any candidate. He did not deny that money had been contributed. The next day Mr. Roosevelt wrote Mr. Cortelyou, referring to the Standard Oil Company's reported gift of $100,000, and ordered that if any such sum had been contributed it should be sent back. To like effect he wrote again on October 27th and telegraphed two days later. The money had been received in September and spent. It was not sent back.

Eight years after 1904 the leaders of the riven Republican party, denounced by Mr. Roosevelt as "highway robbers," were not averse to revealing the secrets of the Roosevelt-Cortelyou fund. From the testimony of John D. Archbold, of the Standard Oil; of J. Pierpont Morgan; of George R. Sheldon, who succeeded Cornelius N. Bliss as Treasurer of the Republican National Committee; of Elmer Dover, an employee of the Committee, and others, many facts were elicited by the Clapp Senatorial Committee.

The Standard Oil contribution of 1904 was paid in cash, handed personally by Mr. Archbold to Treasurer Bliss.

Beside this $100,000 Mr. Archbold gave $25,000 to Senator Penrose for use in Pennsylvania. Before giving the $100,000 Archbold insisted that Bliss should assure him that Mr. Roosevelt would "appreciate" the help, and would not be radical in treating the tariff. Mr. Bliss afterward begged for $150,000 more, and when refused intimated that Archbold was making a mistake. Later, when the administration was prosecuting the Standard Oil Company, Archbold reproached Bliss, who replied that he had no influence with the President.

Did Mr. Bliss let President Roosevelt know that Standard Oil had contributed the $100,000, and upon what terms? His friends would accept his unsupported word; but he is dead. Did Mr. Roosevelt upon October 29th or upon November 4th, when he issued his denial of Judge Parker's charge, know that the money of the Standard Oil had not been sent back, could not be sent back, would not be sent back? In any case the contribution supports Judge Parker's statement as to the acts of the trusts and the motives of those acts.

Of Mr. Roosevelt's order that the Standard Oil money be returned the *New York Press*, which supported him for President in 1912, remarked:

Roosevelt prepared his alibis as he went along so that when the time came he could show that he had ordered the return of any protection money he knew about, could prove that he was told the money had been returned, and could demonstrate by the record and testimony that anybody who imagined he was buying Government favors from him with campaign contributions was "either a crook or a fool."

What the Republican campaign fund of 1904 amounted to perhaps no one living knows. Chairman Cortelyou, examined by the Clapp Committee, thought it was less than two millions. If Treasurer Bliss thought a single trust should be assessed $250,000 this estimate seems low. Whatever the sum, it was in greater part given by a few men of wealth. Among the contributions revealed after eight years of denial and evasions, some of those of greatest consequence were:

G. W. P. (Perkins)	$100,000
G. W. P. (Perkins)	250,000
George J. Gould	100,000
E. H. Harriman	100,000
C. S. Mellen, President	50,000
C. H. Mackay	15,000
E. T. Stotesbury	136,000
B. T. Wainwright	101,700
H. H. R. (Rogers) and J. D. R.	100,000
R. F. Rose, International Harvester	20,000
G. W. P. (Perkins)	100,000
J. P. Morgan & Co.	100,000
Chauncey M. Depew	100,000

The Stotesbury contributions were for the Philadelphia Committee; the Wainwright contributions for the Pittsburg Committee. George V. L. Meyer acted for the Boston Committee. James Stillman, of the National City Bank in New York—the "Standard Oil Bank"—gave several sums of $5,000 each. Depew's money was for the New York Central—and for his own menaced Senatorship. Whitelaw Reid, Jacob H. Schiff, James Speyer, J. F. Dryden, Andrew Carnegie, Roswell Miller, the Cuba Mail Steamship Company, William Nelson Cromwell, the American Can Company, Robert Bacon, and the Clarke Manufacturing Company were among the contributors.

Finally, the Harriman fund, late in the campaign, called out additional sums from J. P. Morgan, James H. Hyde (who wished to be Ambassador to France), C. N. Bliss, James Stillman, E. H. Harriman, H. C. Frick, D. O. Mills, H. McK. Twombly, E. T. Stotesbury, G. W. Perkins, Jacob H. Schiff, and Isaac Seligman. Mr. Frick stood ready, as Mr. Roosevelt testified, to make good any sum the Campaign Committee might lose by returning a Standard Oil contribution.   There was no such loss.

Stotesbury, Bacon, and Perkins were partners of J. P. Morgan.   Bacon afterward became Assistant Secretary of State and Ambassador to France.   Meyer was rewarded with conspicuous office.

Upon the Democratic side the situation, as it was disclosed eight years later, was equally disheartening, though less of a public menace since smaller sums were being spent for an end impossible.   August Belmont gave about $250,000 and Thomas F. Ryan as much as $450,000 —the largest single contribution of the campaign—without hope of success, as he afterward testified, but with the purpose of "holding the organization together."   Of the Republican fund seventy-three and one-half per cent., according to Treasurer Sheldon, was contributed by corporations and trust interests.   Fully as large a proportion of the Democratic fund must have been provided by a few wealthy men.   How far Judge Parker was aware of the financial operations of his Campaign Committee has not been revealed.

It was only after 1904 that *The World's* long fight for honest elections began to show results of the first importance.   The real beginning of any corrupt-practice legislation in this country which was anything more than a mere formal setting forth of public aspiration for honest elections unsupported by penalties for corruption was contained in the insurance code of the state of New York, forced by *The World's* philippics in 1906 from a reluctant governor and legislature.

Then for the first time in American history a state forbade any contribution whatever by corporations for political purposes.   The New York law also enforces publicity of campaign funds and expenditures.   New Jersey passed in 1911, under Governor Wilson's urging, an act, the Geran law, that is almost a model, providing for publicity, limiting the amounts that candidates may spend, and forbidding campaign contributions. Other states are rapidly falling into line.

The shocking insurance disclosures were also the beginning of forward action in Washington. They gave force to the sentiment which had long been growing there that the nation itself should not lag behind its states in frowning upon corruption; and in the early days of 1907 Senator Culberson's proposed amendment to the railway-rate bill, providing that no corporation engaged in interstate commerce should contribute to any federal campaign fund, and the Tillman bill, forbidding national banks to make such gifts, were combined in the law of January 26th, which forbids all corporations to contribute.

The campaign of 1908 was an improvement in decency upon all its predecessors since the Civil War. Said *The World* on October 10th:

For the first time in the history of American politics, the sources of a National Committee's campaign fund have been voluntarily disclosed. This action marks the beginning of a new era. . . . When George R. Sheldon was made Treasurer of the Republican National Committee he declared that inasmuch as he was a resident of this State the publicity laws of New York would apply to the Republican campaign fund. That act requires a sworn statement of expenditures as well as of receipts. Herman Ridder having been elected Treasurer of the Democratic Committee to succeed Governor Haskell, the publicity laws of New York apply to him as well as to Mr. Sheldon.

So publicity in a national election was practically forced upon the campaign treasurers of both parties by the laws of a single state.

The Rucker bill, passed by Congress in August, 1911, was the next step. This provides for publicity of campaign funds and limits the amounts that may be spent in Congressional elections. It was during its energetic advocacy of the bill that *The World* received from ex-Judge Parker this letter, which it printed with comment:

PUT THEM IN JAIL

TO THE EDITOR OF THE WORLD.

Your editorial of yesterday served to remind me of the masterful campaign you have waged for years against the corrupt use of money at the polls.

Others, at the outset in sympathy with the movement, either grew weary after a time, or else jumped, as does the trout at the angler's fly, at the new "isms" dangled before the people that the truth might not be seen and understood.

But The World never faltered, and for this effective service as to the most important of all latter-day public questions the people owe you a debt that can never be measured.

Yet I venture to ask you to continue your work until the act of Jan. 26, 1907, be so amended as to provide imprisonment for the officers of corporations devoting corporate funds to political ends.

The act imposes a fine.

The punishment was not intended to hinder contributions.

It was intended to deceive the general public, not the corporation bargainer with government for the right to levy toll upon the people. To him the act was to, and does, mean: "Contribute if you wish, for the only risk you run is a possible fine, which you can take out of the corporate treasury as easily as you took out the contribution."

Very sincerely yours,

ALTON B. PARKER.

ROSEMOUNT, ESOPUS-ON-THE-HUDSON, *August 15, 1911.*

Judge Parker is right. The law should provide that the "corporation bargainer with government for the right to levy toll upon the people" must go to jail; and to that end the true friends of honest elections will continue their efforts.

Nor need they despair of soon achieving success, seeing how great an advance has been made, in the seven years since the crowning debauchery of 1904, in repressing the purchase of elections.

Little need be said of campaign funds in 1912. They were of modest size compared with those furnished during so many campaigns. The combined expenditures of the three parties were probably not far from the sum spent by the Republicans alone in 1904.

The Democrats had the largest provision, 91,000 persons contributing $1,100,000. There was a substantial residue not spent.

The Progressive fund amounted to $790,682, as accounted for under the laws of New York, including money given by the National Committee to the State Committee in that state, but not funds in other states; and here again was a surplus. Something like $700,000 was also used before the Republican national convention, as testified to before the Clapp Committee, in the vain attempt to secure the nomination of Mr. Roosevelt on the Republican ticket. George W. Perkins gave $122,500 to the earlier fund, $130,000 to the later, and $10,000 for New York; a total of $262,500. Frank A. Munsey gave $118,000 to the pre-convention fund, $112,250 to the campaign fund proper, and $10,000 in New York; a total of $240,250. Dan Hanna gave $177,000 to the pre-convention fund.

The Republican National Committee reported the receipt of $904,828, and again a surplus. The largest contributor was President Taft's brother, Charles P. Taft, who gave $150,000. J. P. Morgan & Co. and Andrew Carnegie put in $25,000 each, and other contributions seem to have been scaled down to modest figures.

The laws governing the use of money in campaigns are still far from perfect. There are loopholes; evasion is possible; enforcement has not always teeth; penalties for infraction are often slight. But a revolutionary advance has been made in thirty years, *The World* aiding it by a fight that has been continuous from the day of its birth.

XXIII

AGAIN MR. ROOSEVELT

1881–1911

The Early Career of a Great Politician—Mr. Roosevelt and the Edmunds Campaign—He Leaves the Independents to Support Blaine—His Troubled Presidency — Congress and the Secret Service Moneys — The Roosevelt Corporation Policy—"The World" Nominates Him for Senator—His Trip to Africa—Rushing to Defeat in the Stimson Campaign—Governor Dix's Vari-colored Administration—The Birth of the Progressive Movement—Mr. Roosevelt Takes Possession.

In the autumn of 1881 a slender young man of nervous temperament wearing eye-glasses and a moustache with side-whiskers was elected to the New York Assembly as a reforming Republican. He quickly became prominent and was intrusted with the chairmanship of a legislative committee to investigate conditions in New York City.

In 1884 Theodore Roosevelt appeared as one of the delegates-at-large at the National Convention, where he was active in urging Senator Edmunds of Vermont for the Presidency. Blaine was chosen. A conference of Edmunds men was called in New York, and such leaders as Carl Schurz and George William Curtis repudiated Blaine and Logan as unfit, and resolved that "it is our conviction that the country will be better served by opposing these nominations than by supporting them." Mr. Roosevelt, after some hesitation, said: "I intend to vote the Republican ticket. . . . I did my best and got beaten, and I propose to stand by the result."

Upon Mr. Roosevelt's public activities up to this point *The World* in the summer of 1884 made sarcastic comment:

Young Mr. Roosevelt started well in the Legislature as a municipal reformer. When he was turning up the soil of our city government he came across outrageous irregularities in the Taxes and Assessment Department and blackmail offenses in the Surrogate's office. As the President of the Tax Department and the Surrogate are Republicans young Mr. Roosevelt quickly threw in the dirt again and turned in another direction.—*July 24, 1884.*

The first necessary step toward reform in this city was to remove Johnny O'Brien, whom the Tribune had denounced as the embodiment of the most corrupt machine methods, from the head of the Election Bureau. . . . We found that Roosevelt sold out to O'Brien [and] accepted from his machine an election as delegate-at-large to Chicago.

Then we denounced young Mr. Roosevelt as a reform fraud and a Jack-in-the-box politician who disappears whenever his boss applies a gentle pressure to his aspiring head. . . . What an exhibition he makes of his reform professions at the present moment, when he signifies his intention to seek by his vote to elect as President of the United States a man he admits to be venal and corrupt, and for whom he blushes to speak!—*August 26, 1884.*

The World did not lack further opportunities to comment upon the activities of the young reformer who turned politician in that early crisis of his career. It opposed him for Mayor in the Henry George campaign of 1886. It denounced his headstrong course as Police Commissioner, which discredited reform by assailing personal liberty. It sustained the cause he represented in the Civil Service Commission. It opposed his election as Governor in 1898, but without enthusiasm for Augustus Van Wyck, whom Tammany stupidity set up to check his eager onrush. As Governor it found him often aiding its policies for reform; sometimes, as in the franchise-tax legislation, muddling good causes. It praised him in 1905 for his courage in standing ready, like Cleveland, to suppress with federal troops labor riots affecting interstate commerce, the mails, and national property. It commended his administration for dissolving the Northern Securities merger, and heartily praised him for his energy in ending the coal-strike menace. It admired his courage in undertaking to make peace between Russia and Japan. It supported him when attacked for having Booker Washington, a negro, at luncheon in the White House. It scored his injustice in dismissing a body of negro troops for the misdeeds of an unidentified few at Brownsville, Texas.

With Mr. Roosevelt's slow progress as President in punishing crimes of high finance *The World* was soon dissatisfied. In December, 1907, it was prodding him for failing to prosecute, as he had promised, "crimes of cunning no less than crimes of violence." Said *The World*:

It was nearly four years ago that Judson Harmon and Frederick N. Judson, in their report to the President on the Santa Fe rebate cases, informed Mr. Roosevelt that guilt is always personal. The same idea is presented in Woodrow Wilson's plea that the best way to discourage wealthy malefactors is to send the one responsible man to jail. . . . Yet in spite of all Mr. Roosevelt's burning words about crimes of cunning, great railroad wreckers and malefactors of great wealth, in no case has the one responsible man been sent to jail; in no case has the one responsible man been criminally prosecuted; in no case has the one responsible man even been indicted. . . . Was Punch right, after all, when it cartooned President Roosevelt as a rocking-horse crusader, brave, dashing and dauntless, but never getting anywhere?

Earlier in the year *The World* had commented upon "the most far-reaching claim of federal power ever advanced by any President of the United States"—President Roosevelt's Decoration Day address in Indianapolis, in which he claimed federal control of carriers, "whether their business is or is not interstate," under the power to establish post-roads. Of this dream of centralization *The World* said:

> If this contention be admitted, no city can control its own public streets. These thoroughfares are used by mail-carriers and mail-wagons and the power of regulation rests in the Congress of the United States. No State can control its own wagon-roads if these roads are used by rural-free-delivery carriers. No city can regulate its own traction companies. These companies in New York City and in many other places carry United States mail. . . .
>
> Mr. Root, in his speech before the Pennsylvania Society warned the States that they could preserve their authority only by a vigorous exercise of their powers for the general public good. But there is no salvation by good works in Mr. Roosevelt's scheme of theology. Under the clause empowering Congress to establish post-roads the States were predestined to be extinguished.

Of Mr. Roosevelt's Provincetown speech calling like the daughters of the horse-leech for more law, and ever more law, *The World* said, under the heading "More Muddling of Government":

> The grave defect of Mr. Roosevelt's corporation policy is that he has no policy. He has advocated a constitutional amendment to enable the Government to suppress the trusts; he has advocated publicity as the first essential step in controlling these corporations and secured the agencies of such publicity; he has promised the strictest enforcement of the Sherman law; he has explained why "good" trusts should not be prosecuted at all; he has advocated Federal licenses for all corporations engaged in interstate commerce; he has undertaken to have receivers appointed for corporations that violate the law; he has advanced the astounding doctrine that

under the post-roads clause Congress can control any common carrier that transports the mails; he has demanded and obtained the power through a commission to fix railway rates; he has declared that no criminal, high or low, whom the Government could convict would escape punishment; he has explained why the criminal prosecution of these criminals is generally inexpedient—and now he has arrived at Federal incorporation as the sovereign remedy.

Mr. Roosevelt advances one new scheme after another until the business mind is bewildered in the mazes of Presidential experimentation.

No part of Mr. Roosevelt's programme was more bitterly denounced than his attempt to use secret-service funds to compel Congress to support his policies. He sought to persuade the country that, owing to the machinations of Congressmen who "did not themselves wish to be investigated by Secret Service men," the machinery of justice had been crippled, and that Congress, when it questioned an appropriation for secret-service purposes, was legislating to protect "criminals."

Congress answered the President by passing the Perkins resolution. This declared that the Secret Service paragraph of his message was "unjustified and without basis in fact" and a "breach of the privileges" of Congress. Of this famous dispute *The World* said:

Other Presidents have quarreled with Congress; but no other President ever attacked in a message the integrity of the entire law-making branch of the Government, or insinuated that "the Congressmen" were practically the accomplices of criminals.

Yet not for all its criticisms of the President was *The World* willing to contemplate the loss to public life of his talent and energy. On November 9, 1908, it advocated his election as United States Senator from New York to succeed Platt. "Better," says an Eastern proverb,

22

"a wise enemy than a foolish friend." The advice tendered in these passages would, if accepted, have provided Mr. Roosevelt a far better route of re-entry into public life than the Stimson débâcle of 1910:

Theodore Roosevelt should succeed Thomas C. Platt as United States Senator from New York.

The World would infinitely prefer a Democrat of proved ability, integrity and character, but no Democrat can be elected. The Legislature is Republican; Platt's successor will be a Republican, and the choice narrows to the Republican best qualified to represent the State of New York. That man, in our opinion, is Theodore Roosevelt. . . .

Mr. Roosevelt's faults would be far less conspicuous in the Senate than in the White House. In the United States Senate no man is supreme. However energetic, however impulsive, however ambitious, he must conform to the traditions of the greatest deliberative body in the world. . . .

Any man who has been President of the United States has gained an experience that is invaluable to the nation and should not be lost.

The World's farewell to Mr. Roosevelt as President was a full-page editorial on March 4, 1909, entitled "Seven Years of Demagogy and Denunciation." For a little there was a breathing-space for Mr. Roosevelt; politics was dropped for the production of some extremely readable articles upon his hunting-trip in Africa. The condition of American parties during his absence—the lull before the reawakened storm—was described in December, 1909, in a remarkable article called "The Twilight of the Gods":

Democrats and Republicans alike are divided. In the House, Speaker Cannon faces an insurgent revolt; but Champ Clark, the Opposition leader, cannot command the unanimous support of the Democratic Representatives, Senator Culberson has resigned the thankless task of leading the Democratic minority in the Senate, and Senator Aldrich finds his own leadership sharply challenged by radical Senators from the West. Republican Senators and Representatives can be found who are no less radical than Mr. Bryan and Mr. Clark, and there are Democratic Senators and Representatives who are no less conservative than Mr. Aldrich and Mr. Cannon.

Party demoralization in Congress is no accident. It is the inevitable result of a political discontent that is struggling to find a voice. Mr. Bryan expressed it in a way; but neither of them ever got to the heart of things. . . .

As The World sees it, to find the genesis of this present-day discontent we must go back nearly twenty years, when public opinion, inflamed by the aggressions of great combinations of capital, compelled the enactment of the Sherman Anti-Trust law. But no law is self-enforcing. Least of all one that strikes at privilege and plutocracy. Before sufficient pressure could be brought to bear upon the Executive to compel a vigorous enforcement of the Anti-Trust act the silver question had become acute. Attention was diverted from the trusts, and the Sherman law was temporarily forgotten in the struggle to save the nation from the consequences of free silver.

What the country most needs politically is a new alignment of parties, in order that they may again represent the principles and ideals of their members; but this is too much to hope for at present. There are thousands of Republicans who are really Democrats, and thousands of ·Democrats who are really Republicans; but they are held to their ancient party allegiance by habit, sentiment, tradition and prejudice. Instead of seeking a party that better expresses their views, they are seeking to mold their own party over to their changing principles, and the growing spirit of independence makes the issues only the more confusing. . . .

The old battle-cries fall on deaf ears. The old standards arouse little enthusiasm. The old prophecies excite no reverence. A new order is seeking to establish itself politically. This is the twilight of the gods.

Mr. Roosevelt's return to America on June 18, 1910, was like the triumph of a Roman general. He was welcomed by a huge outpouring of the people.

It was expected that the ex-President would remain for a time quiet. He may have intended to do so, but his restless temperament forbade him to stay inactive at the edge of a fight. He had surrounded Governor Hughes's path with difficulties, had driven him to the Supreme Court, out of the road to the Presidency, and thus had paved the way for the Republican schism of 1912 which the progressive Hughes might have avoided. A new campaign for Governor of New York was near. The hunter plunged into the fray by his discovery in Osawatomie, Kansas, August 31, of the "New Nationalism." Showing a belated concern for the dangers of corruption in campaign contributions by corporations, he put forward as a remedy the control of corporations by the government, and fathered such a policy of federal power as to disconcert the disciples of Hamilton scarcely less than those of Jefferson.

As the state convention in New York drew near it became apparent that the hunter had bagged the party. He overturned the machine plan, by which Vice-President Sherman was to have been permanent chairman of the convention, and took command. The old-line leaders, who by helping Roosevelt to crowd Hughes off the course had shown themselves less skilful politicians than he, stood back to "watch Teddy run things." Their allegiance in the campaign that followed was little more than nominal.

For Governor Mr. Roosevelt selected Henry L. Stimson.

Mr. Stimson was the former United States Attorney for the Southern District of New York. He was an able lawyer, an effective speaker; he was not known to the voters, but Mr. Roosevelt overlooked this weakness.

The platform was timid. Mr. Roosevelt was willing to make radical speeches in Kansas, but in drawing up a policy for New York, Progressivism roared gently. The Taft administration, which two years later the Rooseveltians were to assail so furiously, was "enthusiastically indorsed." The Payne-Aldrich tariff was praised. The platform was silent on the income tax, which Presidents Taft and Roosevelt had both urged; on the workmen's compensation law; on initiative and referendum and the direct election of Senators. As for direct-primary action, the rock on which the Hughes administration had split, it called for the extension of the signature-registration law to primaries, but otherwise went into no detail.

So much for leader and fighting-call. For tactics Mr. Roosevelt reverted to the old Parsons-Odell plan of joining forces with Mr. Hearst.

In 1906 Elihu Root had denounced Mr. Hearst with President Roosevelt's authority as the instigator of the murder of McKinley. Mr. Roosevelt had held responsible for that crime "those who on the stump and in the public press appeal to the dark and evil spirits of malice and greed, envy and sullen hatred." Mr. Root, repeating these words in a speech at Utica at the end of the Hughes-Hearst campaign, had added: "I say, by the President's authority, that in penning these words, with the horror of President McKinley's murder fresh before him, he had Mr. Hearst specifically in mind. And I say, by his authority, that what he thought of Mr. Hearst then he thinks of Mr. Hearst now." That unflattering opinion was soon modified, for on November 16, 1908, Mr. Hearst was a caller upon President Roosevelt at the White House. On September 7, 1910, he published in his newspaper this appeal:

Come home to New York, Mr. Roosevelt, and honestly take the war-path against the bosses. We Independents are whetting our tomahawks for the fray. There is no jealousy in our ranks. We do not care who leads, if he only leads aright.

We do not care who gains the glory as long as the people gain the victory.

Drive the Republican bosses out of the Republican party, Mr. Roosevelt, and if one of them deserts to the Democratic party fifty thousand Independents will take his place.

On the following day Mr. Roosevelt replied: "I am going back to New York State, as mentioned by Mr. Hearst, to fight the bosses. I will welcome the support of any man who wishes to aid in that fight."

An interview with Mr. Hearst was cabled from Paris on September 26th in which he said: "Certainly I would support Mr. Roosevelt upon a properly progressive platform, but frankly I would much prefer to support some other man in whose sincerity and stability I have more confidence."

Support was given indirectly by the nomination of a third ticket. Mr. Roosevelt had the satisfaction of conducting the fight of the first Republican candidate for Governor of New York defeated in sixteen years. The Hearst nominee, John J. Hopper, received 48,470 votes, 59 fewer than the Socialist. Stimson was beaten by 67,401. In the following year, while he thought it still possible to prevent a Republican schism, the amiable Mr. Taft made him Secretary of War.

The Democratic candidate, John A. Dix, was supported by *The World* on the sole ground that his election was necessary to prevent a third term of Rooseveltism more violent and unrestrained than ever before. However dissatisfied it may later have been with his administration, it never expressed regret for its choice in 1910. Mr. Dix suffered greatly in comparison with Governor Hughes. Where Hughes had fought the bosses and often beaten them to their knees, Governor Dix compromised. He purchased support for his measures by the approval of boss-drawn bills, like the Levy election law to prevent independent voting, which was riddled by the courts. He bought confirmation of his personal nominees by throwing "patronage" to Tammany. Where he followed his own choice Governor Dix as a rule made good selections of public officials; he forced the ratification of the income-tax amendment by New York; and upon the financial side his administration made a record of progressive legislation. On the other hand, corruption and waste crept swiftly into the public service of the state, so that at the end of Governor Dix's term *The World* was obliged to disclose demoralization in the Good Roads service, the chief interest of political bosses; in the Architect's office, and in other departments of state activity.

A fight broke out after Mr. Dix's inauguration upon the election of a Senator; Boss Murphy, fulfilling a preelection promise, swinging his support to William F. Sheehan. With all the power it possessed *The World* denounced this cynical bargain to deliver a great office to the ex-boss of Buffalo, and it heartened the Democratic "insurgents" in the Legislature to resist. Here aid was given by the late Edward F. Shepard, of Brooklyn. Before becoming openly a candidate for Senator Mr. Shepard consulted *The World* and offered to leave with it the decision whether he should make a public statement. He was advised to do so; he might be beaten, but even in defeat he would serve his state. Mr. Shepard took this view of his duty; was defeated; died soon afterward— he was of delicate frame and health—and was followed to the grave by public sorrow and appreciation. He made many good fights, filled no high office, but served his city and his state.

The Senatorial deadlock was ended by the election of Supreme Court Justice James A. O'Gorman, an admirable choice with which *The World* was well satisfied.

The defeat inflicted upon Mr. Roosevelt in 1910 extended far beyond New York:

Theodore Roosevelt and the New Nationalism have gone down to their Waterloo. Mr. Roosevelt will not be the Republican candidate for President in 1912.

When The World made Mr. Roosevelt the issue in this campaign he gaily accepted the challenge and spread himself over the political map, from the Rocky Mountains to the

Atlantic Ocean. He elbowed Mr. Taft and the Republican Administration aside while he conducted a sky-rocket campaign for a third term and his own political apotheosis. Mr. Roosevelt has been speaking for many weeks. Now the people have spoken, and the people have repudiated Rooseveltism.

He is beaten decisively in his own State, where his personally conducted candidate is overwhelmed, and the Republicans have lost the Governorship for the first time in sixteen years.

He is beaten in his own Congress district.

He is beaten in his home district in his own town, which was carried by John A. Dix.

He is beaten in Massachusetts, where he viciously assailed Mr. Foss, and the people elected Mr. Foss Governor.

He is beaten in Connecticut, where he viciously assailed Judge Baldwin, and the people elected Judge Baldwin Governor.

He is beaten in Ohio, where he viciously assailed Judson Harmon, and the people have re-elected Judson Harmon Governor.

He is beaten in New Jersey, where Woodrow Wilson made an Old Nationalism Democratic campaign against the vagaries of the New Nationalism.

He is beaten in Indiana, where he campaigned for Senator Beveridge on a fake tariff reform of false pretenses.

He is beaten in Iowa, where a Republican majority of 74,000 is nearly if not completely wiped out.

And wherever Mr. Roosevelt has been beaten, he has been beaten by Republican votes.

Republican victory would have been a Roosevelt victory. Republican defeat is a Roosevelt defeat. When the Republican Convention in 1912 looks for this mysterious Moses whom Elihu Root has so eloquently described, it will not look in the direction of Oyster Bay.

Such a defeat would have disheartened most men. One thing that endeared Mr. Roosevelt to his countrymen was that he did not know when he was whipped. The campaign of 1912 was begun on the field of the rout of 1910. The fulsome praise in the New York platform of 1910 for the failing administration of Mr. Taft could not be forgotten in a day; but mounting discontent soon helped Mr. Roosevelt to attack what he had lauded. The great Progressive movement in Congress, which developed such logical leaders as Senators La Follette, Cummins, and Bristow, was left for a time to plow and harrow and sow the Colonel's field. But in the spring of 1912 it became apparent that, foiled by Stimson's defeat of gaining the Republican nomination, Mr. Roosevelt was holding in reserve a schismatic candidacy.

Senator La Follette has told how he was encouraged by the Roosevelt group to believe that he had a clear road for a Progressive nomination. Why should he not believe his road was clear? Had not Mr. Roosevelt, after his re-election in 1904, on November 8th made this pledge with the people?

On the 4th of March next I shall have served three and a half years, and this three and a half years constitute my first term. The wise custom which limits the President to two terms regards the substance and not the form, *and under no circumstances will I be a candidate for, or accept, another nomination.*

Had not Mr. Roosevelt more than three years later, on December 11, 1907, amplified the pledge?

I have not changed and shall not change that decision thus announced.

Mr. La Follette further tells how, later, the impatient Nimrod thrust him aside and took possession of his undertaking. The election of 1911 aided the plan. Though not an important contest, it showed the people still dissatisfied. New York reverted to the Republican side in disgust at Tammany; California went overwhelmingly Republican but with progressive intent; New Jersey returned a narrow Republican legislature through the treachery of Democratic bosses to Gov. Woodrow Wilson. But Indiana remained Democratic; Ohio continued to support Governor Harmon with a Democratic legislature; Massachusetts again elected the Democratic Governor Foss, and Maine for the first time in years chose a Democratic Governor and legislature, and later a Democratic Senator.

Gloomy indeed was the situation of the Republicans. The country was in revolt. The enemy had invaded the citadels of privilege. President Taft's administration was a failure; the failure of a man respected and beloved, but still in public esteem a failure. Progressivism was demanding its rights in a West which could no longer be deceived or cajoled.

Add to this the portent of Rooseveltism upon the horizon, and the party horoscope, as 1911 drew to its close, was heavy with warnings of fate.

XXIV

"ARMAGEDDON"

1912

The "Seven Little Governors" Invite Mr. Roosevelt into Action—He Throws His Hat into the Ring—Attempts to Grasp the Republican Nomination and is Defeated—"The World" Demands the Nomination of Woodrow Wilson—Mr. Bryan's Great Services at the Baltimore Convention—Crushing Defeat of Boss Murphy and the Reactionaries—Nomination of William Sulzer for Governor—Philosophy of Politics—Barren Results of the Bull Moose Campaign—"A New Birth of Freedom."

THE debut of Theodore Roosevelt as a candidate for a third Presidential term was skilfully stage-managed.

On the 10th of February, 1912, seven Governors addressed to him a letter of invitation. They stated that they believed after investigation that " a large majority of the Republican voters of the country favor your nomination, and a large majority of the people favor your election, as the next President of the United States." The seven Governors were Stubbs, of Kansas; Carey, of Wyoming; Glasscock, of West Virginia; Aldrich, of Nebraska; Osborn, of Michigan; Bass, of New Hampshire, and Hadley, of Missouri.

Mr. Roosevelt did not at once reply. On February 24th, however, he "threw his hat into the ring" with the statement, "I will accept the nomination for President if it is tendered to me," and began an open campaign for the Republican nomination. He secured 450 delegates to the national convention who would stand by him to the end, and a collection of 78 contested cases, involving 254 seats, which were desperately fought in the national committee before the Chicago convention met.

Mr. Roosevelt reached Chicago, amid scenes of frenzied enthusiasm, on Sunday preceding the convention. On Monday night he made the famous speech that bore the message, "If they ask for the sword they shall have it," and closed with the lilting line, "We stand at Armageddon and we battle for the Lord."

The Roosevelt delegates were excited; Illinois was a Roosevelt state; Roosevelt enthusiasm in the galleries was certain. Many observers predicted bloodshed, but the convention did not prove more tumultuous than is the rule with these vast, unwieldy gatherings. The test came quickly in the vote for permanent chairman. The Roosevelt forces supported Governor McGovern of Wisconsin, a La Follette delegate, who received 502 votes; Senator Root, the Taft champion, was elected by 558 votes, and handled the gathering with extraordinary parliamentary skill. Governor Hadley of Missouri was the able floor leader of the Roosevelt hosts. Mr. Roosevelt's adherents cast 510 votes upon the motion to admit the contesting delegations, and this showed their greatest strength. Before the nomination was made they had agreed to withdraw, and in the selection of a nominee only 107 participated by voting for their candidate. La Follette received 41 votes; Cummins, of Iowa, 17. Six delegates were absent, 344 did not vote—making with the 107 a total Progressive strength of 451. Mr. Taft had 561 votes, but three more than on the first test, so closely held was the battle-field.

That night was held in Orchestra Hall one of the most excited political meetings ever known in this country. Mr. Roosevelt's speech was inferior to his Armageddon effort; but what it lacked in phrasing was supplied, to an audience worked up almost to frenzy, by his impassioned energy of utterance. The movement to nominate a third ticket was definitely under way.

The World, meanwhile, had surveyed the battle-scene with impartial philosophy. With the collapse of the La Follette movement it welcomed the nomination of Mr. Roosevelt by the Republicans, which then seemed not unlikely: "The issues involved in his political activities might as well be settled now as at any other time. If he is not nominated in 1912 he will be a candidate for the nomination in 1916. That will mean four years more of Rooseveltian agitation, Rooseveltian denunciation, Rooseveltian clamor and Rooseveltian intrigue. And to what good? Why not meet this Roosevelt question now and dispose of it once for all?" Nevertheless it soon predicted that Mr. Roosevelt would not be nominated by the Republicans. On March 16th it gave the reason:

American politics has witnessed nothing more extraordinary than Mr. Roosevelt's loss of strength since the announcement of his candidacy.

Up to that time he was a formidable figure, occupying a position of impregnable strength. He was professedly fighting for a principle. His opposition to Mr. Taft was ostensibly the opposition of thousands of other Republicans who believed the Taft Administration had not been sufficiently progressive.

Had Mr. Roosevelt been able to maintain this attitude it is by no means certain that he would not have been nominated. Mr. Taft was growing steadily weaker. He himself admitted the possibility of his defeat at the polls in November. . . .

The turn came when Mr. Roosevelt announced his candidacy. He was no longer disinterested. The mask had been removed. The so-called Progressive movement was revealed as a political conspiracy against Mr. Taft. . . . Mr. Roosevelt may have a large following in the Chicago Convention. Populistic States like Oklahoma will send delegations that are instructed for him, but the Roosevelt men will be in a minority.

The prophecy was fulfilled, but rather by the strength of the Republican machine than by the voice of the rank

342 THE STORY OF A PAGE

and file. Had there been Presidential direct primaries throughout the country Mr. Roosevelt would almost certainly have been nominated. His strength in the Chicago convention came from states where Presidential primaries were held. His opponents came from states where the old convention plan was still in force and the conspicuous leaders were in control. The smaller leaders of the party quite generally favored Roosevelt because with him they felt they had a gambler's chance of electing town and county officials, while with Taft nominated and a divided party their cause in many localities was hopeless. A majority of the rank and file also probably preferred Roosevelt.

Hard upon the heels of the Republican convention followed that of the Democrats in Baltimore.

Six years earlier Mr. Pulitzer in a memorandum for his editors had compared Dr. Woodrow Wilson, president of Princeton, to Dr. Eliot of Harvard as "a political thinker of the very first rank; far above ordinary politicians and more of the statesmanlike cast of thought than the President of the United States; perhaps because he is not a politician nor a partisan but an independent thinker"; and had said: "This is the type of man the Democrats should nominate, ridiculous though the suggestion will probably appear." The suggestion began to appear less ridiculous in 1910 when Dr. Wilson was elected Governor of New Jersey after a masterly campaign and proceeded to give that state an admirable administration.

Yet Governor Wilson was by no means the leading candidate in the number of his supporting delegates at Baltimore. He was, on the other hand, the candidate most obnoxious to certain financial interests that formed something like a conspiracy to prevent his nomination or that of any man too conspicuously progressive to suit their purposes. The first candidate of these men was

Governor Harmon of Ohio, an admirable executive. Governor Harmon has suffered some injustice in popular estimation from this support. He was worthy of a better following. His age and the fact that he represented the Cleveland Democracy, against which the old feeling still existed among the Bryan element, handicapped him further. The second choice of the reactionaries was Representative Oscar Underwood, chairman of the Ways and Means Committee of the House. Mr. Underwood had the public confidence, but his unbidden friends did not help his chances. There was also a general feeling that he could be most useful to the party and the country in Congress.

When it became apparent that neither Harmon nor Underwood could win the conspirators shifted their strength to Speaker Champ Clark, who had a large popular following, and whose column of pledged delegates, with the help of his new allies, put him in the lead.

Support of Clark in such conditions was impossible to *The World*. Of that it had given fair warning. On May 30th it nailed Governor Wilson's name to the masthead in an article entitled, "For President—Woodrow Wilson":

Like a twentieth-century Genghis Khan, Theodore Roosevelt, with his horde of prairie Populists and Wall-street Socialists, is sweeping down upon the Republican National Convention. Mr. Taft seems as powerless to check him as the degenerate Romans were to check the descent of the Goths and the Vandals. The historic party of Lincoln and Seward and Chase and Sumner and Conkling and Chandler and Blaine and Garfield and Harrison and Sherman and McKinley is apparently in the death-throes. This is the twilight of the gods, and the Democratic party must rise not only to its opportunity but to its responsibility.

How can it do its duty better than to match sanity against lunacy; statesmanship against demagogy; the historian against the Rough Rider; the educator of public opinion against the debaucher of public opinion; the first term against the third term; the tariff-reformer against the stand-patter; the man who would prosecute trust magnates against the man who protects trust magnates; the man with clean hands against the man who draws his campaign fund from Wall Street; the supporter of constitutional government against the champion of personal government; law against lawlessness; Americanism against Mexicanism; the Republic against the dictatorship?

Who better represents these issues than Woodrow Wilson?

The "conservatives" in the Baltimore convention planned to show their strength by making Alton B. Parker the temporary chairman. *The World* pointed out to Mr. Bryan, who as a delegate from Nebraska was to be a potent figure in the convention, his opportunity to use his great power for the party. The handicap under which he labored was "the growing cloud of suspicion that he is secretly planning his own nomination." Boss Murphy and the Wall Street Democracy were trying to force Parker upon the convention on the plea that if Bryan was not beaten he would seize the nomination for himself. By taking his "great patriotic opportunity"— by announcing that he was not a candidate—Bryan could crush the Wall Street-Tammany coalition, force the adoption of "a platform that squares with the principles and convictions of the rank and file of the party," secure the nomination of Wilson or another as satisfactory, and "make himself the architect of a Democratic victory in November that will pave the way for twenty years of Democratic administration in Washington."

Of the candidates only Woodrow Wilson was bold enough to protest in advance against the selection of Mr. Parker as temporary chairman, as an unwise yielding to men whose domination of the party would invite if not insure defeat. When on June 25th the convention met, Mr. Parker was seated by a vote of 579. Mr. Bryan, who ably fought against Parker and consented to stand for the post instead of his nominee, Senator Kern, received 510 votes. The test was a triumph for the conservatives, but a costly one.

On Thursday night, June 27th, Mr. Bryan introduced his famous resolution beginning: "We hereby declare ourselves opposed to the nomination of any candidate for President who is the representative or under any obligation to J. Pierpont Morgan, Thomas F. Ryan, August Belmont, or any other of the privilege-hunting or favor-seeking class," and demanding the withdrawal of delegates representing such interests.

The second part of the resolution was resented on behalf of Virginia, under whose banner Thomas F. Ryan had appeared as a delegate, and was withdrawn. The resolution as quoted was then passed, Charles F. Murphy, of New York, casting 90 votes for it, although August Belmont was one of the Tammany delegates. The reactionaries smiled at having, as they thought, taken the sting out of the resolution by supporting it.

On Friday balloting began, with Mr. Clark in the lead. He was supported by his own state, by Mr. Bryan, and by many others of the progressive wing. Late that night, on the tenth ballot, Murphy swung the solid New York column of 90 votes from Harmon to Clark. Clark's strength rose to 556, more than half the convention, two-thirds of which was necessary to a nomination. Wilson's vote was 354½. But the Tammany accession was far from causing a stampede; Clark's vote fell on the next ballot to 554, while Wilson's continued rising. This showed what the convention thought of the stencil-plate delegates from New York who had sat, wincing but dumb, under Mr. Byran's invective.

Balloting continued on Saturday with a gradual loss to Clark and a steady gain to Wilson; and when on the forty-third vote the convention adjourned over Sunday Wilson was well in the lead.

23

Monday morning *The World* published, in the most conspicuous manner its editorial typography has ever assumed, a strong article headed "Wilson—No Compromise with Ryan and Murphy":

Compromise was possible until the Ryan-Murphy conspiracy was fully revealed and the Tammany boss carried out the terms of his bargain with the Clark managers by throwing New York's ninety votes to Champ Clark. Compromise was possible until Mr. Bryan was compelled by the inexorable logic of events to repudiate Champ Clark's candidacy and vote for Woodrow Wilson. Compromise was possible until it became apparent to every intelligent man that the Ryan-Murphy-Belmont-Hearst coalition had set out to strangle progressive Democracy, destroy Mr. Bryan politically and prevent the nomination of Woodrow Wilson at any cost.

Compromise is no longer possible. There can be no Democratic harmony, there can be no Democratic unity, there can be no Democratic integrity, until the convention overwhelms this shameful alliance between corrupt finance and corrupt politics. . . .

The Ryan-Murphy coalition will now accept anybody except Wilson. If the convention yields to the plea for a compromise candidate, it will be a Ryan-Murphy victory.

A thousand Roosevelt orators will be thundering from the stump their denunciation of Democracy's surrender to Wall Street.

The issue that is vital to Roosevelt's campaign for a third term will come to his hand ready-made. The Democratic party might as well retire from the contest as to go before the country with the Ryan-Murphy taint upon its ticket. . . .

As Stephen A. Douglas once said, "There can be no neutrals in this war—only patriots or traitors."

When the convention reassembled Wilson received the nomination on the forty-sixth ballot.

The World predicted Governor Wilson's election. He would be "the first President of the United States in a generation to go into office owing favors to nobody except the American people. No political boss brought about his nomination. No political machine carried his candidacy to victory. No coterie of Wall Street financiers provided the money to finance his campaign. The American people have set out to regain possession of their government, and Woodrow Wilson was nominated for President because he embodies that issue." The share which Mr. Bryan had taken in the struggle was gratefully acknowledged:

Whether in all things wisely, whether in all things unselfishly, whether in all things loyally devoted to Gov. Wilson, it was his courage, his clearness of vision, his knowledge of the forces with which he had to contend, and his splendid mental and physical endurance that gained the day. . . .

It has seemed at times that Mr. Bryan's purpose was not to strengthen Democracy, but to strengthen himself. That suspicion attached to him at Baltimore and it delayed his triumph. Indeed, the glory of his achievement is doubled by the fact that it was brought about at last as much by foes convinced as by friends who never doubted.

In this record of a political success that has few parallels, we find but a single flaw. If at any stage, Mr. Bryan had emphatically put aside personal ambition, the outcome would never have been in doubt and his disinterestedness would have made him speedily invincible. This he did not do, and we shall always regret it. It was an opportunity lost.

Politicians will long debate whether Mr. Bryan had well-defined hopes of securing the nomination himself. If in a year when any popular Democrat was sure of election the leader who had borne the banner of Democracy in three defeats now wished to bear it to victory, it was not strange. But the fact remains that Governor Wilson's nomination was made possible by the brilliant battle which Mr. Bryan waged in the Baltimore convention against the bosses of the party and their financial allies.

As in 1892, *The World's* chief service to Democracy

twenty years later was rendered before the convention, in forcing forward the strongest candidate, and the result fully vindicated its judgment.

The campaign was put upon a high plane by Governor Wilson. No one had been more bold than he showed himself in addressing popular audiences in such terms as one might use before small groups of educated men; and his method was successful. Mr. Roosevelt specialized in denunciations of the men who had "stolen" the Republican nomination; but many of his supporters were of the social-worker class—agents of public charities, settlement residents and those in sympathy with them—who welcomed the opportunity to discuss sanitation, education, working-men's insurance, and other topics more fitting to state than national campaigns. With much of their doctrine Governor Wilson was in accord; he had done much for it in New Jersey; but he argued that workers for "social justice" would get more help from a practical party in Constitutional ways than from a rump of a party of privilege, itself committed to the governmental license of Big Business.

But the great issue was the tariff. The Republicans complained that the Democratic platform denied the Constitutional right to levy duties, save for revenue; in this position the Bull Moose party, as the Progressives came to be called, were equally emphatic. As no tariff had ever been passed except as a revenue measure, and as Governor Wilson was pledged to respect the interests of the community in restraint of violent measures, the point was not important.

Of the speech of acceptance by Governor Wilson *The World* said:

The same vicious system that is responsible for tariff extortion is largely responsible for the high cost of living. "The high cost of living is arranged by private understanding," as Gov. Wilson truly says. The same vicious system is responsible for the trusts and for all the evils that they represent. "The trusts do not belong to the period of infant industries." On the contrary, "they belong to a very recent and sophisticated age when men knew what they wanted and knew how to get it by the favor of Government."

The same vicious system is responsible for the so-called money power; for "the vast confederacies" of banks and railroads and express companies and insurance companies and manufacturing companies, all banded together by small and closely related boards of directors. "There is nothing illegal about these confederacies" which are now "part of our problem." They have never wanted anything from the Government except immunity from interference and they know how to get that immunity.

Because of the identification of Govenor Dix's administration more and more closely with Tammany Hall the campaign for the Democratic nomination for Governor of New York attracted wide attention.

The chief candidate, besides Governor Dix, was William Sulzer, a Representative in Congress from a strong Democratic district in New York City. Though Mr. Sulzer was a Tammany man, his personal strength in his district had enabled him to show occasional independence of the Boss, a circumstance that added greatly to his popularity in the rural districts of the state.

The World had no candidate; it was determined that the Boss should not be permitted to force the nomination of Governor Dix, thereby handicapping Governor Wilson and at the same time menacing New York State with the continuance of a nerveless and boss-controlled administration. Therefore it gave prompt warning:

The World will not support a Murphy candidate for Governor.
The World will not support John A. Dix for re-election.
The World will not support a candidate for Governor who owes his nomination, directly or indirectly, to the sinister power of the Tammany Boss.

We are unalterably opposed to Murphy's domination of the Democratic party in this State and we intend to make that opposition as effective as possible. Murphy must keep his unclean hands off the Democratic State Convention.

The nomination by the Republicans of Job Hedges as an unbossed candidate who "won without the help of the old guard," and the wild enthusiasm in the Progressive state convention which forced the candidacy of Oscar Straus, led *The World* to predict that "Unless the [Democratic] State Convention nominates a candidate for Governor who is publicly known to be an anti-Murphy Democrat, the next Governor of New York will be Oscar S. Straus or Job E. Hedges. Either of them would make a very good Governor."

Murphy played in convention a part less brazen than in Baltimore. He kept his hands off; he himself voted for no candidate; in these conditions Mr. Sulzer won with comparative ease. *The World* supported him with a warning:

Mr. Sulzer was the undoubted choice of the rank and file of the Democratic party. He would have been nominated for Governor in a direct primary, and the delegates who named him at Syracuse only carried out the wishes of their constituents. That much must be admitted by friend and foe alike.

Whether the delegates acted wisely or unwisely will depend upon Mr. Sulzer's own attitude toward his candidacy. He must first make it plain that he is a free man who recognizes no obligation to any boss or any machine. . . . He must make it plain that as Governor he, and not Charles F. Murphy, will be the leader of the Democratic party in this State.

The country remained calm during the campaign, since of the outcome there could be no doubt. The attack upon Mr. Roosevelt in Milwaukee by the unbalanced Schrank gave the contest its thrilling moment; but he was not seriously injured; and as Governor Wilson out of

courtesy canceled his engagements for speeches while
Mr. Roosevelt was recovering, argument by the candidates ended a month before election.

The occasion was therefore favorable for editorial
articles in a field which *The World* has always favored,
the deeper philosophy of politics. Such was its long
study of October 21st entitled "Monopoly is Slavery."

The men who thought that the Government of the United
States could safely legalize and regulate slavery were greater
statesmen than now exist in any country of the world. They
were undoubtedly the wisest, the most disinterested, the most
inspired body of statesmen known to the whole history of human
civilization.

Yet slavery was the rock upon which they split the Republic.
The attempt to legalize and regulate slavery was the one stupendous blunder of the Constitution, which led to civil war
and the most momentous conflict of modern history. . . .

The vital truth that Woodrow Wilson is now seeking to impress upon the minds of the American people is that monopoly
is slavery. It is not only economic and industrial slavery
but it is political slavery. The Government does not regulate
monopoly and cannot regulate monopoly. It is monopoly that
regulates the Government.

The Republican party has no clear and definite policy of
dealing with this great evil. The Progressive party purposes
to regulate and control monopoly. But the Democratic party,
under the leadership of Woodrow Wilson, purposes to extermi-
nate monopoly.

This country wants no favored monopolistic class established
and maintained by law. It wants no great mass of citizens
condemned forever to be hewers of wood and drawers of water
because a legalized monopoly has shut the door of opportunity
in their faces.

On the Saturday before election *The World* contained a
full-page editorial called "Democracy—or Despotism,"
which drew the contrast between two systems of govern-

ment, the one based on Roman, the other on English law, and argued that men of our Republic are better suited to thrive under the English type of administration. This was *The World's* final comment upon the vision of paternal coddling raised before the American voter by Theodore Roosevelt's "New Nationalism," with its lengthening vista of government control of business:

Under Roman law the citizen exists for the benefit of the state. Under English law the state exists for the benefit of the citizen. Under Roman law the affairs of the people are an active concern of government. Under English law the affairs of government are an active concern of the people. Roman law is an institution of imperialism. English law is an institution of democracy.

The best modern example of government under Roman law is Prussia. The best modern example of government under English law is the United States. These two conflicting systems cannot be permanently reconciled. . . .

Under the Prussian form of government all the activities of the citizens are regulated by an all-wise and all-powerful bureaucracy. At every step of his life a highly centralized Government tells him what he may do, what he must do and what he must not do. By the agency of its tariffs and its subsidies the Government decides what industries it will discourage. By means of its cartels it opens or closes the gates of opportunity at will. Production and consumption are alike regulated by its decrees. Competition or monopoly hinges upon the word of the bureaucrat. The Government guarantees the manufacturer his profit and it tells the consumer what he shall contribute toward the enrichment of industry. Its peasants are supposed to remain peasants and till the soil dutifully for the landlord classes that own the estates. Its workmen are supposed to remain workmen and assist the employer in conquering the markets of the world. . . .

As exemplified in the case of Prussia, government under Roman law is necessarily a government under which individual opportunity is inevitably circumscribed and limited. It is a government which rules a nation founded on the military principle—a few officers and a great army of privates who can never rise from the ranks. It is a government capable of development into a wonderfully organized machine which performs its functions with amazing precision. It is a government under which a whole people may be molded to suit the purposes of those in authority. It is a government under which one directing mind can shape the destinies of an army; but it is a government which has never been tolerated by a free people, and which no people could tolerate and remain free.

In the name of "social justice" it is now proposed to erect a replica of Prussian institutions upon American soil. It is proposed that a government of bureaucrats shall regulate the activities of ninety-five million people. It is proposed to make the National Government a priceless prize for Plutocracy to take possession of and administer for its own profit. It is proposed to turn a great Republic into the theater of a class war, and every election into a battle for wages, dividends and spoils. . . . At the head of this system is to be a President of the United States clothed with greater power than any other living man except the Czar of Russia, and he is to hold the liberties, the welfare and the progress of the nation in the hollow of his hand.

We know from long experience with the tariff what happens when great aggregations of capital are at the mercy of government. They step in and control the government. For more than a generation the protected industries have been united in a common conspiracy to name Presidents, to name Representatives in Congress and to name United States Senators. For more than a generation this conspiracy has been successful. . . .

The National Government has not regulated the tariff; the tariff has regulated the National Government, and to-day the tariff-taxing industries, under threat of panic, defy the American people to interfere with their special privileges.

This is the condition to which the country has been brought by a single experiment in paternalism. What would be the result if the profits of every corporation hinged on the action of government?

Does any sane human being who knows the history of tariff manipulation doubt what the result would be? Is there the faintest shadow of question that organized Plutocracy would seize upon all the machinery of national authority? . . . That it would make Presidents and Congresses and courts and rule the country by the sheer brute force of money? . . .

We are suffering already from too much personal government, from too much privilege, from too much favoritism. We have not kept the faith with our own traditions. We have not kept the faith with our own institutions. The way out is not to rush headlong into centralization, despotism and plutocracy, but to return to first principles. . . .

It is possible that this Republic was founded in error. It is possible that the Declaration of Independence was a mistake and the Constitution a blunder. It is possible that the Washingtons, the Franklins, the Jeffersons, the Madisons, the Adamses, the Jacksons and the Lincolns were wrong, and that the Roosevelts, the Perkinses, the Johnsons, the Flinns, the Jane Addamses and the Munseys are right; but The World, for one, still holds to the faith of the fathers.

The popular vote gave indication of distrust and uncertainty. It revealed such a fermentation of new ideas and new party alignments as had not been witnessed since 1860.

The total was but slightly larger than in 1908. The Debs vote grew from 420,793 to 900,672, although Socialists had feared defections to the Progressives. Wilson's vote, 6,293,454, was 115,650 smaller than Bryan's in 1908; Democratic losses to the Progressives were not balanced by Republican aid. A more amazing fact was that the Taft vote, 3,484,980, and the Roosevelt vote, 4,119,538, were together 74,390 smaller than the Taft vote of 1908. Considering the added thousands of newly enfranchised women, there must have been many stay-at-home Republicans.

The Wilson electoral vote was 435, that of Roosevelt 88, that of Taft 8. The Progressive party failed to appear in Congress in strength to determine public action. There the political division was mainly upon the old lines, as

Democrats and Republicans, though Progressive policies were certain to divide or weaken the Republican vote. The House was Democratic by 147 members, the new Senate proved to be Democratic by six, but the situation as affecting action upon the tariff was more complicated than the mere count revealed. Not quite all the Democratic Senators could be relied upon for a thorough tariff revision.

In not one state legislature were the Progressives put into control. In but few were they in position to hold the balance of power. In but two states did a Roosevelt candidate for Governor run even second. Women voters in six states showed no especial gratitude to Mr. Roosevelt for his support of suffrage.

The Roosevelt states were Michigan, Minnesota, Pennsylvania, South Dakota, and Washington; California was divided, eleven electors for Roosevelt, two for Wilson. The Taft states were Vermont and Utah.

One service remained after the election which an independent press could perform for Governor Wilson's administration. As if by secret understanding there arose a cry for the postponement of action upon the tariff. The friends of Privilege, routed in the field, sought to delay action by forebodings of disaster if that policy upon which the American people had decided were carried out at once.

In this emergency *The World* demanded an extra session of the new Congress; not only an extra session, but the immediate pledge of an extra session, so that business men might not be distracted by uncertainty. Other Democratic newspapers and citizens voiced the same views, and Governor Wilson, upheld in his own opinion, delayed not long to make his position clear in this statement of November 15, 1912:

I shall call Congress together in extraordinary session not later than April 15. I shall do this not only because I think that the pledges of the party ought to be redeemed as promptly as possible, but also because I know it to be in the interest of business that all uncertainty as to what the particular items of tariff revision are to be should be removed as soon as possible.

So closed the battle of 1912 in the rebirth of hope. The fruit of thirty years of fighting since Joseph Pulitzer re-established *The World* seemed fair upon the tree. For the first time since the civil war the people had taken control of their own government. As *The World* had said before election: "Sometimes protected industry had lost control of the Presidency. Sometimes it had lost control of the House of Representatives. Sometimes it had lost control of the Senate." But for fifty years "there had been no time in which it had lost complete control of all the branches of government." Now the change in the federal government was complete in both the executive and legislative departments.

Not in the sense in which Mr. Roosevelt had used the word, it was indeed Armageddon.

And thus, as "A New Birth of Freedom," *The World* hailed it on the morning of November 6, 1912, when the magnitude of the victory first broke upon the vision of the waiting country:

Under the leadership of Woodrow Wilson the Democratic party has won its greatest victory since 1852.

But this victory is no tawdry partisan triumph. It is no vote of confidence in the Democratic party as a party. It is a mandate from the people, and woe be unto the leaders of this Democracy if they falter in obedience to that mandate.

The country is seething with political discontent in spite of its unparalleled material wealth and prosperity. This discontent is confined to no particular class or section. Rich and poor alike, children of fortune and children of poverty, have begun to lose faith in the efficacy of their Government to establish justice and promote the general welfare. They are not sure where the fault lies; they are not united as to the remedy; but this they know—that their institutions have been seized by privileged interests and turned against them; that subtle, mysterious forces operating unseen have proved time after time that their power over public affairs was greater than the power of the people as a whole, and they demand that their Government be emancipated from this partnership.

This is the great work that confronts Woodrow Wilson and the Democratic party—to restore popular confidence in the institutions of the Republic and re-establish a government of the people, by the people and for the people.

For sixteen years the Republican party has been in continuous control of national affairs. In 1896 it polled 7,104,799 votes. In 1900 it polled 7,207,923 votes. In 1904 it polled 7,623,486 votes. In 1908 it polled 7,678,908 votes. But suddenly this seemingly invincible organization came crashing down to ruin because it had not kept the faith. The Democratic party in turn will go crashing down to ruin if it does not keep the faith.

The American people are no longer hypnotized by party labels and party emblems. They are concerned with principles of government and with parties as a means of translating those principles into action. They have made Woodrow Wilson President because they believe that his ideals are their ideals; that his courage is their courage, and that he will find a way to right the wrongs against which they have protested.

A man of lesser character, of lower ideals, of smaller ability, could not have won the victory that Governor Wilson won yesterday. He could not have appealed to the imagination of the country as Woodrow Wilson appealed to it. No man has ever been elevated to the Presidency who was more fully the people's President than this college professor who scorned alike the support of the bosses and the support of Plutocracy. It is a tremendous compliment that the voters have paid to him, but the responsibility is equally great.

If he should fail, the consequences must be doubly disastrous. If he succeeds, as The World believes he will, a new era will have begun in American history, with a new vindication of Republican institutions and a new vindication of the immortal principles of the Republic. This Nation will indeed have a new birth of freedom.

INDEX

THE END